REMOTE VIEWING:
BRIDGING SCIENCE, INTUITION & HEALING

BY Dr. Irina Webster

Copyright © 2025 Dr Irina Webster

All rights reserved.

No part of this book may be reproduced in any form or by any electronic or mechanical means including information storage and retrieval systems, without permission in writing from the Publisher.

Publishers:
Inspiring Publishers
PO box 159 Calwell ACT 2905, Australia.
Email: inspiringpublishers@gmail.com

National Library of Australia Cataloguing-in-Publication entry

Author: Webster, Irina

Title: **Remote Viewing**

ISBN: XXXX

Table of Contents

Key Insight
Dedication 8
Preface 9
Introduction 11
My Journey and Credentials 13
What You'll Find in This Book 13
Learning from the Experts 14

1: What is Remote Viewing? 17
   History and Evolution of Remote Viewing 17
   Difference Between Remote Viewing and
      Other Psychic Abilities 19
   Why Is It Important to Learn Remote Viewing Today? 21
   My Experiences with Remote Viewing 21
   My First Adult Experience with Remote Viewing 24
   Historical Background of Remote Viewing 25

2: Remote Viewing in Health and Wellness 35
   Medicine: How Remote Viewing Enhances Healing 35
     - "Sleeping Elena" – A Story of Remote Viewing with
       Intuitive Healing
     - Remote Viewing of Gallstones - A Life-Saving Insight
     - Remote Viewing in the Children's Rehab Centre
   Psychology: Stories of How Remote Viewing
      Transforms Mental Health 40

Weight Loss: How Remote Viewing Can Help You Achieve a
Slimmer You 42

3: Influential Figures in Remote Viewing **46**
Prominent Russian Individuals who Contributed
   to the Development of Remote Viewing 46
   - *Grigori Rasputin*
   - *Helena Blavatsky*
   - *Nina Kulagina*
   - *Anatoly Kashpirovsky*
   - *Wolf Messing*
   - *Alexei Yurievich Savin*
   - *Boris Ratnikov*

4: Group Exploration of Remote Viewing............................... **53**
Remote Viewing Experiments
   by Russian Research Centres and Universities.........................53
Private Research Groups: Independent Studies
   with Significant Impact 55
How to Set Up Your Own Remote Viewing Group.......................57

5: Scientific Theories Behind Remote Viewing **59**
Quantum Mechanics and Consciousness......................................63
Quantum Entanglement..64
The Role of the Observer..65
Non-locality and Information Transfer 66
The Role of the Subconscious Mind in Remote Viewing............67

6: The Process and Stages of Remote Viewing........................ **71**
Steps for Effective Remote Viewing..71
Different Methodologies and Protocols 74
Examples of Each Methodology...

7: My Approach to Remote Viewing..79
   Blending Medical Intuition with Remote Viewing......................79
   Holographic Nature of Life 79
   Remote Viewing Ethics...82
   A Simple Exercise to Calm Your Mind..82

8: Practical Applications of Remote Viewing 84
   Remote Viewing Exercises at Home..84
   Remote Viewing a Person Using Their Name................................87
   Remote Viewing of Food 89
   Everyday Applications for Remote Viewing Targets 90

9: Remote Viewing of Your Body.. 246
   How Remote Viewing Can Support Your
      Health and Healing 247
   How to Use This Guide to Remote View
      Organs and Body Parts.. 247

10: The Future of Remote Viewing 320
   The Most Important Question: *"What is right for me?"*.............. 320
   Integration with Other Disciplines 321
   Developing Consciousness and the Mind 322
   The Role of AI and Technology in Remote Viewing 322
   Striking a Balance Between Intuition and Technology 323
   Misuse of Technology in Remote Viewing 323
   Conclusion: Remote Viewing as a

11: Reflecting on Your Progress 325
   Assessing Your Growth and Achievements 325
   What Actions Should You Take? 325
   Setting Goals for Continued Practice 326

12: Appendices 328
Glossary of Terms: 329
Recommended Resources 333
Sample Exercises and Templates 335
Setting Up Practice Groups and Sessions 338

Available from Dr. Irina Webster: 340
Membership Program: *Remote Viewing with Intuitive Healing*
11-Week Intuitive Healing Practitioner Course
11-Week Empath Practitioner Course
Intuitive Healing and Remote Viewing Meditations
Dr. Irina's Published Books and Resources

KEY INSIGHT

"Remote Viewing reminds us that the boundaries between the physical and the intuitive are illusions—we are all connected in infinite ways."

Purpose:
Introduce remote viewing as a practice for unity, interconnectedness, and the absence of duality.

DEDICATION

This book is dedicated to everyone working to unite people and move beyond division and duality in the world. Your efforts to create unity and understanding are an inspiration. Through remote viewing, we explore the idea that everything in the world is interconnected. Remote viewing interconnects people through *energy* by tapping into the universal field of consciousness, enabling the transfer of information and awareness beyond physical boundaries.

PREFACE

Thank you for picking up this book. I hope that the insights within will help you as profoundly as they've helped me and countless others. In fact, I hope this book transforms your life.

Now, more than ever, it is essential to understand the interconnectedness of all things. Remote viewing reveals the unity of all things, emphasizing the *energetic* connections that bind the universe together. It invites us to experience a world where all parts come together as one. Through remote viewing, we tap into the universal field of consciousness and discover that, *energetically*, there is no separation between anything or anyone.

"We are all One"
– The Guiding Principle of Remote Viewing

Remote viewing serves as a gateway to the *oneness of the universe*, allowing anyone to access the vast *energy field* that extends beyond physical boundaries. By tapping into this field, you can move beyond the limits of space and time.

The guiding principle of "All is One" teaches that separation is an illusion—people, places, objects, and locations are energetically interconnected. Your unconscious mind already knows the energetic imprint of any target you seek. During a session, all you need to do is *align yourself with its energy field*.

Remote viewing is not a special gift or an innate talent limited to a select few. It is a skill that anyone can learn through practice and dedication.

Why I Teach Remote Viewing with Intuitive Healing

My journey began in conventional medicine and later shifted to intuitive healing. Over time, I have come to see these disciplines as deeply interconnected. Early in my career as a medical doctor, I explored Psychoneuroimmunology—the science of the mind-body connection. The discipline taught me to perceive organs and body parts energetically. During this process, I realized that this method of energetic perception could extend beyond the body to any object or target in the universe.

Because of this realization, I now teach remote viewing integrated with intuitive healing, emphasizing its benefits not only for connecting with external targets but also for reconnecting with and healing our bodies and minds. My goal is to teach remote viewing as a path to self-healing, as it allows us to connect with the universal field of oneness, which is inherently healing.

In this book, you will find a blend of theory and practical guidance designed to make remote viewing accessible to all. Whether you are new to these concepts or have experience in intuitive work, this journey will deepen your understanding of both the universe and yourself. Remote viewing provides a way to reach beyond the physical realm, and integrating it with intuitive healing opens pathways to a richer, more unified experience of existence.

As you move through these pages, may you discover your own connection to the universal energy that binds us all. May you find within yourself the power to heal and the wisdom to navigate the mysteries of life, knowing that you are part of a greater whole. This book is my offering to you—a guide to harnessing remote viewing and intuitive healing in a way that transforms both inner and outer worlds.

Irina Webster

INTRODUCTION

Imagine having the ability to see beyond the visible world—to sense what is concealed from view and gather insights from distant places, as if the boundaries of space and time no longer exist.

Now is the perfect time to embrace this, as we have entered a new era—the energetic era. It's truly a remarkable time to be alive. Never before have there been so many possibilities and opportunities for you to become who you aspire to be, achieve your goals, and contribute to a better world. In fact, you might feel as if you're drowning in options. With countless paths to choose from, the ability to make decisions becomes a crucial factor in what you accomplish in life.

If you're like many people today, you may feel overwhelmed by the sheer volume of tasks and the limited time available. How do you determine what truly matters? How can you decide what to prioritize now and what can wait? How do you look beyond the physical realm to uncover what is hidden yet profoundly significant?

Remote viewing may be the key to accessing information that remains invisible yet essential.

My first encounter with this extraordinary ability came during a medical training session in Russia, where I found myself amidst an unconventional group of doctors and scientists. Among them were two Russian practitioners who had developed a rare skill during the Cold War: *remote viewing*—the art of perceiving distant locations, objects, and events with the mind alone.

As they shared stories of success and accuracy, it felt like science fiction, yet the connection was undeniable, even tangible. They weren't just observing objects or locations; they were seeing beyond the physical realm into an energy field that unites us all. I realized that remote viewing was more than an ability—it was a window into the oneness of existence, and I was standing on the edge, ready to see for myself.

The Current Reality: How It Is

Today, most people live with a limited understanding of reality, one that only acknowledges the visible, physical world. We're taught to believe in the separation between ourselves and everything else around us—other people, countries, distant places, and even our own physical bodies. However, the notion of interconnectedness is quietly gaining traction, with studies in quantum mechanics and consciousness suggesting that this separation may be an illusion.

In medical practice, I observed how psychological states affected patients' physical health, and as I studied Psychoneuroimmunology, I discovered that our minds and bodies are not separate entities but parts of a larger whole. What could we achieve if we recognized this interconnectedness in a more direct, practical way?

What Could Be: Exploring Limitless Potential

Imagine a world where distance and time don't limit you. You could reach across continents, connect with loved ones, or find answers to questions that seem out of reach. Remote viewing offers precisely that possibility – a tool that brings us closer to the unity underlying everything. With it, you can observe events across the globe, gain insight into your health, or connect with the energy of someone far away. Remote viewing offers a bridge between science and spirituality, a way to actively experience the universal oneness that we're all a part of.

Science and spirituality unite in Remote Viewing, proving their connection through the universal field of consciousness.

My Journey and Credentials

This book represents a unique fusion of my experiences and expertise as a medical doctor, healer, medical intuitive, and remote viewer. Born and raised in Russia, I have always been attuned to the energies around me, and this sensitivity guided me to explore both medicine and the human psyche. I graduated in 1993 as a medical doctor from Northern State Medical University and pursued further specialization in immunology and allergy at the Medical University of St. Petersburg. It was here, through my study of psychoneuroimmunology, that I first encountered the idea of remote viewing.

In an informal group of Russian medical practitioners, I was introduced to a once-secret skill, refined during the Cold War to uncover hidden information. This skill was rooted in telepathy—the ability to transfer consciousness across time and space.

As members of this informal group, we used these telepathic abilities to energetically connect with the bodies and organs of others, as well as ourselves, from a distance.

I continue to use these skills in my practice today and teach others how to do the same. By applying remote viewing in medical settings, I developed a unique approach that addresses not only physical ailments but also the deeper, unseen layers of energy and consciousness.

What You'll Find in This Book

This book is both a guide and an invitation. It will introduce you to the principles and practices of remote viewing and show you how to harness this ability for personal growth, healing, and expanded understanding. Here's what you can expect:

1. **Foundations of Remote Viewing** – Explore the core principles, science, and telepathic elements of remote viewing, providing a grounded understanding of its roots and methodologies.

2. **The Practice of Intuitive Healing** – Discover how remote viewing and intuitive healing come together to offer insights into physical and emotional health.
3. **Stages and Protocols** – Follow a step-by-step guide to the structured process of remote viewing, with methods you can learn and practice.
4. **Historical Insights and Real-life Accounts** – Read stories from CIA-funded programs, Russian scientific experiments, and personal insights from renowned remote viewers.
5. **Ethical Considerations and Responsible Practice** – Understand the ethical responsibilities involved, emphasizing neutrality and kind intentions.
6. **Applications and Transformative Power** – Learn how remote viewing can enhance personal growth and awareness, including its role in medical intuition.
7. **Connection to Oneness** – Delve into the philosophical exploration of how remote viewing taps into the universal oneness that links us all.

Each chapter builds upon the last, offering a complete roadmap from understanding the fundamentals to exploring complex applications in healing and beyond. As you engage with this material, you'll find a guide not just to remote viewing but to a deeper, more connected experience of life itself.

I invite you to take this journey with an open mind. Through the practice of remote viewing, may you uncover the invisible threads that bind us all and find your place in the vast, interconnected tapestry of existence.

Learning from the Experts

Over the years, I've studied the work of numerous experts in remote viewing. Many were involved in pioneering programs during the Cold War, such as the CIA-funded Stargate Project in the United States and similar initiatives in Russia. These early practitioners honed their skills under strict secrecy, yet their impact has lasted far beyond those original programs. In recent years, new generations of remote viewers have emerged, bringing fresh perspectives and insights.

One trend stands out among all these experts: once they truly experienced remote viewing, they never stopped practicing, even long after those government projects ended. For many, remote viewing transformed from a skill into a calling. They became dedicated teachers, driven by a mission to share the message of oneness. To them, remote viewing isn't simply a tool or technique; it's a way to promote unity and help others recognize the interconnectedness of all things.

In this chapter, I've gathered quotes from both American and Russian practitioners, reflecting on remote viewing as a powerful tool for connection and understanding. Their words reveal the profound and transformative impact remote viewing can have on our perception of reality and our place within it.

Quotes from American Practitioners

"Remote viewing is a powerful tool for accessing information beyond ordinary perception. It allows us to explore hidden dimensions of reality, offering insights that can transform our understanding and decision-making."
— Dr. Russell Targ, physicist and remote viewing researcher.

"Remote viewing reveals the interconnectedness of all things, offering a unique perspective that can guide personal and professional choices with greater wisdom."
— Joe McMoneagle, former military remote viewer and author.

"Remote viewing can be seen as a bridge between the conscious and unconscious mind, providing clarity and guidance in navigating life's complex decisions."
— Dr. Edgar Mitchell, Apollo astronaut and remote viewing proponent.

"By tapping into remote viewing abilities, one can gain access to a broader spectrum of information and possibilities, enhancing personal growth and strategic decision-making."
— Major Ed Dames, former military remote viewer.

Quotes from Russian Practitioners

"The practice of remote viewing opens doors to hidden realms, enabling us to gather information that transcends conventional limits of time and space."
— Dr. Vladimir Kotelnikov, Russian scientist and remote viewing expert.

"Through remote viewing, we can access information that is not readily available to the senses, offering a deeper understanding of both our environment and ourselves."
— Dr. Alexander Kozlov, Russian remote viewing researcher.

"Remote viewing is a method for tapping into the collective unconscious, allowing us to gain insights and solve problems that might otherwise remain elusive."
— Dr. Andrei Tsvetkov, Russian scientist and remote viewing researcher.

"Remote Viewing demonstrates that consciousness is not bound by space or time, revealing the inherent interconnectedness of all existence,"
— Nikolai Kozyrev, Russian astronomer and astrophysicist.

Chapter 1:
What is Remote Viewing?

A modern dictionary defines remote viewing as follows:
"Remote viewing is *the ability to acquire accurate information about a **distant** or **non-local** place, person, or event without using your physical senses or any other obvious means.*"

The concept of remote viewing has ancient roots, with similar practices evident in various cultures throughout history. In ancient civilizations, such as Egypt, Greece, and Rome, seers and oracles used techniques akin to remote viewing to access hidden knowledge and predict future events. However, it wasn't until the 20th century that remote viewing became formalized as a scientific practice.

During the Cold War, the United States government, intrigued by reports of Soviet psychic experiments, initiated research programs like the Stargate Project. These programs aimed to explore the potential of remote viewing for espionage and military intelligence gathering. The most notable research was conducted at the Stanford Research Institute, where physicists Harold Puthoff and Russell Targ worked with renowned psychic Ingo Swann to develop a standardized protocol for remote viewing.

History and Evolution of Remote Viewing

Since its initial exploration during the Cold War, remote viewing has evolved beyond its military origins.

Today, remote viewing techniques have been adapted for civilian use, with individuals and groups around the world practicing and teaching remote viewing for purposes ranging from personal development to exploring consciousness.

Remote viewing is now applied in various fields, including:

- Archaeology
- History
- Forensics and Criminology
- Legal Investigations
- Security and Threat Assessment
- Finding Lost Objects or People
- Financial Forecasting
- Fashion Trends Forecasting
- Medical Research
- Environmental and Ecological Studies
- Creative Industries
- Science (e.g., cosmology, quantum physics)
- Spirituality and Psychology
- Research on Consciousness and Mind
- Personal Development

Remote viewing has gained popularity among those intrigued by the metaphysical, who see it as a pathway to unlocking human potential and exploring deeper layers of reality. While some scientists remain sceptical, the practice continues to attract interest and research, bridging the realms of science, spirituality, and human consciousness.

In Russian, remote viewing is often referred to as "**дистанционное видение**" (distantsionnoye videnie) or "**дистанционное восприятие**" (distantsionnoye vospriyatie), which translates to "remote vision" or "remote perception."

During the Soviet era, remote viewing was studied under the umbrellas of parapsychology and psychotronics as part of military and intelligence research. Soviet scientists and military personnel explored psychic abilities, including remote viewing, for espionage and national defence. This research often emphasized practical applications, including medical uses.

Difference Between Remote Viewing and Other Psychic Abilities

Remote viewing differs from other psychic abilities primarily in its structured and teachable nature. It **can be learned** through specific protocols, while psychic abilities are generally considered innate.

Psychic abilities like clairvoyance and mediumship often rely on spontaneous insights and unique talents. In contrast, remote viewing follows a disciplined protocol allowing nearly anyone to develop the skill with practice. It involves focusing the mind to perceive details about a distant or unseen target without using the physical senses.

Picture1: Remote Viewing and other Psychic abilities.

Key Differences:

Conscious Control: Remote viewing requires conscious effort to gather information, unlike clairvoyance, which often provides random or unbidden visions.

Teachability: Remote viewing can be taught and practiced systematically, while psychic abilities often depend on natural sensitivity.

Verification: Remote viewing results can be documented, repeated, and verified, whereas psychic phenomena are typically harder to validate.

Scientific Approach: Remote viewing is studied in controlled settings, offering a more scientific framework compared to the mystical perception of other psychic abilities.

Table 1. Comparison chart between Remote Viewing and Psychic Ability.

Criteria	Remote Viewing	Psychic Ability
Structure	Follows specific protocols and methods	Generally spontaneous and unstructured
Teachability	Can be taught and learned by most people	Relies on innate talents or natural abilities
Conscious Control	Requires conscious effort to gather information	Often occurs without conscious control
Verification	Results can be documented, repeated, and verified	Difficult to verify or replicate
Focus	Directs awareness to specific targets	May provide random or unbidden insights
Psychic Sensitivity	Less reliant on natural psychic sensitivity	Strongly reliant on the individual's psychic gifts
Purpose	Often used for specific, practical tasks	Can be used for a variety of purposes, often less defined
Connection to Science	Has a more scientific approach	Viewed as mystical or spiritual, with less scientific backing

Why Is It Important to Learn Remote Viewing Today?

On a collective level, remote viewing bridges science and spirituality, blending two perspectives critical to navigating the complexities of modern life. Science helps us understand the physical world, while spirituality connects us to deeper meanings—our purpose and our sense of being part of something greater.

On a personal level, remote viewing facilitates a profound transformation, guiding individuals from a purely physical, materialistic perspective—focused solely on the tangible—towards a more spiritual or energetic understanding of life. This shift aligns with the new paradigm that emphasizes the interconnectedness of energy and consciousness.

By combining these two approaches, remote viewing offers a more complete picture of life. This balance fosters holistic solutions to challenges and encourages both personal and societal growth.

Remote Viewing Benefits:
- Expands human potential.
- Enhances personal growth and awareness.
- Provides unique perspectives.
- Facilitates problem-solving beyond the physical level.
- Elevates consciousness and perception.
- Encourages exploration beyond the physical realm.
- Improves focus and discipline.

By integrating science and spirituality, we move beyond duality and embrace the interconnectedness of all things, fostering a more compassionate and meaningful existence.

My Experiences with Remote Viewing

Remote viewing skills have profoundly contributed to my personal growth, enabling me to adapt and transform in alignment with life's ever-changing demands.

My Introduction to Remote Viewing

Have you heard of the Stargate Project? During the Cold War, this secret U.S. operation used remote viewing to gather intelligence on the Russians. Interestingly, the Russians had their own team of remote viewers conducting similar operations. I was fortunate to meet two members of this Russian team, Alex and Oleg, who shared intriguing details about their experiences and techniques.

However, my sensitivity to remote viewing dates back even further—to my childhood.

Growing up in Russia, I was deeply sensitive and intuitive. As a child, I often described people in colours, saying things like, *"Aunt Galina is green today,"* or *"Grandad feels so brown."* These perceptions, dismissed by my parents as imagination, often turned out to reflect real truths. These early experiences laid the foundation for my journey into remote viewing.

My Childhood Experiences with Remote Viewing

I clearly remember certain situations from my childhood that revealed my intuitive viewing sensitivity.

When I was six years old, I had a strong feeling about our neighbour, Ivan. I often played in the park next to his house and chatted with him during our encounters. One day, I told my mum, Nina, that I sensed something was wrong with Ivan—that he was feeling very sad, even though he hadn't mentioned anything troubling.

My mum, though sceptical, decided to check in on him. To her surprise, she discovered that Ivan's sister had just passed away from cancer. My feeling had been accurate. This deeply impressed my mum and showed me, even at a young age, how attuned I was to others' emotions.

When I was about nine, our neighbour's dog, Rex, went missing. The entire neighbourhood searched for him, but he was nowhere to be found. One day, I had a sudden, strong feeling that Rex was trapped somewhere. I told my mum that I had a sense he might be stuck in an old shed near the edge of the field.

Although doubtful, my mum agreed to check it out. When we arrived, we found Rex trapped inside, wedged between some old crates. He was frightened but unharmed. I felt immense relief and pride, knowing that my intuition had led us straight to him. That experience reinforced my belief in the power and accuracy of our feelings, even as children.

Now I understand that highly sensitive people like myself are naturally inclined toward telepathy, which forms the basis of remote viewing.

However, sensitivity isn't a prerequisite for practicing remote viewing. Many well-known remote viewers are not particularly sensitive but are often highly intellectual—scientists, physicists, engineers, psychologists, and other professionals. Look at this story...

Transformation of an Intellectual Through Remote Viewing: The Story of Dmitri Ivanov

During my postgraduate studies in Immunology and Allergy at St. Petersburg University, I came across a fascinating story about an intellectual and sceptic whose life was transformed by remote viewing.

The Transformation of an Intellectual and a Non-Believer

Dmitri Ivanov, a respected professor of physics, was known for his logical mind and scepticism toward anything unscientific. However, his former student, Elena, demonstrated her ability to accurately "see" hidden objects through remote viewing, which piqued Dmitri's curiosity. Intrigued but doubtful, he decided to research the practice and conduct his own experiments.

Initially, Dmitri struggled to make sense of his experiences, but as he persisted, he began achieving increasingly accurate results. He perceived distant places and events with clarity that surprised him. Gradually, Dmitri theorized that remote viewing might be connected to the principles of quantum mechanics, suggesting that consciousness could transcend the boundaries of space and time.

Through this journey, Dmitri's understanding of the universe shifted dramatically. What once seemed impossible became a gateway to a new perception of reality, revealing the vast interconnectedness of existence.

As a result of this transformation, Dmitri completely reimagined his approach to teaching. His lectures began to integrate a spiritual and energetic perspective alongside factual, scientific knowledge. This balanced approach resonated deeply with his students, who found his teachings both insightful and inspiring. Despite facing opposition from some colleagues, Dmitri's openness sparked a shift among a few of them as well. These individuals gradually moved away from rigid, purely scientific viewpoints toward a more balanced perspective, incorporating spirituality and even remote viewing into their teaching and personal lives. Dmitri's journey not only transformed his own understanding but also influenced an entire academic community, bridging the gap between science and spirituality.

My First Adult Experience with Remote Viewing

My first encounter with remote viewing as an adult happened in the mid-1990s when I was working as a junior doctor. After graduating in 1993 with a specialization in paediatrics, I developed a keen interest in immunology and allergies. This led me to pursue a postgraduate course at the Medical University of St. Petersburg, where I discovered the emerging field of psychoneuroimmunology, which studies how the psyche affects the body.

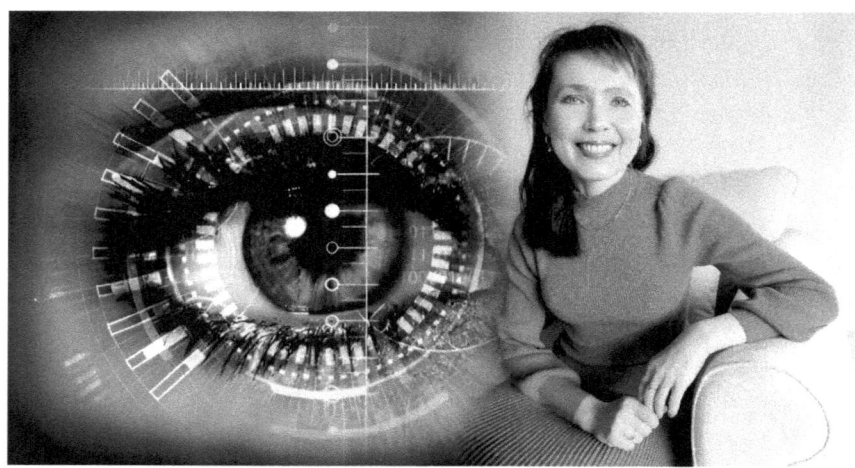

Dr Irina Webster: Remote Viewing

During my studies, I joined an informal group of medical professionals interested in psychoneuroimmunology. We practiced sensing organs and body parts to detect emotions trapped within them and understand how these emotions affected the body. We used telepathy to connect with the energy of these organs.

Word of our group's activities spread, and one day we were visited by Alex and Oleg, former members of a remote viewing team at Saint Petersburg State University during the Cold War. They shared that the techniques they used for espionage were remarkably similar to our telepathic methods for connecting with the human body.

This experience profoundly impacted me and shaped my future path.

From Russia to Australia: Continuing the Journey
When I moved to Australia in 2001, I brought with me the research I had begun in Russia on psychoneuroimmunology. I continued my work by writing a book titled *The Secret Energy of Your Body*. In it, I explored how emotions transform into energy within the body, influencing the development of diseases and symptoms, and how this process can be reversed by shifting emotions and energy.

In Australia, I also discovered the Stargate Project, a U.S. government initiative during the Cold War, which mirrored Russian efforts in remote viewing. Both nations shared a fascination with the potential applications of this practice in science and military intelligence.

Historical Background of Remote Viewing
Remote viewing has deep historical roots.

In ancient Greece, doctors would enter altered, dreamlike states to intuitively access information about their patients' illnesses. These intuitive body scans functioned similarly to modern diagnostic tools like x-rays, MRIs, or CT scans and were reportedly very accurate. Ancient texts suggest that these practitioners were scanning a person's energy and energy centers—techniques that align closely with what we call 'medical intuition' today.

26 | Remote Viewing

Ancient Greek doctors knew about remote viewing.

In Roman times, remote viewing-like practices were closely associated with augury and divination. Seers and priests claimed to perceive distant events or gain knowledge beyond ordinary senses. Augurs, highly respected officials, interpreted the will of the gods by observing natural signs such as the flight of birds or the entrails of sacrificed animals. Although not remote viewing in the modern sense, these rituals often involved gaining insights into **distant or future events**. They were regarded as trustworthy and dependable, playing a crucial role in decision-making.

Historical Evolution of Remote Viewing: From Ancient Times to the 20th Century

Ancient and Classical Practices

Romans believed certain individuals possessed the ability to connect with distant places and foresee the future, offering critical guidance to emperors, generals, and the wealthy. This form of proto-remote viewing was highly valued for decision-making, blending mystical practices with the pragmatic needs of an expanding empire. Predictions guided significant events such as wars, conquests, and the construction of cities and fortifications.

Divination and scrying.

In Medieval times, remote viewing was often intertwined with practices of divination and scrying, although it was not recognized by that name. Mystics and seers were believed to perceive events and locations beyond their immediate presence, using tools like crystal balls, reflective surfaces, or deep meditation. These practices, shrouded in secrecy, were primarily reserved for rulers and military leaders seeking insights into battles or governance. Abilities like these were both revered and feared, forming an integral part of the spiritual and cultural fabric of the era.

The Industrial Revolution and Remote Viewing
The Industrial Revolution, with its rapid technological advancements and emphasis on empirical reasoning, created a dichotomy for remote viewing. Despite the growing emphasis on empirical evidence and rational thought, remote viewing persisted as a clandestine practice among those who believed in the power of the mind to transcend physical limitations. While mainstream society focused on mechanization and industrial growth, a small but dedicated group of practitioners continued to explore remote viewing, often in secret, seeking insights beyond the material world. This period saw

a tension between the rise of industrial science and the enduring fascination with the metaphysical, with remote viewing serving as a reminder of the human quest for knowledge beyond the tangible.

These figures and events demonstrate how the Industrial Revolution contributed to the eventual emergence of remote viewing as a studied phenomenon.

Franz Anton Mesmer and Hypnosis (Late 18th Century):

Mesmer's work with "mesmerism," later known as hypnotism, sparked interest in the power of the mind to influence the body. While not remote viewing, it laid the foundation for later exploration of extrasensory perception (ESP), which would include remote viewing.

Spiritualism (Mid-19th Century):

The rise of spiritualist movements brought attention to mediums and claims of perceiving events beyond the physical senses. This idea of accessing unseen realms influenced later concepts of remote viewing, even if the two are not identical.

Scientific Exploration of Consciousness:

Intellectual advancements during the Industrial Revolution, like Charles Babbage's work in early computing, fostered a broader interest in the potential of the human mind. This curiosity around mental abilities would eventually lead to modern studies of psychic phenomena, including remote viewing.

These ideas contributed to a growing belief in the power of the mind to access information beyond the physical world, paving the way for the formal study of remote viewing in the 20th century.

The Victorian Era (1837-1901)

The Victorian fascination with the occult and spiritualism created a fertile ground for remote viewing practices. Despite the period's strong emphasis on science and rationality, many Victorians were captivated by the mysteries of the unseen world. Séances, mediumship, and other forms of paranormal exploration became popular, particularly among the upper classes. Remote viewing, though not widely recognized by that name, was practiced in various forms by those seeking to tap into hidden knowledge or explore distant places without physical travel. This era saw the blending of mysticism with emerging scientific inquiry, as some intellectuals and spiritualists attempted to legitimize such abilities through studies and experiments. The Victorian fascination with the supernatural kept remote viewing alive, albeit often in secret or within niche circles, as society grappled with the boundaries between the material and spiritual worlds.

Remote Viewing During the World Wars

World War I

Remote viewing, while not formalized, captured the interest of military and civilian circles. The war period saw an increased interest in various forms of psychic phenomena, as both sides sought any advantage they could find. Remote viewing, though often intertwined with other psychic practices such as telepathy and clairvoyance, was explored discreetly by some military and intelligence personnel seeking to gain insights into enemy plans and locations.

This era also saw the rise of various paranormal research organizations and the continued work of individual practitioners who were interested in understanding and harnessing psychic abilities for strategic purposes. Despite the focus on empirical and technological advancements in warfare, the quest for knowledge beyond conventional means persisted, reflecting a complex interplay between scientific progress and metaphysical exploration during the tumultuous years of the First World War.

Interwar Period (1920s-1930s)

The years between the wars saw a mix of scepticism and curiosity as researchers and enthusiasts delved into the study of psychic phenomena. During this period, remote viewing was explored in the context of broader paranormal research, often alongside telepathy and clairvoyance. Although formal recognition and scientific validation remained elusive, the 1920s and 1930s witnessed the rise of influential figures and organizations dedicated to studying the mind's potential. This era also saw increased public interest in spiritualism and occult practices, which fuelled ongoing investigations into remote viewing. The interwar period laid important groundwork for future research, reflecting a persistent intrigue with the capabilities of the human mind even as the world prepared for another global conflict.

World War II
Both Allied and Axis powers discreetly experimented with psychic phenomena, including remote viewing, as part of espionage efforts. Both sides experimented with various forms of extrasensory perception in hopes of uncovering enemy plans and gaining tactical insights. Although these efforts were often shrouded in secrecy and met with scepticism from mainstream scientific communities, they contributed to the growing body of knowledge about psychic abilities. The war's demands for innovation and edge in intelligence led to increased funding and interest in parapsychological research, which would later influence the development of more structured programs in the Cold War era. The wartime exploration of remote viewing reflected a broader trend of seeking novel methods to address the challenges of global conflict.

Soviet and Nazi Interest in Psychic Research
The Soviet Union, after the war, became deeply invested in studying psychic phenomena, which later included remote viewing. However, some reports suggest that Nazi Germany had also explored the potential of psychic abilities for espionage and military advantage during the war. Some accounts claim that German occultists and SS officers were involved in experiments related to remote viewing and other paranormal activities, though much of this is speculative. After the war, both the USSR and the U.S.

began more formal investigations into these abilities during the Cold War.

The U.S. and Allied Interest

During World War II, the U.S. military began investigating unconventional methods, including psychic phenomena, in the belief that it could offer a strategic advantage. The **Office of Strategic Services (OSS)**, the precursor to the CIA, was reportedly interested in exploring the use of psychic abilities for intelligence-gathering. This included the study of psychics who claimed to have the ability to see remote locations or events. Some of the early research into psychic phenomena in the U.S. during this time would later lay the groundwork for the **Stargate Project**, a more formalized study of remote viewing during the Cold War.

While the full extent of these programs during World War II is not entirely clear, the war acted as a catalyst for governments to explore the potential military applications of psychic phenomena, including remote viewing. These early investigations into "psi" abilities continued into the post-war period and were further developed during the Cold War.

Post-War Developments and the Cold War

The post-war period, marked by the development of nuclear weapons and heightened geopolitical tensions, accelerated the exploration of remote viewing and psychic research. Both the United States and the Soviet Union sought to leverage these abilities as part of their broader intelligence strategies.

Soviet Union:
The Soviets conducted extensive research into psychic phenomena, often in secretive environments like Moscow and Leningrad. Figures such as Nina Kulagina, a psychic who reportedly demonstrated psychokinetic abilities, became central to these efforts. Her feats were studied in controlled experiments, although skeptics questioned their authenticity. Soviet research revealed that trained individuals

could accurately describe distant locations and events, providing valuable intelligence about Western military activities and technological developments.

United States:
In the 1970s, the CIA launched the Stargate Project, a classified program dedicated to investigating remote viewing for intelligence gathering. One of its most notable participants, Ingo Swann, impressed officials by accurately describing distant locations and objects. Swann's work helped establish protocols still used in remote viewing practices today, cementing its reputation as a tool for military and intelligence purposes.

Stargate Project: blending science and the mystical

Cold War Exploration of Remote Viewing

The Cold War, characterized by rapid advancements in nuclear technology and intense competition between superpowers, created an environment ripe for exploring unconventional intelligence methods. Remote viewing emerged as a significant focus, blending scientific innovation with the fringes of human perception.

Applications in Intelligence and Strategy

Both the Soviet Union and the United States demonstrated the practical potential of remote viewing. Trained individuals provided insights into military strategies, technological developments, and even classified sites. These capabilities were seen as tools to mitigate threats and maintain strategic superiority.

Intersection with Science and Medicine

In the Soviet Union, remote viewing research extended beyond espionage, with medical professionals using these abilities to explore healing and deepen their understanding of the human mind. This multidisciplinary approach highlighted the broader applications of psychic phenomena.

Key Figures and Programs

Nina Kulagina (Soviet Union):
A prominent psychic, Kulagina's reported abilities to move objects with her mind drew significant attention during the 1960s and 1970s. She became a symbol of Soviet interest in the potential of psychic research for both scientific and military purposes.

Ingo Swann (United States):
Swann's contributions to the Stargate Project were pivotal in legitimizing remote viewing as a tool for intelligence operations. His work demonstrated the ability to perceive remote targets with remarkable accuracy, bridging the gap between psychic phenomena and structured scientific inquiry.

Global Impact and Legacy

The exploration of remote viewing during the Cold War demonstrated a willingness among governments to investigate unconventional methods for gaining intelligence and addressing strategic challenges. These efforts not only advanced the understanding of psychic phenomena but also showcased the enduring human quest to explore the limits of perception and consciousness.

The research conducted during this period laid the foundation for modern studies of remote viewing, blending ancient practices with scientific rigor. Programs like the Stargate Project and their Soviet counterparts reflected the complex interplay of competition, innovation, and the persistent intrigue surrounding the capabilities of the human mind.

Chapter 2:
Remote Viewing in Health and Wellness

Medicine: How Remote Viewing Enhances Healing
In Russia, it was more common than in the West for doctors to rely on knowledge beyond conventional understanding, often using unconventional methods to diagnose and treat patients, including remote viewing.

Here, I share stories from my personal experiences as a doctor, highlighting the profound insights gained along the way.

"Sleeping Elena"
- A Story of Remote Viewing with Intuitive Healing

This story takes me back to my university years. As a medical student specializing in pediatrics at Northern State Medical University, I studied under Professor Elena Nikolaevna, a neonatologist who worked with newborns. At first glance, she seemed like a typical professor: accredited, knowledgeable, and dedicated to teaching and conducting practical work in the children's hospital. Yet, there was something unique about her. People quietly referred to her as "Sleeping Elena" due to the unusual way she treated critically ill infants who weren't responding to conventional care.

Elena's approach was simple yet remarkable. She would sit alone in a room with a severely ill newborn, wrapping her arms around the child without actually touching them. Breathing deeply for a few moments, she would enter a timeless, almost trance-like state, disconnecting entirely from the outside world. Her eyes would fixate on a single spot, or sometimes she'd close them, appearing frozen yet fully awake. It was as if she was in a different dimension of consciousness, beyond the logical mind, allowing her to connect deeply with the infant's energy.

She would sit like this with a child for 40 minutes, an hour, or even longer, maintaining an intense, silent presence. When she was finished, she'd quietly leave the room, allowing the nurses to continue their care. The effects of these sessions were often profound, with many babies showing marked improvement afterward. No one could explain these transformations logically, and Elena rarely spoke about it openly. Though parents would approach her, even offering money to repeat this technique with their sick children, she never accepted payment, preferring to keep her practice private and low-key. People spoke about her work with a sense of reverence, as if whispering could somehow preserve its mystery.

I remember her as a brilliant, compassionate doctor who carefully separated her conventional duties from her "sitting method." Looking back, it seemed like she was tapping into the energy field around these infants, perhaps even practicing a form of remote viewing that brought about genuine change.

I share this story not to suggest that Western doctors should sit quietly with their patients but to show that when a healer believes in what they are doing and commit their energy fully, powerful results can sometimes occur, even without a clear explanation.

To add to Elena's story, her journey into the "sitting method" began with profound challenges with her own children. She had two daughters: the older child was healthy, but her second was born premature with Down Syndrome. This diagnosis included not only developmental delays but also a congenital heart defect. Her younger daughter often turned blue from heart insufficiency and struggled to breathe, requiring frequent artificial respiration. With a weakened immune system, she frequently caught colds and infections, which made her "blue spells" even worse.

Her prognosis was grim, and as a neonatologist, Elena was devastated that she couldn't save her own child. Desperate, she began her "sitting" practice, cradling her daughter without touching her and entering a state of timeless stillness for hours until someone would come in and interrupt. Astonishingly, after one of these sessions, her daughter's condition began to improve. Though the full details remain unknown, Elena likely continued this practice with her daughter.

I personally met Elena's younger daughter when she was six, as Elena brought her in to demonstrate to medical students how to care for a child with Down Syndrome. While she still had Down Syndrome, she was well-adjusted and in good health, with no blue spells, respiratory issues, or frequent infections. She was thriving, a child who had once been expected to die.

This experience transformed Elena, inspiring her to become the "sitting doctor" or "sleeping doctor" for her critically ill patients, offering a unique, deeply compassionate practice that brought comfort and healing to many.

Remote Viewing of Gallstones: A Life-Saving Insight

Anna's story demonstrates the transformative power of remote viewing in self-healing. Anna had suffered from debilitating gallstone attacks for years, often requiring hospitalization and morphine to manage the pain. While her doctor recommended surgery, Anna sought an alternative approach.

I taught her to perform a body scan—a technique similar to remote viewing of an organ, where you tune into your body's subtle energy to observe it deeply.

As Anna practiced this form of remote viewing on her gallbladder, she made a surprising discovery: a day or two before an attack, her abdominal area would feel bloated and warm. This sensation only appeared just before her episodes, serving as an early warning.

With this newfound awareness, Anna took medication as soon as she sensed these signs.

Over time, her attacks became less intense and eventually stopped entirely. By using body scans as a form of remote viewing, Anna connected deeply with her own body's signals, breaking the cycle of pain before symptoms could fully set in. This skillful self-observation through organ-focused remote viewing was a game-changer in her healing journey.

Empowered by her experience, Anna began practicing remote viewing on all her organs, tuning into her body's signals regularly, and even taught her children how to do it. This skill has become a powerful tool for them, helping each of them safeguard their health in remarkable ways.

Remote Viewing in the Children's Rehab Centre

When doctors envision a desired outcome and set clear goals while working with children, it leads to positive and impactful results, promoting better health outcomes and overall well-being.

After graduating from medical school and completing my specialization, I worked as an immunologist-allergist in a children's hospital, specifically in a department called the Rehab Centre for Frequently Sick Children in northwest Russia. This center brought together a variety of specialists and facilities to offer treatments, primarily focusing on alternative therapies. Children would undergo courses of treatment lasting from 30 to 60 days.

A Holistic Approach to Healing

The center provided treatments such as:
- Daily massages and physiotherapy tailored to specific conditions.
- Herbal therapy, including inhalations and supervised consumption, guided by a herbalist.
- Breathing techniques, such as Buteyko.
- Psychological support, including child psychologists and mind therapists.

- Art therapy, vocal therapy, and dietary plans to support emotional and physical well-being.
- Specialized gymnastics and other non-traditional methods.

Each day, children arrived with their parents for these treatments, typically staying for half a day or longer as needed, before returning home and coming back the next morning.

Remote Viewing for Future Health
Doctors' expectations and the visualization of the desired outcome play a crucial role in achieving the results they anticipate.

As an immunologist-allergist, I worked primarily with children suffering from conditions such as asthma, allergic dermatitis, eczema, atopic dermatitis, respiratory allergies like allergic rhinitis (hay fever), and food allergies. While we prescribed conventional treatments like inhalers, antihistamines, allergy shots (immunotherapy), and steroids, I noticed a remarkable trend: after completing a 30- to 60-day course of non-traditional treatments, many children showed significant improvements in their conditions—even with reduced medication or none at all.

Before starting these alternative treatments, **we set clear goals for what we hoped to achieve in each child's health**. We envisioned the desired improvements before they occurred. Then, as the child went through the treatment course under our supervision, we continuously guided them toward these improvements. It was akin to performing remote viewing of a patient's future state and actively monitoring their progress—what I refer to as *remote viewing of the future state*.

I observed significant health improvements in the children after these courses. Some even experienced a complete cessation of asthma attacks for an entire season, a year, or longer. Afterward, we would often repeat the course.

Other health conditions in children showed similar outcomes when specialists set goals for what to expect after 30 to 60 days, leading to notable improvements. These conditions included neurological disorders, musculoskeletal issues, paralysis, ear-nose-throat problems, brain-related issues, digestive disorders, and more. It's worth mentioning that these courses were government-funded, with only a few treatments requiring additional fees from parents.

As I reflect on my experiences while writing this book, it becomes clear that we were effectively conducting remote viewing of children's health within the rehab center. During my time as a doctor in Australia, I didn't encounter a comparable approach. There, alternative treatments were kept completely separate from conventional medicine, and the concept of a 30- to 60-day rehab program was virtually nonexistent—unless it involved addiction treatment funded by celebrities themselves. I believe that remote viewing of our health represents the future of medicine—an approach we will be guided to embrace in this new era. I'm excited by this idea, seeing its vast potential to help us improve our health naturally.

Psychology: Stories of How Remote Viewing Transforms Mental Health

Mark's Journey to Mental Clarity

To heal, you must create a new, healthier version of yourself. The first step is to be able to visualise it. Remote viewing helps you see a future version of yourself...

Mark, a 35-year-old graphic designer from Los Angeles, had been struggling with severe anxiety and depression for over a decade. Despite years of therapy and medication, he felt trapped in a cycle of negative thoughts and overwhelming emotions. A friend recommended he explore remote viewing as a complementary approach to his treatment, particularly for its potential to help him reimagine his future self beyond his mental struggles.

Mark worked with a psychologist who was also a certified remote viewing instructor, who specialized in integrating this technique into psychological healing. In their first session, she guided Mark into a meditative state to quiet his mind. She then introduced him to the idea of visualizing a "future version" of himself—one where he no longer experienced anxiety or depression.

Creating a New Vision
Using remote viewing techniques, Mark was encouraged to:

1. **Seeing himself healthy**: In his mind's eye, he visualised a version of himself waking up refreshed, free from anxious thoughts, and ready to face the day with enthusiasm.
2. **Feeling his future emotions**: Mark imagined the emotions he would feel as this healthier version—confidence, peace, and joy.
3. **Transforming his body**: He saw his posture improve, his shoulders relaxed, and his face brighter with a genuine smile.
4. **Envisioning daily activities**: He imagined himself jogging in the park, cooking healthy meals, and engaging in meaningful conversations with friends and family.

The psychologist emphasized neutrality throughout the process, reminding Mark that this visualization wasn't about denying his current struggles but about giving his mind a blueprint for change.

The Timeline and Commitment
Mark practiced this visualization for 20 minutes daily, combining it with journaling his insights after each session. Initially, it was difficult—his negative thoughts often intruded, and he doubted the effectiveness of the process. However, by the third week, he began noticing subtle shifts.

- **Week 4**: Mark started feeling more hopeful. He reported fewer intrusive thoughts and a growing belief in his ability to change.
- **Month 2**: His visualization became vivid and detailed. He began incorporating actions into his daily life that aligned

with his future self, such as taking morning walks and eating healthier.
- **Month 6**: Mark experienced a significant improvement in his mental health. While he continued therapy, he noticed that remote viewing had given him a new sense of direction. His anxiety episodes reduced, and he described feeling more "anchored" in his vision of himself as a confident, capable individual.

Results

A year later, Mark was thriving. He credited remote viewing as the turning point that helped him break free from his mental prison. By regularly visualizing his healthy future self, he had rewired his mindset to focus on possibilities rather than limitations.

He reflected:

> *"For years, I felt like I was stuck in the same story. Remote viewing helped me write a new one. It allowed me to see the version of me I wanted to be—and eventually, I became that person."*

Weight Loss: How Remote Viewing Can Help You Achieve a Slimmer You

Key points: You create the image of yourself that you envision.

Case Study: Judy's Weight Loss Journey Through Remote Viewing

Judy, a 42-year-old teacher, had struggled with her weight for most of her adult life. She tried countless diets and exercise plans, but none brought lasting results. Her weight issues weren't just physical; they were tied to emotional struggles, stress, and self-doubt. Desperate for a change, she joined a wellness program where remote viewing was introduced as a unique method to help participants reimagine themselves and align their mindset with their goals.

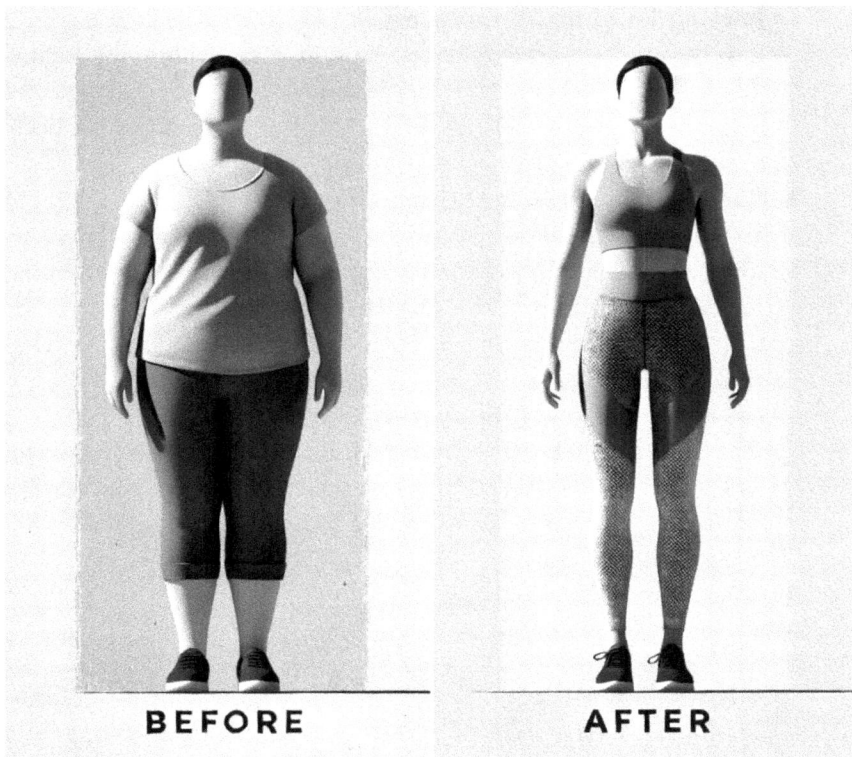

Remote viewing for Weight Loss

The Remote Viewing Process

In her first session, Judy worked with a coach to use remote viewing to *project herself into the future—a version of herself that had achieved her ideal weight and a healthy, confident lifestyle.* This process was not just about seeing her future self but also feeling, thinking, and acting like her.

1. **Visualizing the Slim Version of Herself**:
   Judy closed her eyes and envisioned her future self standing in front of a mirror—slimmer, with glowing skin, a relaxed, confident posture, and clothes that fit beautifully.

2. **Feeling Her Future Emotions**:
   She focused on the emotions tied to this vision—joy, pride, and a sense of accomplishment. Her coach encouraged her to embrace these feelings fully, helping her mind and body recognize this version as achievable.
3. **Foreseeing Her New Habits**:
   Judy then imagined the daily routines that this healthier version of herself followed—eating balanced meals, enjoying regular walks, and managing stress with mindfulness rather than overeating. She saw herself enjoying these habits rather than dreading them.
4. **Creating a Mental Blueprint**:
   The final step was to anchor this vision in her mind, using it as a roadmap for her weight loss journey. Judy practiced this visualization every day, allowing her mind to align with her body's transformation.

Results

Week 1:
Judy noticed small but meaningful shifts in her mindset. She felt more motivated to make healthier choices and reported a sense of calm she hadn't experienced before.

Month 2:
By now, Judy had lost 10 pounds. While she acknowledged that progress was gradual, the daily remote viewing sessions helped her stay focused and resilient. When faced with cravings or emotional triggers, she would close her eyes and reconnect with her future self for strength.

Month 6:
Judy had lost 35 pounds and was well on her way to achieving her goal. More importantly, she felt like a different person—one who believed in herself and found joy in the process rather than

frustration. Her coach noted that her transformation wasn't just physical but emotional and mental as well.

A Year Later:
Judy maintained her weight loss and continued to thrive. She credited remote viewing for giving her the mental clarity and emotional alignment she needed to succeed.

Her Reflection:
"I didn't just lose weight—I gained a vision of who I wanted to be. Remote viewing gave me the power to step into that vision and make it my reality."

Chapter 3:
Influential Figures in Remote Viewing

Prominent Russian Individuals who Contributed to the Development of Remote Viewing

Growing up in Russia, I was deeply influenced by stories of extraordinary individuals who demonstrated abilities that defied conventional understanding. These figures, including mystics, scientists, and healers, showcased the profound potential of Remote viewing and its connection to health, healing, and human consciousness.

My mindset was influenced by stories of remarkable Russians with extraordinary psychic abilities.

Notable Russian Figures and Their Contributions

1. **Grigori Rasputin,** a Russian mystic and advisor to the Romanov family, was well-known for his extraordinary abilities that went beyond conventional understanding. Rasputin's methods, though not officially recorded as remote viewing, involved various telepathic practices. He was famous for his healing abilities, often said to perform miraculous cures through prayer and touch.

Grigori Rasputin, a Russian mystic.

Many believed he had a strong sense of foresight, predicting future events with surprising accuracy.

Here are some events often mentioned as proof of his telepathic abilities:

Prediction of World War I: Rasputin allegedly predicted the outbreak of World War I. He is said to have warned the Romanovs about the coming war and the possible fall of the Russian monarchy. While his exact predictions weren't always recorded in detail, many people at the time saw his warnings about political instability and conflict as important.

Foretelling the Fall of the Romanov Dynasty: Rasputin reportedly predicted the fall of the Romanov dynasty, foreseeing that the family's reign would end in disaster. This prediction was made well before the Russian Revolution of 1917, and many viewed his foresight as a chilling reflection of his intuitive grasp of the political climate.

Guiding Political Decisions: Rasputin's intuition was believed to have influenced several political decisions made by Tsarina Alexandra. His advice was sought on various matters, including appointments of government officials and military strategies. Although his specific intuitive insights were not always recorded, his ability to sway significant decisions suggested a level of influence that many attributed to his perceptive and intuitive abilities.

2. Helena Blavatsky was a telepathic intuitive and co-founder of the Theosophical Society, renowned for her influential work in esoteric spirituality, including her detailed writings in "The Secret Doctrine" and her claims of accessing hidden spiritual knowledge through remote viewing and psychic abilities.

Helena Blavatsky: contribution to remote viewing.

Helena Blavatsky is recognized for her remote viewing abilities such as:

Perceiving Distant Events: Blavatsky reportedly had the ability to gain information about events occurring far from her physical location, often providing details that could not be easily explained.

Accessing Hidden Knowledge: She claimed to receive insights into esoteric and occult knowledge, which were said to be revealed through her remote viewing and spiritual communication.

Describing Locations and People: She was known to describe distant locations and individuals with remarkable accuracy, based on her remote viewing experiences.

Demonstrating Psychic Phenomena: Blavatsky's abilities were part of her broader repertoire of psychic phenomena, including telepathy and precognition, which were central to her work and teachings.

3. Nina Kulagina: She was a famous Soviet psychic in the 1960s and 1970s, known for her supposed ability to move objects with her mind. She reportedly showed several skills, like moving or levitating small items. She is famous for:

Psychokinesis: She claimed the ability to move objects with her mind without physical interaction.

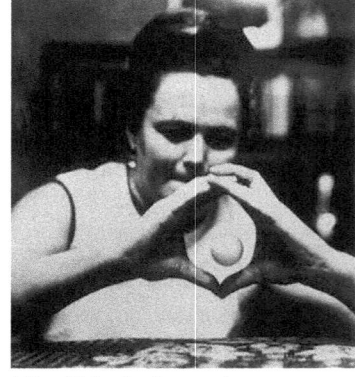

Nina Kulagina's experiments.

Remote Viewing: She could perceive and describe distant or unseen objects and locations.

Influencing Objects: She was reported to have influenced the movement of objects from a distance, such as making small objects levitate or change direction.

Medical Perception: Kulagina claimed to diagnose health conditions and influence physiological processes in people.

Telepathic Abilities: She was said to have telepathic communication skills, allowing her to transmit thoughts or information over distances.

Energy Manipulation: Her demonstrations included claims of manipulating energy fields around objects and people.

4. Anatoly Kashpirovsky is a Russian psychic, healer, and hypnotist who became famous in the 1980s for his televised sessions of psychotherapy. He is known for his work in remote viewing and related phenomena. His abilities include:

A. Kashpirovsky worked with remote viewing.

Remote Viewing: He claimed the ability to perceive and describe distant or unseen locations and objects.

Psychic Healing: Kashpirovsky reportedly used his abilities to heal individuals by influencing their physical and emotional states from a distance.

Telepathy: He was said to have telepathic skills, allowing him to receive and transmit thoughts or information across distances.

Influencing Biological Processes: Kashpirovsky was known for his attempts to influence physiological processes, such as helping in recovery from illness or pain through remote influence.

Energy Manipulation: He claimed to manipulate energy fields to bring about healing and affect outcomes.

Aura Reading: Kashpirovsky reportedly could read and interpret a person's aura or energy field to gain insights into their health or emotional state.

5. **Wolf Messing,** a renowned Russian psychic and performer, is known for his extraordinary remote-viewing abilities. His abilities include:

Remote Viewing: He claimed to perceive and describe distant or hidden objects and locations.

Telepathy: He supposedly had the ability to read minds and transmit thoughts to others over distances.

Wolf Messing worked with remote viewing.

Psychokinesis: Messing was known for his ability to influence and move objects with his mind.

Precognition: He reportedly could foresee future events or outcomes.

Aura Reading: He was said to have the ability to read and interpret a person's aura to gain insights into their health and emotional state.

Influencing Behaviour: Messing claimed to influence people's actions and decisions through mental suggestions or commands.

Medical Perception: He purportedly had the ability to diagnose health conditions and influence physiological processes from a distance.

6. **Lieutenant General Alexei Yurievich Savin**, a Russian military officer and researcher, was known for his involvement in studying and applying psychic phenomena, including remote viewing. His reported skills and contributions in this area include:

Remote Viewing: Savin was involved in research and experimentation related to perceiving and describing distant or unseen objects and locations.

Alexei Yurievich Savin worked with remote viewing.

Telepathy: He investigated the ability to transmit thoughts and information mentally between individuals across distances, as well as how one person can influence the mindset of another from afar.

Clairvoyance: Savin investigated the capacity to gain information about objects or events without direct sensory input.

Precognition: He studied the ability to foresee or predict future events before they occur.

Influencing Outcomes: Savin conducted research on using psychic abilities to remotely influence events or decisions. He emphasized that the energy of an individual or group can significantly impact the outcome of an event.

7. **Boris Ratnikov,** a Russian psychic and researcher, retired major-general of the reserves of Russia's Federal Security Service, was known for his work in remote viewing and related phenomena. His reported skills and contributions include:

Remote Viewing: Ratnikov had the ability to perceive and describe distant or hidden objects and locations.

Boris Ratnikov contributed to remote viewing.

Telepathy: He presumably had skills in transmitting and receiving thoughts or information over distances without traditional sensory means.

Clairvoyance: Ratnikov was known for his ability to gain information about distant or unseen events and objects.

Precognition: He reportedly had the ability to predict future events or outcomes before they happened.

Energy Manipulation: Ratnikov explored the ability to influence and manipulate the energy fields surrounding people and objects, emphasizing that these energy fields play a crucial role in health and overall well-being.

Remote Influence: He claimed to affect or influence events and outcomes from a distance through his psychic abilities.

Ratnikov's work was part of the broader exploration of psychic phenomena in Russia, contributing to the field of remote viewing and related studies.

These individuals had a profound impact on my mindset, and their knowledge may have even contributed to shaping who I am today. They gave me the foundation to start my journey. As you can see from the examples, the successful practitioners of remote viewing in Russia often integrated health, body, and mind into their research. None of them separated the body from the equation, as some may do by focusing solely on external objects or others without considering what's happening within their own bodies. This is not how remote viewing works. It works by uniting the viewer with what they are observing—there is no energetic separation between things and people.

This holistic mindset greatly influenced me and inspired me to teach remote viewing combined with intuitive healing. It's this integration of body, mind, and energy that defines my approach and the work I do today.

Chapter 4:
Group Exploration of Remote Viewing

Remote Viewing Experiments by Russian Research Centres and Universities

My research reveals that not only individual Russians were interested in remote viewing, but many universities and research centres also conducted studies on the topic. Medical doctors, scientists, physicists, engineers, psychologists, and other professionals were involved, exploring how remote viewing could be used for human health and other purposes. Some of the notable institutions include:

1. Moscow State University (MGU)
- **Involvement**: Moscow State University, one of Russia's leading academic institutions, was involved in research on consciousness, telepathy, and related phenomena, which included remote viewing. Some departments and researchers at MGU explored the theoretical aspects of psychic abilities and consciousness.
- **Key Researchers**: Prominent figures like Dr. Leonid Vasiliev, who later worked at the Institute of the Brain, were connected to MGU's academic circles.

2. Leningrad State University (now Saint Petersburg State University)

- **Involvement**: Leningrad State University was a hub for research on parapsychology and psychotronics during the Soviet era. Researchers there were involved in exploring the mechanisms of remote viewing, telepathy, and other psychic phenomena.
- **Key Researchers**: Dr. Leonid Vasiliev, who conducted pioneering work on telepathy and remote viewing, was closely associated with this institution.

3. Moscow Institute of Physics and Technology (MIPT)

- **Involvement**: MIPT, known for its cutting-edge research in various fields of science and technology, had departments and researchers interested in psychotronics, the study of the interaction between consciousness and matter. This included remote viewing as part of broader research into the capabilities of the human mind.
- **Key Research Areas**: Research focused on the potential applications of remote viewing in areas such as intelligence, defence, and understanding human consciousness.

4. Saratov State University

- **Involvement**: Saratov State University engaged in psychotronics and parapsychology research, including studies related to remote viewing. The university's work in these areas often intersected with military and intelligence interests.
- **Key Studies**: Researchers at Saratov explored the influence of consciousness on physical systems, including remote viewing as part of their investigations.

5. Russian Academy of Sciences (RAS)

- **Involvement**: While not a university, the Russian Academy of Sciences played a crucial role in parapsychological research in Russia. Various institutes under the RAS umbrella, such as

the Institute of the Brain and the Institute of Psychology, conducted research into remote viewing.
- **Key Research**: The RAS focused on the physiological and psychological underpinnings of psychic phenomena, aiming to understand the scientific basis of remote viewing.

These institutions were part of a broader Soviet-era interest in exploring psychic phenomena, often driven by military and intelligence motivations. The research was often classified, contributing to a mix of scientific inquiry and speculative study.

Private Research Groups: Independent Studies with Significant Impact

Independent research groups in Russia have also contributed significantly to the development of remote viewing. Operating outside traditional academic frameworks, these organizations often blend scientific inquiry with spiritual and esoteric practices. Notable private research groups include:

1. Institute of Applied Mysticism (Moscow)

Focus: This organization blends mystical and esoteric practices with scientific research into remote viewing, telepathy, and other psychic abilities.

Activities: The institute offers training, workshops, and research into the development of psychic skills, including remote viewing. It emphasizes the spiritual and meditative practices that enhance these abilities.

2. Moscow Society for Psychical Research

Focus: This society is dedicated to the study and promotion of parapsychology, including remote viewing. It aims to explore the scientific and philosophical aspects of psychic phenomena.

Activities: The group organizes lectures, seminars, and experiments related to remote viewing, telepathy, and other parapsychological phenomena.

3. Russian Association for Instrumental Psychotronics (RAIP)

Focus: RAIP is a private group that researches psychotronics, which includes the study of the interaction between consciousness and matter. Remote viewing is a key area of interest.

Activities: The association develops and tests psychotronic devices believed to enhance or measure psychic abilities. They also conduct research into the practical applications of remote viewing.

4. Centre for Bioinformation Technologies

Focus: This centre explores bioinformation technologies, which include remote viewing as a means of accessing and manipulating information through non-traditional means.

Activities: The centre conducts research, offers courses, and provides consultancy services in areas like remote viewing, energy healing, and biofeedback.

5. Sfera Group (Moscow)

Focus: Sfera Group specializes in research and training related to remote viewing, telepathy, and psychokinesis, often focusing on their applications in business and personal development.

Activities: The group offers remote viewing courses, personal coaching, and research into the practical uses of psychic abilities in everyday life and decision-making processes.

6. Cosmoenergetics Research Institute (Moscow)

Focus: This institute blends energy healing practices with remote viewing and other psychic phenomena. They explore how cosmic energies can be harnessed to enhance psychic abilities.

Activities: The institute conducts research, holds workshops, and offers certifications in cosmoenergetics, which includes elements of remote viewing.

7. The Russian School of Transpersonal Psychology (Moscow)

Focus: Although primarily focused on transpersonal psychology, this school includes remote viewing in its curriculum as part of broader research into altered states of consciousness.

Activities: The school offers courses, seminars, and research opportunities that explore the connection between consciousness, psychic phenomena, and spiritual development.

These private research groups often operate in a space where scientific inquiry intersects with esotericism, and they attract individuals interested in developing and applying psychic abilities like remote viewing in various contexts.

As you can see, remote viewing has been a significant topic in Russia for many years. It has evolved and developed through both individual and group efforts, including government-funded universities, specialized schools, and research centres. While not all of these institutions have always been publicly acknowledged, they are now entering a new phase of rapid development. These centres recognize the interconnectedness of individual and collective consciousness, emphasizing that both are inseparable.

However, to create a better world, we must focus on the individual consciousness first. Each individual must align with their divine purpose and become the person they are meant to be. When most individuals are healthy and in alignment with their true selves, we can collectively create a better world for all.

How to Set Up Your Own Remote Viewing Group

You can create your own Remote Viewing group to practice together and enjoy the experience as a fun and collaborative activity.

Steps to set up your group:
   1. **Define the Purpose:**

Decide on your group's focus—learning Remote Viewing, exploring specific topics, or contributing to societal causes like missing person cases.

2. **Recruit Members:**
Invite 5-10 like-minded individuals through social media, friends, or local communities. Host an introductory session to explain Remote Viewing.

3. **Set a Schedule:**
Choose a consistent time and venue (in-person or online) to meet regularly.

4. **Plan Sessions:**
Structure meetings with relaxation exercises, practice targets, sharing results, and teaching new skills. Start simple and progress gradually.

5. **Emphasize Ethics:**
Foster kind intentions, neutrality, and respect for privacy to maintain a safe and trusting environment.

6. **Reflect and Improve:**
Document sessions, track progress, and encourage members to journal their experiences.

7. **Keep it Fun:**
Incorporate themed sessions, friendly challenges, and celebrate successes to keep members engaged.

Benefits of a Remote Viewing Group

- **Personal Growth:** Develop intuitive skills and mindfulness.
- **Community:** Build meaningful connections.
- **Learning:** Explore new topics and perspectives.
- **Societal Impact:** Assist with real-world issues like environmental or rescue efforts.
- **Enjoyment:** Relieve stress and find joy in collaboration.

Starting a Remote Viewing group offers discovery, connection, and a chance to make a positive impact on society.

Remote Viewing Group.

Chapter 5:
Scientific Theories Behind Remote Viewing

How do you explain remote viewing to someone new to the concept?

Remote viewing is a fascinating combination of science and the psychic realm. By harmonizing these two seemingly opposite areas, we gain a deeper understanding of reality's interconnected nature. As Albert Einstein once said:

"Science without religion is lame, religion without science is blind."

Albert Einstein

This reflects Einstein's belief in the complementary relationship between science and spirituality, emphasizing that both are essential to understanding the universe and our place within it.

Albert Einstein also reminded us,

> *"Imagination is more important than knowledge."*

This quote shows that imagination drives discovery in both science and spirituality, reaching beyond the limits of knowledge.

He also said,

> *"The intuitive mind is a sacred gift and the rational mind is a faithful servant. We have created a society that honors the servant and has forgotten the gift."*

This quote highlights the imbalance in society, emphasizing that we prioritize logic over intuition, neglecting the deeper wisdom and creativity that intuition offers.

Remote viewing connects the spiritual and scientific into a unique blend.

When we combine science with intuition, we can see the world as a unified whole. Remote viewing is a technique that helps us achieve this vision, and it's available to anyone open to exploring it.

Remote viewing is a technique that allows a person to access information about a distant location, object, or event without using their physical senses. The five primary physical senses are:

1. Sight (Vision)
2. Hearing (Audition)
3. Touch (Tactile)
4. Smell (Olfaction)
5. Taste (Gustation)

Remote viewing relies on the *sixth sense*, which can be experienced through the five physical senses or beyond them, often described as an "inner knowing."

The sixth sense is connected to remote viewing

During remote viewing, a person may perceive information through sensations that aren't physically present.

For example, they may feel a touch without any actual contact, smell a scent that isn't physically there, taste something in their mouth without any substance, or see a vision of something that exists elsewhere but not in their immediate surroundings.

These experiences highlight how remote viewing taps into non-physical forms of perception, where the mind accesses information beyond the five senses. Think of it like using your mind to see or sense things that are far away or hidden from view. It involves focusing your consciousness and tapping into a deeper level of awareness to gain insights that wouldn't normally be available through traditional means. While it may sound mysterious, remote viewing has been practiced and studied for years, and it's something anyone can learn with practice and focus.

Science, like quantum mechanics suggests that our consciousness can go beyond the usual limits of space and time, allowing us to access information that isn't physically present. The idea of entanglement indicates that particles can be linked, affecting each other instantly, which could be similar to how our minds connect.

Additionally, the subconscious mind can pick up on information we aren't consciously aware of, helping us retrieve insights during remote viewing. These ideas challenge our typical understanding of reality and suggest that remote viewing might tap into a deeper, shared consciousness that goes beyond what we can see.

Quantum Mechanics and Consciousness

One explanation for how remote viewing works lies in the connection between quantum mechanics and consciousness.

Quantum mechanics, the study of particles at the tiniest scales, has completely changed how we see reality. It shows us a world that's full of possibilities, deeply connected, and much more intricate than traditional physics suggests. Some researchers believe that the ideas from quantum mechanics could help explain how remote viewing works.

This real story may illustrate the connection between quantum mechanics and consciousness.

Maria, a psychologist interested in remote viewing, led a workshop where participants were asked to think of a specific object in a distant location. As the group focused, Maria suddenly envisioned a large blue vase filled with flowers. Unsure if this image was her imagination, she asked the participants to share their thoughts.

To her astonishment, several of them described the same blue vase she had seen. In that moment, Maria realized their shared focus had created a powerful connection, allowing their consciousnesses to intertwine and access information from afar. This experience transformed her understanding of remote viewing, highlighting how quantum mechanics might explain the deep links between human consciousness, revealing a world filled with possibilities and interconnections that science is just beginning to explore.

Quantum Entanglement

Another explanation for how remote viewing works is through quantum entanglement. It is one of the most discussed aspects in relation to remote viewing. This phenomenon occurs *when two particles become entangled*, meaning their states are linked regardless of the distance between them. Changes to one particle instantaneously affect the other, no matter how far apart they are. Some scientists believe that remote viewing could be facilitated by a form of *mental entanglement*, where the consciousness of the viewer becomes entangled with the target, allowing for instantaneous perception.

I really resonate with this explanation because it captures exactly how I feel when I do remote viewing – my consciousness seems to merge with the target, even if just for a moment.

Here's another practical example related to quantum entanglement.

I recently heard a story from a friend that illustrates *quantum entanglement*.

Anya, a talented artist, felt a sudden urge to reach out to her best friend, Dmitry, who lived far away. They hadn't spoken in weeks, but she sent him a quick message, asking how he was doing. To her surprise, Dmitry replied almost immediately, revealing that he had been feeling down and really needed someone to talk to.

Later, during a video call, Anya mentioned how they often seemed to sense each other's feelings. "It's like we're entangled," she said excitedly. Dmitry nodded, sharing that he often felt happier whenever Anya was working on a new painting, even from afar.

Feeling inspired, Anya began to paint, pouring her emotions into her artwork. As she worked, she realized their connection was more than just friendship; it was a powerful bond that linked their thoughts and feelings, regardless of the distance between them. This sense of entanglement made their friendship feel even stronger, demonstrating how true connections can transcend miles and create an unbreakable link between people.

The Role of the Observer

Quantum physics introduces the concept of the observer effect, suggesting that simply observing something can alter its outcome. This idea implies that our consciousness plays a vital role in shaping reality. In remote viewing, it's believed that a person's consciousness may interact with the quantum field, gaining access to information beyond the reach of our usual senses. I believe this explanation may also clarify how some individuals can influence physical objects through focused intention. The observer's directed awareness appears to shift the energy of objects, at least on a subtle level.

In my experience working at a children's rehabilitation centre for frequently ill children in Russia, we saw the power of this observer effect in action. We prescribed 30- to 60-day courses of natural remedies to children with chronic conditions and consistently observed remarkable improvements in their health. Our positive expectations seemed to influence the outcomes, helping us achieve the results we envisioned for these children.

A related story about the observer effect from someone I know involves a scientist named Alex, who conducted an experiment on sunflower growth.

He planted two identical groups: one listened to classical music, while the other remained in silence. Each day, Alex lovingly tended to the music group, adjusting the volume and talking to them, convinced they would thrive. In contrast, he neglected the silent group, checking on them only occasionally.

Weeks later, Alex was amazed to find that the music group had grown tall and vibrant, while the silent sunflowers struggled and remained small. He realized that his attention and positive energy had influenced the outcome. This experience taught him a valuable lesson: as an observer, his beliefs and actions shaped the reality of what he studied, highlighting the powerful connection between intention and result.

Non-locality and Information Transfer

Another explanation for how remote viewing works involves non-locality and the transfer of information across space and time.

Non-locality refers to the phenomenon where particles can instantaneously affect each other, regardless of the distance between them. This means that changes in one particle can instantly influence another, even if they are far apart. For remote viewing, this concept suggests that people might access information about distant places or objects without any physical link. If our consciousness works on a quantum level, it could move beyond the usual limits of space and time, making remote viewing possible.

I agree with this explanation and believe it helps to explain how some people can receive random information about future events or distant places. For instance, many people reported dreaming about an airplane hitting a tower before the events of September 11, though they didn't have details like the exact date or location—just the general storyline. This information seemed to come to them spontaneously, illustrating the concepts of non-locality and information transfer.

Another story I heard a few years ago perfectly illustrates non-locality and information transfer.

A man named Ivan was at home in Los Angeles when he suddenly felt the urge to call his old friend, Lena, who lived in Boston. Although they hadn't spoken in a while, something inside him compelled him to reach out.

When Ivan called, Lena answered, surprised. "I was just thinking about you!" she said, her voice shaky. She shared that she was struggling at work and feeling completely overwhelmed. In that moment, Ivan sensed a deep connection between them, revealing how information transfer can occur even over great distances.

*As Ivan listened and offered his support, their conversation flowed easily, filled with laughter and shared memories. After they hung up, Ivan reflected on the timing of his call. It felt as though he had tapped into **a moment of non-locality**, where their thoughts and emotions intertwined despite the miles between them.*

*This experience reinforced Ivan's belief in the profound connections we can have with others, demonstrating how our minds can communicate beyond physical boundaries. It showed that through **non-locality and information transfer**, we can support one another, no matter how far apart we are.*

The Role of the Subconscious Mind in Remote Viewing

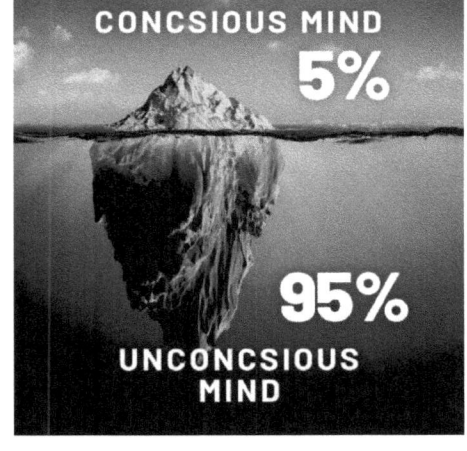

The subconscious mind plays a significant role in the ability to perform remote viewing. In fact, it's the subconscious that connects with the remote object or target during the process.

How does this work? To understand, let's first look at the structure of the mind.

If you think of the mind as 100%, the Conscious Mind, or Logical Mind, only makes up about 5-10% of its total capacity.

The Subconscious Mind, on the other hand, occupies a vast 90-95%. This hidden part of our psyche influences our repetitive thoughts, emotions, behaviours, and perceptions, operating beyond our logical awareness and processing information that the conscious mind can't access.

Most of the functions in both our body and mind occur at the subconscious level, without our awareness.

Remote viewing taps into this realm, granting access to processes that are usually concealed from our conscious mind.

To effectively connect with the subconscious, it's essential to first **quiet the Logical Mind.**

There are many ways to calm the Logical Mind, such as deep breathing, meditation, and relaxation. However, I recommend Intuitive Healing meditations, where we connect to and become attuned to the **subtle energy within the body**. From my experience, this technique is particularly powerful because it aligns us with the fundamental essence of our existence—energy—and facilitates the remote viewing process more effectively than other methods.

How the Subconscious Mind Assists in Remote Viewing?

Accessing Deep Cellular Memory: The subconscious mind has access to a deeper, more expansive (so-called Cellular) memory system. This system might include information from the past, present, and even potential futures. Remote viewing could be a process where the subconscious mind taps into this reservoir of information, bringing it to the conscious awareness of the viewer.

Example: Sarah's Journey into Cellular Memory.

Sarah sat in her quiet Paris apartment, preparing for her remote viewing session. Her focus was on the Baths of Caracalla, the ancient Roman ruins she had always been fascinated by but never physically visited. As she entered a meditative state, images began to form, not just of the ruins themselves, but of an overwhelming sense of familiarity. The deep cellular memory that surfaced seemed to transcend her personal experience—it was as if she had been there before, not just as an observer but as someone who had once walked the very halls she now visualised. The arches, the marble, the smell of the warm steam—it all felt strangely intimate, as though her cells were unlocking a memory from a past life. The deep cellular memory wasn't just an intellectual recollection—it was visceral, connecting her not only to her own memories but to the broader tapestry of human experience. In this quiet moment, Sarah realized the possibility that she might have actually been in this place before, in another lifetime, experiencing the baths in their full Roman glory. It was as if her subconscious mind had tapped into the ancient well of deep cellular memory, a layer of awareness that carried the wisdom of past lives, waiting to be uncovered...

Intuition and Symbolism: The subconscious mind often communicates through intuition, symbols, and metaphors. In remote viewing, a viewer may receive impressions that are not literal but symbolic representations of the target. Interpreting these symbols requires an understanding of the language of the subconscious mind, which is often more abstract and less linear than conscious thought.

Example: The Golden Key
I once heard a story from a friend who had been practicing remote viewing for a while. He was attempting to view a distant location but kept receiving an image of a **large, golden key** *in his mind. At first, he dismissed it, thinking it was irrelevant to the target. But as he continued to focus, the symbol of the key began to take on more significance. It wasn't just a physical object; it seemed to represent something much deeper. The key symbolized access—unlocking something hidden or closed off, like a deeper understanding or a new opportunity. Later, when he learned more about the location, he discovered that it was a place with restricted access—an old, private estate that had recently been opened to the public.*

The key was a perfect metaphor, drawn from his subconscious mind, symbolizing the opportunity to access something that had been previously closed off. This experience illustrated how intuition and symbolism work together in remote viewing. The subconscious doesn't always deliver literal impressions but often communicates through abstract symbols that require careful interpretation. Understanding these symbols, as my friend learned, is crucial to deciphering the deeper messages from the subconscious mind, which is often more abstract and nonlinear than our conscious thinking...

Hypnosis and Altered States: Techniques such as hypnosis or deep meditation are often used to access the subconscious mind more directly. In these altered states, the barriers between the conscious and subconscious minds are reduced, allowing for a freer flow of information. Remote viewers frequently use relaxation and meditation techniques to enter a state where their subconscious mind can take the lead, potentially accessing information beyond ordinary sensory experience.

Example: Claire's Vision of The Big Tree during meditation

A few years ago, Claire, a beginner in remote viewing, decided to use deep meditation to explore a location she had never seen. As she relaxed and entered a meditative state, images began to form in her mind—at first abstract, but gradually becoming clearer. She saw a large, ancient tree with expansive roots and branches. As the vision sharpened, Claire realized the tree was **The Big Tree** *in* **The Grampians National Park***, Victoria, Australia. Though she had never visited, the tree felt familiar, symbolizing strength and grounding. This experience showed Claire how deep meditation could help bypass the conscious mind, allowing her subconscious to reveal information, even about a place she had never consciously encountered...*

Chapter 6:
The Process and Stages of Remote Viewing

Remote viewing involves structured stages to help the viewer from initial perception to a detailed description of the target. These stages are designed to help the viewer tap into their subconscious mind, where the information about the target is believed to reside, and then bring that information into conscious awareness.

The main principle:

> ... **My Subconscious Mind Already Knows What I'm Looking For** ...

Steps for Effective Remote Viewing
Step 1: Adopting a Mindset for Success
Before you begin remote viewing, recognize that your subconscious mind already knows the target ... Your task is to **align yourself with the energy of the target** by embracing the principle of "oneness and interconnectedness of all there is."

I recommend using the following affirmation five minutes before remote viewing any object or target:

"My subconscious mind already knows the target I am about to connect with."

This practice helps to align your mind and open the channels of communication with your deeper subconscious, reinforcing the belief that the information you seek is already available within you.

Step 2: Relaxation

Before the actual remote viewing session begins, the viewer prepares mentally and physically. This might involve relaxation techniques, meditation, or deep breathing exercises to calm the mind and body. *The goal is to enter a focused, receptive state of consciousness, free from distractions. Typically, this step takes about 5 to 10 minutes.*

Step 3: Target Acquisition

The viewer is given a target, which could be anything from a specific location to an object, person, or event. You can also select your own target, but it should be clearly defined.

Step 4: Sketching First Impressions

The viewer quickly creates a simple sketch, capturing their instinctive reaction to the target called "first impressions".

Goal: Capture instinctive reactions to the target, such as shapes, textures, or emotions.

Timing: The process should take no more than 30 seconds to prevent interference from the logical mind.

Outcome: A raw, intuitive glimpse into the target, bypassing conscious analysis.

Step 5: Deep Breathing

After finishing with the first impressions, the viewer disconnects from the target and focuses on deep breathing for 2 to 5 minutes.

Step 6: Sensory Data Collection

After deep breathing, focus intensifies as the viewer delves deeper into the target, noticing additional details such as size, shape, temperature, and sounds.

Goal: Expand on initial impressions without overanalysing.

Duration: Typically 5-10 minutes, though it may vary depending on the target and flow of information.

Step 7: Deeper Perception

The viewer perceives more intricate aspects of the target, such as dynamics, interactions, and structural elements. At this stage, the viewer may even 'smell, taste, or feel the target.'

Goal: Delve deeper into the target's essence while maintaining intuitive focus.

Duration: This stage can take longer depending on the viewer's persistence and the complexity of the target, typically lasting another 5 to 10 minutes.

Step 8: Analytical Overlay and Summary

The viewer begins organizing data into a coherent picture. While guesses or conclusions may emerge, the viewer should recognize and set aside analytical overlay.

Goal: Compile findings into detailed sketches, maps, or descriptive notes.

Outcome: A synthesized representation of the target based on raw impressions.

Step 9: Feedback and Review

After the session, the viewer is often provided with feedback about the actual target, allowing them to compare their perceptions with the **target's reality**. This feedback is **crucial** for honing the viewer's skills, helping them to recognize when their perceptions were accurate and when they were influenced by analytical overlay or other factors.

Conclusion: These stages, when mastered, can be adapted and modified based on the target, the viewer's desire to continue, the speed of their perceptions, and other factors. The time spent on each stage may also vary depending on the specific situation and circumstances.

Different Methodologies and Protocols

I have been researching over the years different methods to create a unique approach to remote viewing that incorporates intuitive healing. Over time, various protocols have been established to make remote viewing more effective and consistent. While these methods aim to help viewers better access and describe distant or hidden targets with minimal interference from their conscious mind, my focus has been on integrating medical intuition, telepathy and remote viewing. This combination allows viewers not only to perceive distant locations but also to sense and address energetic imbalances and emotional states related to health. My goal is to develop a method that enhances both the accuracy of remote viewing and the potential for healing.

Let's explore the remote viewing strategies that have been developed and practiced in recent years.

Controlled Remote Viewing (CRV)

Developed by Ingo Swann and other researchers for the U.S. military's Stargate Project, CRV is one of the most well-known methodologies. CRV is a structured, step-by-step process that guides the viewer through different stages of perception, from initial ideograms to detailed target descriptions. The CRV process emphasizes the importance of separating raw perceptions from analytical overlay.

Remote Viewing | 75

Example of CRV:

One famous example of Controlled Remote Viewing (CRV) comes from the work of the U.S. military's Stargate Project in the 1970s. In one case, a remote viewer named Pat Price was tasked with locating a secret Soviet military base. After entering a relaxed, focused state, Price described a location in the Soviet Union, noting a large complex surrounded by fencing and a distinctive structure, which he identified as a "large, round building." When intelligence analysts later reviewed satellite images, they confirmed that Price's description matched a previously unknown facility in the Soviet Union. This demonstrated how CRV can be used to access accurate, detailed information from a distance, offering a powerful tool for intelligence and remote exploration...

Extended Remote Viewing (ERV)

ERV is a more unstructured approach compared to CRV. It involves the viewer entering a deep, meditative state, often through relaxation techniques or self-hypnosis, and allowing perceptions of the target to emerge naturally. ERV relies heavily on the viewer's ability to access and interpret subconscious information without the strict stages of CRV.

Example of ERV:

A real example of Extended Remote Viewing (ERV) comes from the work of remote viewer and psychic, Joseph McMoneagle, who was part of the U.S. military's Stargate Project. In one well-documented case, McMoneagle was tasked with describing a Soviet missile base in the 1980s. Rather than using the structured protocols of Controlled Remote Viewing (CRV), McMoneagle employed ERV, which involves a deeper, more passive meditative state. During the session, McMoneagle described the target with such detail that analysts were able to confirm his findings later through satellite imagery and intelligence reports. He described the layout of the missile base, its location in a remote region, and even noted the presence of large concrete structures that were later verified by photos. ERV allows *the viewer to access information in a relaxed, less focused state, providing a more spontaneous flow of impressions, as McMoneagle's experience demonstrated...*

Associative Remote Viewing (ARV)

Associative Remote Viewing (ARV) is a specialized technique within the practice of Remote Viewing (RV) that is used to predict outcomes that involve two or more possible choices or results. It is commonly applied in areas like predicting the outcome of financial markets, sports events, or other future decisions.

Example of ARV:
Imagine you want to predict the winner of a basketball game between Team A and Team B. To do this, you use ARV:
1. **Set up Targets:** *You assign two random images as targets:*
   o *Image 1: A picture of a mountain for Team A.*
   o *Image 2: A picture of a beach for Team B.*
2. **Conduct the Remote Viewing:** *A Remote Viewer is asked to describe a target associated with the actual outcome of the game, without knowing about the teams or the images. They write down impressions like "calm, blue, sandy," which match the beach image (Image 2).*
3. **Make a Prediction:** *Since the viewer described the beach, you predict Team B will win.*
4. **Confirm the Outcome:** *After the game, if Team B wins, the viewer is shown the beach image as feedback to reinforce their accuracy. If not, the process can be refined for future attempts.*

This method helps bypass direct prediction by focusing on associated targets, allowing intuition and subconscious insights to guide the result.

Coordinate Remote Viewing (also known as CoRV or Geographical Remote Viewing)

Similar to CRV, this method involves providing the viewer with geographic coordinates or a reference number as the target identifier.

The viewer then follows a structured process to perceive and describe the target, often focusing on physical locations or sites.

Example of CoRV:
One real example of Coordinate Remote Viewing (CoRV) involving non-professionals comes from the work of remote viewing practitioners who have used the technique to find missing persons or objects. A notable case occurred in the 1990s, where a group of amateur remote viewers was asked to locate a missing hiker in the dense forests of Oregon. The viewers were given only the geographic coordinates of the area where the hiker was last known to be, and through CoRV, they described a series of landmarks that helped search teams pinpoint the hiker's location. One viewer described a small clearing near a stream, which turned out to be accurate, and another viewer mentioned a large fallen tree, which helped to guide the search team toward the hiker's position. The search ended successfully, and the hiker was found within hours of the remote viewing session, demonstrating the potential of Coordinate Remote Viewing in real-life situations, even when practiced by non-professionals...

Technical Remote Viewing (TRV)

Developed by former military remote viewers, TRV is a commercialized version of CRV that emphasizes a highly disciplined, data-driven approach. TRV focuses on rigorous training and precise documentation of perceptions, with an emphasis on practical applications such as business intelligence and problem-solving.

Example of TRV:
A well-documented case of Technical Remote Viewing (TRV) comes from the work of remote viewer Lyn Buchanan, a former military remote viewer who later taught others how to use TRV techniques. In the early 2000s, Buchanan was part of a project to locate a missing plane in a remote area. The task was complex and required TRV's systematic process, where viewers use distinct stages to gather and analyse detailed information.

Buchanan's target was a plane lost in the mountains of the Pacific Northwest. Using TRV, he focused on the target coordinates and described not just the plane's location but also its condition and surroundings. He provided highly specific information about the terrain, including trees, elevation, and nearby rock formations. His remote viewing session helped guide the search teams to a region where the wreckage was eventually found, exactly as he had described it.

This case illustrates how TRV, with its emphasis on structured methodology, allows for detailed and actionable information to be obtained from distant or hidden locations, even outside military applications...

Chapter 7:
My Approach to Remote Viewing

There are numerous approaches to remote viewing, each offering its own methods and insights. My approach focuses on using remote viewing in daily life and enhancing health, blending and simplifying all different techniques into an easy, practical method.

Principle No 1:
Blending Medical Intuition with Remote Viewing
The method I use focuses on promoting health and healing; I am simply not interested in anything else.

Everything is energy, and the energy behind each step should be pure and kind. Medical intuition helps reveal where we deviate from our true nature, often leading to problems. For this reason, it is a valuable tool for guiding your practice during remote viewing.

All remote viewing sessions should always be approached with ethics, integrity, a neutral mind, and kind intentions.

Principle No 2:
Holographic Nature of Life
The way I teach remote viewing starts with understanding the holographic nature of life. When you connect to a target, you observe its hologram—an energetic representation of a body, object, or entity.

The holographic view is based on the concept that everything is energy.

Take the human body, for example. It's composed of cells, which can be broken down into molecules and then into atoms. Atoms, in turn, can be further reduced to energy, as demonstrated by processes like nuclear fusion.

Everything can be represented as a hologram. In science fiction movies, the concept of a holographic view of life is a recurring theme, often showcasing holographic transportation to move humans or objects. What we see in these films may very well become a reality in the future.

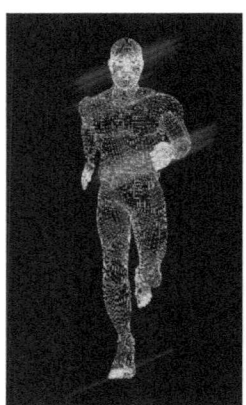

Holograms of a human and a car.

A hologram provides a 5D perspective, incorporating energetic dimensions, while conventional viewing offers a 3D perspective, focusing on physical and material aspects.

The difference between a holographic view (5D) and a conventional view (3D) lies in their perspectives.

The 3D view focuses on physical, material aspects, perceiving objects as solid and tangible. In contrast, the 5D holographic view considers everything as energy, recognizing interconnectedness and existence beyond the limits of physical space and time. Remote viewing taps into this energetic, 5D perspective to access information beyond normal sensory perception.

Practical Examples: Differences Between 3D and 5D - Viewing of a Person

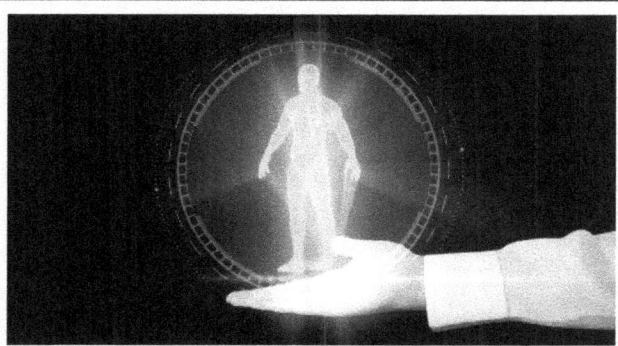

For instance, if I view my friend Peter from a conventional 3D perspective, I might describe him as a middle-aged Caucasian man with grey eyes, an average build, average height, and wearing blue jeans and a black shirt. While this gives a basic physical description, it doesn't capture much about Peter's unique identity.

However, if I describe Peter from a 5D perspective, I would include a richer array of details: his life experiences, traumas, thoughts, emotions, and attitudes about life and himself—all as recorded in his energetic system. This approach provides a far more comprehensive and nuanced understanding of who Peter truly is.

Practical Examples: Differences Between 3D and 5D - Viewing of a Burger

If you examine a burger from a 3D perspective, you would focus on its physical attributes like size, taste, and the ingredients listed on the label, including the amounts of protein, fat, sugar, minerals, and additives.

> From a 5D perspective, however, you would delve deeper into the energy of the burger: how it was prepared, the attitudes and intentions of those who made it, any hidden chemicals not listed on the label, and its true level of organic content compared to what's claimed. Additionally, you could assess whether the energy of the burger aligns with your own personal energy.
>
> This approach provides a more holistic way to make food choices, helping you avoid potential allergies or intolerances by ensuring that the food you consume is in harmony with your own energetic system.

Principle No 3: Remote Viewing Ethics

Ethics are vital for ensuring that this powerful tool is used responsibly and with integrity. The most important principle is to approach remote viewing with kind intentions and a calm mind—free from emotions and thoughts. A neutral mindset is key, as it allows you to be like an "empty vessel," simply observing **without influencing the target.**

Many people ask me, *"Do I need to get another person's permission to connect with them during remote viewing?"*.

The answer is *"no, you don't need to ask their permission"* but practicing remote viewing ethics is essential.

What is Remote Viewing Ethics?

In our daily lives, **we connect with others all the time** without explicit permission—when we think about someone, talk about them, or even gossip.

For instance, when you think about someone in an emotional way, like sexually, you don't ask their permission, yet your thoughts can affect them. Similarly, when you gossip negatively about a friend, you don't ask for their permission, but you still transmit negative energy to them.

The reality is that when we think about others with strong emotions, we inevitably influence them. The only way to avoid this influence is by reaching a state of neutrality, becoming an "empty vessel" when connecting with them.

The core ethics of remote viewing revolve around emotional awareness and maintaining a "calm mind." This practice calls for cultivating kind intentions and sustaining a neutral, serene mindset. A calm, neutral mind ensures no energy is transmitted, keeping remote viewing respectful and free from unintended influence on others.

It's important to differentiate between a "calm" mind and a "happy" mind. Society often emphasizes the importance of being happy, but a "happy" mind is frequently forced or artificial, carrying emotional charge. While a "happy" mind is influenced by emotions, a calm mind remains steady and unaffected. Forcing happiness can be as stressful as negative emotions, as it conceals underlying insecurity. In remote viewing, a "happy" mind leads to false impressions, contaminated by emotional influence.

Ultimately, a calm mind is essential for fostering self-healing, self-regulation, intuition, and higher perception. In remote viewing, the priority should always be on maintaining a calm mind over simply striving for happiness.

A Simple Exercise to Calm Your Mind

To calm your mind, try this simple breathing exercise:

- Take seven slow, deep breaths.
- Focus on the sensation of air entering through your nose, filling your belly, and exhaling fully.
- Count each inhale and exhale from 1 to 7, ensuring every breath is deep and intentional.

This practice can help soothe your mind almost immediately. Try it and notice the difference!

Chapter 8:
Practical Applications of Remote Viewing

Remote viewing can be used to explore many different things, with no limits to what you can look into. This includes checking out faraway places, uncovering hidden treasures, or even learning about medical conditions and food products. The key is to use remote viewing ethically. This means approaching your targets with a calm mind, being neutral, and not letting personal feelings or expectations influence you. Your goal should be to use remote viewing for positive and respectful purposes, always keeping in mind that you need to respect others' privacy and use your skills responsibly.

Remote Viewing Exercises at Home
Exercise 1: Remote Viewing with a Partner

This simple exercise allows you to practice remote viewing at home with a partner. To begin, prepare 5-10 cards using white paper with pictures on one side that will serve as the targets for remote viewing. You can cut out images from magazines—any common pictures of objects such as people, buildings, household items, clothing, flowers, mountains, geographic locations, or food. On the blank side of the card, write numbers (1, 2, 3, 4, etc.).

Place the cards in a manila envelope, face down, and prepare several sets of envelopes with different cards inside so you can switch roles with your partner. Choose someone who is interested in remote viewing to do this exercise with you.

Steps for Remote Viewing Practice:
1. Select a Range of Targets (5-10)
   Use the envelope with the cards inside as your target deck.
2. Release and Let Go
   Before you begin, write down the date, time, and any distracting thoughts or ideas you wish to release. Once you've written them, say: "I am letting these go now." Visualise yourself loosening your grip and setting them free.
3. Quiet Your Mind
   Settle into a calm, neutral state by practicing meditation or deep breathing. Let your mind gradually quiet down. This process may take anywhere from 5 to 20 minutes, depending on your initial state of mind.
4. Partner Prompts
   Your partner will draw a card, keeping the picture side down so you can't see it, and ask you to view it.
5. Record first impressions
   Start writing down your first impressions of the target, spending only 30 seconds on each. Alternatively, you can use sketching. Have your partner set a timer. Within those 30 seconds, focus on describing the key features: Is the target natural or man-made? Do you sense land, water, air, or specific colours? Quickly jot down your initial impressions...
6. Don't Second-guess Yourself
   Note the first thing that comes to mind, no matter how faint. The key is to trust your initial perceptions and describe them without judgment.

7. Connect Unconsciously
   Information flows from your unconscious mind, which already knows the target. It communicates through subtle sensations and feelings in your body.
8. Describe the Basics
   Record sensory details like visuals, smells, tastes, or temperatures. You may also start to perceive dimensions, shapes, and patterns. Emotional reactions to the target may arise—just observe and note them.
9. Draw a Sketch
   Sketch the target without worrying about accuracy or artistic quality.
10. Bird's-eye View
    Imagine floating a few hundred feet above the target. Can you perceive anything surprising? Make a note of your final impressions.
11. End the Session
    Write down the time and summarize what you perceived.
12. Get Feedback
    Pull the top card from the envelope and compare the picture to your notes. Take your time observing the colours, shapes, and details of the image. You might be surprised by the results.

When your mind is still, you naturally enter a state of non-local consciousness, where intuition flows effortlessly. The only barrier to this connection is the constant chatter in your brain.

This exercise can be easily practiced by anyone, and with regular practice over a few months, your perceptions will become surprisingly clear and accurate. The only thing that separates you from your target is the incessant noise of your thoughts. *Release that noise, and you will already know the target.*

Exercise 2: Remote Viewing a Person Using Their Name

You can connect to a person using just their name. Names carry energy. When working with clients, I often connect with them remotely before we even meet, using just their first name. Many people ask why the first name is enough, especially with so many Peters or Karens in the world. How can you be sure you're connecting with the right person? In remote viewing, the energy naturally aligns with your intention, and you'll be connected to the person you're focused on. The process simply works this way.

Steps to Remote View a Person

1. Close your eyes, take a few slow, deep breaths, and focus on your breath moving along your spine for about 30 seconds to a minute.
2. Shift your attention to your forehead, and as you exhale, imagine pushing the air through your forehead as if you're breathing through it.
3. Keep focusing on your forehead, breathing through it until you feel subtle sensations, like a light tingling. This is your subtle energy.
4. Begin repeating the first name of the person you want to connect with aloud, ensuring you can hear your own voice. For example, "Peter, Peter, Peter..."
5. Continue repeating their name while staying aware of your body's energy. Notice any shifts—do you feel a sudden wave of anxiety, anger, happiness, or excitement? Do you experience aches or pains that aren't your own? Do you smell something, hear a word, or see a flash of an image? These are your first impressions, coming from the person's energy field.
6. Now, start asking questions like "How are you? What are you up to? Who are you with? Are you OK?" You can ask anything you want to know.

88 | Remote Viewing

Pay attention to the answers. They may come as words, images, scents, tastes, whispers in your ears, or sensations in your body. These are impressions from the person you're connecting with.

Exercise 3: Remote Viewing of Food

Remote viewing food can revolutionize how we approach eating.

Remote viewing of food.

As an immunologist-allergist, I know many people (my former patients and clients) who try to eat healthy, and spend lots of time, attention, and energy on food but still suffer from negative reactions to food – like food allergies or intolerances.

They keep saying "the food didn't agree with me" although the food was bought as organic and fresh.

This means that even though food is labeled as "organic" and should be good, your body may still react badly to it. It happens because **the food's energy is not aligned with your energy.**

What can you do?

The answer is to **do remote viewing of the food before eating**. This involves checking the food's energy from a higher, 5D perspective to see if it matches your own energy. Doing this helps you choose the right food and ensures harmony between your own energy and food's energy.

> **If the energy of the food aligns with the energy of your body, you will not experience allergies.**

Intuitive Eating includes Remote Viewing of Food

The Intuitive Eating method I advocate combines listening to your body's natural signals with the practice of remote viewing of food. Before eating, you perform a quick remote viewing to assess the food's energy and see if it aligns with your own. This method encourages tuning into your internal cues about when, what, and how much to eat, rather than following external diets or rigid rules.

By integrating both physical and energetic aspects, intuitive eating helps you make choices that support your overall well-being and personal energy.

This 5D approach can help eliminate many issues related to the digestive system, allergies, and intolerances. By selecting foods that resonate energetically with you, you reduce the likelihood of negative reactions and make choices that support your overall well-being.

Conventional diets are grounded in 3D principles, whereas intuitive eating embraces the expanded perspective of 5D principles and remote viewing.

A Real-Life Example: Sarah's Healing Journey of Remote Viewing Food

Sarah had long struggled with digestive issues—bloating, fatigue, and discomfort after nearly every meal. She had tried countless diets, but nothing seemed to provide lasting relief. When she learned about the 5D approach to Intuitive Eating, which combines listening to the body's natural signals with remote viewing of food, she decided to try a new method.

Before even stepping into the grocery store, Sarah would first perform a quick remote viewing session on the food she wanted to buy. By scanning the items, she could sense if their energy aligned with her own energy. For example, when she reached for fresh vegetables, she'd quickly assess if the vibrational frequency of these vegetables was in harmony with her body's energy. If an item felt energetically "off," she would simply put it back, trusting that her energy was guiding her toward the best choices.

Note: She stopped relying on the information listed on food labels and instead trusted her ability to sense the energy of the food. By focusing on the food's vibrational frequency, she was able to make healthier, more intuitive choices that aligned with her body's energy needs.

This practice didn't just change how she shopped; it transformed the way Sarah felt after eating. By choosing foods that resonated with her body's energy, Sarah noticed a significant decrease in digestive discomfort. Her bloating and fatigue disappeared, and her allergies seemed to ease. The more she tuned into the energetic properties of food, the more her body flourished.

Through this 5D approach, Sarah discovered that remote viewing of food allowed her to intuitively select foods that were in harmony with her energy. Instead of reacting to foods with discomfort or sensitivities, she was now proactively choosing what would truly nourish her. This process helped her avoid common health issues, from digestive upset to allergic reactions, showing her how much energy alignment with food can impact overall well-being....

Everyday Applications for Remote Viewing Targets

Let's explore how to practice remote viewing of everyday objects, targets, things and situations.

By developing your skills, you can:
- Make decisions with greater clarity
- Gain insight into other people
- Become more attuned to your environment
- Discover what is truly right for YOU
- Understand your body better
- Understand your health better

The most significant application of remote viewing lies in its ability to guide you toward choices aligned with who you are, your purpose, and what resonates with you on a deeper level. Remote viewing helps you achieve all of this.

Below is a comprehensive, alphabetical list of everyday items that people commonly practice remote viewing with.

How to Use This Guide:
- Start by deciding what you want to remote view, then locate the object or target in the list below and follow the provided steps.
- You can view anything—cities, buildings, people, organs (yours or others), stars, planets, and even events from the past or future. The possibilities are limitless.
- Feel free to repeat the process to gain a deeper understanding. Revisiting your first findings can provide new insights with each subsequent viewing.

Start here: choose your target from this list in alphabetical order. Use one target at a time.

Abandoned buildings

Remote viewing abandoned buildings offers a unique opportunity to explore the remnants of history, mystery, and human activity. People are drawn to these targets to uncover their past stories, understand why they were abandoned, or investigate their current energy dynamics. These spaces often carry residual energy, including feelings of stillness, loss, or echoes of past events. However, some abandoned buildings may also surprise viewers with unexpected bursts of vitality, depending on their history or surrounding environment.

Five Steps to Remote View Abandoned Buildings

1. **Clear Your Mind and Set Your Intentions (3–5 minutes)**
   Begin by quieting your thoughts and entering a state of neutrality. Reflect on your goal for the session—whether to explore the building's history, sense its energy, or uncover specific details. Use deep breathing or a brief meditation to centre yourself.
2. **Connect to the Building's Energy Field (5–7 minutes)**
   Visualise the building and let your awareness reach out to its energetic imprint. Focus on its atmosphere and emotional resonance. Take note of areas that feel active, stagnant, heavy, or light. This step helps establish a connection to the target's essence.
3. **Observe the Physical and Energetic Details (7–10 minutes)**
   Spend time exploring the building's physical structure, layout, and surroundings. Allow impressions of specific rooms, objects, or environmental conditions to surface. Pay attention to any sensory details, like textures, colours, or sounds, as well as the emotional energy of the space.
4. **Engage with the Building's History (10–12 minutes)**
   Shift your focus to the building's past. Let images, emotions, or symbolic impressions of people, events, or activities connected to the site emerge. Trust what arises, even if it feels abstract at first, and let the narrative unfold naturally.
5. **Document Your Observations (5 minutes)**
   Conclude your session by writing down or sketching everything you've sensed. Include both concrete details and emotional impressions. Afterward, review your notes to identify patterns or insights, and compare them with any available historical records for validation.

Repeat the Session for Deeper Insights
The next day, revisit the building as your target. Use the information you documented previously to refine your focus. For instance, explore specific areas or delve into lingering impressions that need more clarity. Each session builds on the last, allowing for a more comprehensive understanding of the building's mysteries and energy.

By revisiting the target over multiple sessions, you can uncover layers of details and insights that deepen your connection to the abandoned building and enhance your Remote Viewing skills.

Ancient Artifacts
Ancient artifacts hold a wealth of knowledge, offering connections to long-lost civilizations, cultures, and practices. Remote viewing these objects allows you to uncover their stories, sense their purpose, and explore the energy they carry through time. These targets often evoke feelings of reverence, mystery, and curiosity, making them ideal for those seeking to connect with the past.

Five Steps to Remote View Ancient Artifacts
1. **Prepare Your Mind and Focus on the Artifact (3–5 minutes)**
   Begin by clearing your thoughts and setting your intention for the session. Visualise the artifact or its general concept if you lack specific details. Stay neutral and open to receiving impressions about its history, use, or significance.
2. **Sense the Artifact's Physical Attributes (5–7 minutes)**
   Focus on perceiving the artifact's material qualities—its size, shape, texture, or colour. Imagine holding it in your hands and noting any tactile impressions, such as weight or temperature. This step anchors your awareness to the physical aspects of the target.
3. **Tap into the Artifact's Energetic Imprint (7–10 minutes)**

Shift your focus to the energy surrounding the artifact. Sense any vibrations, emotional tones, or connections to the people who created or used it. Pay attention to the atmosphere it evokes—does it feel sacred, utilitarian, or ceremonial?

4. **Explore the Artifact's Story (10–12 minutes)**
Allow your mind to dive into the artifact's history. Let impressions emerge about its origins, cultural context, or the events it has witnessed. You may perceive images of its creation, its journey through time, or the individuals who interacted with it.

5. **Record and Organize Your Observations (5 minutes)**
Document your findings, including detailed descriptions, sketches, or symbolic impressions. Organize your notes into themes, such as physical details, energetic impressions, and historical narratives.

Repeat the Session for Deeper Exploration

The following day, revisit the artifact as your target. Use your previous notes to guide your focus, exploring areas that felt unclear or incomplete. For example, dive deeper into its cultural significance, its role in specific ceremonies, or its connection to historical events.

Each session builds upon the last, allowing you to peel back layers of time and energy. By repeating sessions, you not only enhance your understanding of the artifact but also refine your Remote Viewing skills, strengthening your connection to history and the universal energy field.

Animals

Finding a Missing Animal

When an animal goes missing, the emotional turmoil and uncertainty can be overwhelming for both the animal and its owner. Remote viewing can be a powerful tool to help locate lost pets, offering insights into their current location, emotional state, and even possible obstacles they may be facing. By tapping into the energetic field surrounding the animal, you can gain clues that guide your search, provide comfort, and bring clarity to the situation.

Five Steps to Remote View Missing Animals

1. **Set Clear Intentions and Calm Your Mind (3–5 minutes)**
   Begin by quieting your thoughts and centring yourself. Focus on your clear intention to locate the missing animal. Visualise the animal's image and connect with their energy. Hold the intent that you will receive accurate, helpful information about their whereabouts.

2. **Establish an Energetic Connection with the Animal (5–7 minutes)**
   Imagine sending out an energetic signal to the animal. Sense their presence, and pay attention to any physical sensations or emotions that arise. Focus on connecting with the animal's unique energy signature, letting it guide you to where they may be.

3. **Scan the Environment for Clues (7–10 minutes)**
   Expand your awareness and begin to sense the environment surrounding the animal. Look for impressions of specific locations or objects that may be significant. You might perceive certain areas—such as streets, buildings, or natural features—or objects that may be near them, such as a tree, fence, or vehicle.

4. **Tune into the Animal's Emotional State (5–7 minutes)**
   While scanning, take note of the animal's emotional state. Are they scared, calm, or seeking comfort? This can give you clues about their behaviour and help guide where they might be hiding or trapped. Pay attention to their body language, which may emerge through impressions or mental images.

5. **Document and Review Your Findings (5 minutes)**
   After the session, record all impressions, including visual details, emotional cues, and any location-based information. Be sure to capture sketches or written notes. Look for

patterns in the information—these will help you narrow down possible search areas.

Repeat the Session for Further Clarity
The following day, revisit the missing animal as your target. Use the information from your previous session to guide your focus. If a location or emotional state feels unclear, explore it further. You might receive new insights that help you refine your search and get closer to finding the animal.

Remote viewing can provide powerful insights into the whereabouts and well-being of a missing animal. By repeating the session, you can continue to receive guidance and clues that lead to a successful reunion, all while deepening your understanding of your intuitive abilities.

Assessing an Animal's Health

Remote viewing can be an invaluable tool for assessing an animal's health, especially when traditional methods of observation or examination are not possible. By tapping into the energetic field of the animal, you can gather insights about physical conditions, emotional imbalances, or underlying health issues that may not be immediately visible. These steps guide you in connecting with the animal's energy and assessing their overall health.

Five Steps to Remote View an Animal's Health
1. **Clear Your Mind and Set Intentions (3–5 minutes)**
   Start by calming your mind through deep breathing or meditation. Set a clear intention to assess the animal's health. Visualise the animal and establish a connection to their energy. Focus on being neutral and open, ready to receive any impressions related to their well-being.
2. **Connect to the Animal's Energetic Field (5–7 minutes)**
   Begin by sensing the animal's energy field. Imagine you are sending out an energetic connection to the animal, tuning into their unique frequency. Pay attention to any areas of

discomfort, blockages, or heightened energy. These impressions will guide you to focus on specific parts of the animal's body or energy system.

3. **Scan for Physical Symptoms or Imbalances (7–10 minutes)**
Expand your focus to explore the animal's physical health. Scan the body for any indications of illness, injury, or pain. Pay attention to sensations such as heat, cold, tension, or lightness in specific areas of the body. These subtle cues can point to underlying physical conditions that require attention.

4. **Examine Emotional and Behavioural Imprints (5–7 minutes)**
As you continue to focus on the animal's energy, assess their emotional state. Are there signs of anxiety, stress, fear, or lethargy? Emotional imbalances often manifest in physical health issues, so it is important to consider how the animal's emotional state could be impacting their health.

5. **Document Your Findings and Areas for Further Exploration (5 minutes)**
After the session, record all the impressions you've gathered, including physical symptoms, emotional cues, and any specific areas of the body that felt significant. If you felt drawn to particular organs or systems, note them for further exploration. This can guide you in addressing specific health concerns.

Repeat the Session for More Detailed Insights

The following day, revisit the animal's health as your target. Use the information from your previous session to refine your focus. If certain health concerns or areas of the body were unclear, explore them further. Additional sessions may provide more in-depth insights into the animal's health, allowing you to gather a fuller picture.

By revisiting the health assessment in subsequent sessions, you can track changes, refine your observations, and deepen your understanding of the animal's energetic and physical state. This process not only helps you assess their health but also enhances your remote viewing abilities for future use.

Archaeological Sites

Remote viewing archaeological sites offers an extraordinary opportunity to connect with the energy, history, and mysteries of ancient civilizations. These sessions can provide insights into the purpose, construction, and cultural significance of sites that hold timeless wisdom. Here are five structured steps to guide you in remote viewing archaeological sites effectively.

Five Steps to Remote View Archaeological Sites
1. **Set Your Intention and Focus on the Site (3–5 minutes)**
   Begin by clearing your mind and setting a clear intention to explore the chosen archaeological site. Visualise its general characteristics, such as its location or cultural background, if known. Open yourself to impressions, ensuring a calm and neutral mental state.
2. **Connect to the Site's Energy (5–7 minutes)**
   Focus on establishing a connection with the energetic field of the site. Sense its atmosphere—does it feel sacred, mysterious, or heavy with history? Pay attention to subtle impressions, such as the presence of structures, people, or natural features. This step sets the foundation for deeper exploration.
3. **Perceive Physical and Structural Details (7–10 minutes)**
   Shift your focus to the physical attributes of the site. Let impressions of shapes, materials, and layouts come to you. Try to identify specific features like temples, roads, walls, or natural formations. Sketch any images that arise to help you organize these impressions.
4. **Explore the Site's History and Use (10–12 minutes)**
   Allow your awareness to dive into the history of the site. Sense its purpose—was it a place of worship, a residential area, or a trade

hub? Visualise the people who built and used it, their activities, and their connection to the site. Impressions of cultural practices or significant events may emerge during this step.
5. **Record and Reflect on Your Impressions (5 minutes)**
   After completing the session, document your findings in detail. Include descriptions of the physical and energetic characteristics of the site, as well as any historical or cultural impressions. Organize your notes and sketches to create a cohesive picture of the site's essence.

Repeat the Session for Deeper Insights

On the following day, revisit the archaeological site as your target. Use the information gathered from your initial session to guide your focus. Investigate areas that felt unclear or intriguing, and aim to fill in gaps in your understanding. Each session provides an opportunity to refine your perception and deepen your connection to the site.

Remote viewing archaeological sites allows you to uncover layers of history, explore the cultural significance of ancient places, and enhance your intuitive skills. By revisiting the target over multiple sessions, you can gain a richer understanding of the site's energy and the stories it holds, contributing to a deeper connection with humanity's shared past.

Art Collections

Remote viewing art collections offers an opportunity to connect with the essence of human creativity, cultural expression, and historical significance. Whether the collection includes paintings, sculptures, or artifacts, remote viewing can help uncover the emotions, messages, and inspirations behind the pieces. Here are five structured steps to guide you in remote viewing art collections effectively.

Five Steps to Remote View Art Collections

1. **Set Your Intention and Focus on the Collection (3–5 minutes)**
   Begin by calming your mind and setting a clear intention to connect with the chosen art collection. Whether it is a specific gallery, museum, or private collection, visualise its general setting or theme. Keep your mind open to the variety of styles, emotions, and energies that the collection may hold.

2. **Connect to the Energetic Field of the Collection (5–7 minutes)**
   Tune into the collective energy of the artwork in the collection. Notice how it feels—is it vibrant, calming, inspiring, or thought-provoking? Pay attention to any emotional impressions or symbolic messages that arise as you establish a connection with the energy field of the collection.

3. **Explore Individual Pieces in the Collection (7–10 minutes)**
   Shift your focus to individual pieces within the collection. Allow impressions of shapes, colours, and textures to come through. Try to sense the themes or stories behind specific works. Sketch or describe any details that stand out, such as a dominant colour palette, recurring symbols, or the artist's energy embedded in the piece.

4. **Uncover Historical and Emotional Contexts (10–12 minutes)**
   Dive deeper into the historical and emotional layers of the collection. Sense the time periods and cultural influences associated with the pieces. Explore the emotions or ideas the artists intended to convey. Reflect on how the collection as a whole resonates with broader cultural or philosophical themes.

5. **Document Your Findings and Insights (5 minutes)**
   After the session, thoroughly document your impressions. Include notes on the overall energy of the collection, details

of specific pieces, and any historical or emotional contexts that emerged. Create sketches or diagrams to support your observations, helping to form a clear understanding of the collection.

Repeat the Session for Expanded Perception

Revisit the art collection in a follow-up session, using your previous findings to guide you. Focus on areas that felt incomplete or pieces that held particular intrigue. Additional sessions can reveal subtler layers of meaning, helping you form a more comprehensive connection to the collection's artistic and energetic essence.

Remote viewing art collections is a way to engage with the profound creativity and cultural expressions that shape human history. By revisiting the collection and refining your observations, you can deepen your appreciation for art while honing your intuitive abilities to perceive its hidden dimensions.

Astronomical Phenomena

Remote viewing astronomical phenomena allows you to connect intuitively with the universe's mysteries, exploring events and objects beyond Earth. Examples of phenomena include **solar eclipses**, **meteor showers**, **auroras**, **black holes**, and **supernovae**. Follow these steps to deepen your understanding of these celestial marvels.

Five Steps to Remote View Astronomical Phenomena

Step 1: Set Your Intention and Focus on the Phenomenon (3–5 minutes)

Begin by clarifying your target—whether it's a black hole, an aurora, a meteor shower, or another astronomical event. Focus on the phenomenon and set an intention to connect with its energy and details. Visualise the vast expanse of space and allow your mind to open to the infinite possibilities of the universe.

Step 2: Tune Into the Cosmic Energy of the Phenomenon (5–7 minutes)

Establish an energetic connection to the astronomical event or object. Visualise its location in the cosmos, and sense the scale, movement, and vibrational energy it emits. For example:

- For a meteor shower, feel the swift motion and fiery energy of particles entering Earth's atmosphere.
- For a black hole, sense the immense gravitational pull and the mystery of its event horizon.

Stay neutral, allowing impressions to come naturally.

Step 3: Observe the Structure and Dynamics (7–10 minutes)

Shift your focus to the physical and energetic details. Ask yourself:

- What does the phenomenon look like in terms of shapes, colours, and movements?
- How does it interact with its surroundings?
- Are there patterns or rhythms that stand out?

Sketch or write down any impressions, even if they seem abstract. For example, you might notice spiralling energies around a galaxy or vibrant streams of light in an aurora.

Step 4: Explore the Phenomenon's Broader Impact (10–12 minutes)

Dive deeper into the phenomenon's significance:

- How does it influence the surrounding environment?
- What role does it play in the larger cosmic system?
- How does it energetically connect to Earth or other celestial bodies?

For instance, you could explore how the solar wind behind an aurora affects Earth's magnetic field or how a supernova contributes to the formation of new stars.

Step 5: Document Findings and Reflect for a Follow-Up Session (5 minutes)
Summarize your observations, including sketches, sensory impressions, and any insights you gained. Reflect on any areas that felt unclear or require further exploration. Plan a follow-up session to revisit the phenomenon, using your initial findings to deepen your understanding.

Repeat the Session
Revisit the target in a new session to refine your impressions and explore aspects you didn't fully uncover. For example, if you focused on the energy of a meteor shower in your first session, you might explore its trajectory or the origin of the meteoroids in the next.

Remote viewing astronomical phenomena connects you to the universe's grandeur and inspires a profound sense of unity with the cosmos. By revisiting and building upon your findings, you deepen both your understanding and your intuitive abilities.

Biological Samples
Remote viewing biological samples—such as cells, tissues, or DNA—offers a unique opportunity to explore the intricate workings of life on a microscopic level. By tuning into the energy and structure of these samples, you can uncover information about their health, function, or even hidden anomalies.

Five Steps to Remote View Biological Samples

Step 1: Define Your Target and Set Intentions (3–5 minutes)
Clarify the specific biological sample you want to remote view, such as a **blood cell**, **DNA strand**, or **tissue biopsy**. Focus on your intention, whether it is to assess the sample's energy, identify anomalies, or gain insights into its condition. Stay neutral and ensure your mind is calm and focused.

Step 2: Establish an Energetic Connection (5–7 minutes)
Visualise the biological sample and connect to its energy field.

- For a **blood cell**, sense its vibrancy, movement, and functionality.
- For **DNA**, tune into its spiral structure and the flow of information it contains.
- For **tissue**, feel its texture and observe any signs of harmony or discord in its energy.

Allow impressions of colour, shape, movement, or even symbolic imagery to emerge naturally.

Step 3: Observe Structural and Functional Details (7–10 minutes)
Focus on the sample's physical and energetic characteristics:

- What is the **shape** and **structure** of the cells or molecules?
- Are there any areas that appear darker, denser, or disrupted?
- How does the energy flow through the sample?

Sketch or write down your observations, noting patterns, textures, or areas of imbalance. For example, a damaged tissue might emit fragmented or chaotic energy.

Step 4: Explore Environmental and Contextual Influences (10–12 minutes)
Expand your perspective to understand the broader context of the sample:

- How does the sample interact with its surrounding environment?
- Are there external factors (toxins, stress, or nutrition) influencing its state?
- Does the energy suggest a connection to a larger system, such as an organ or the body as a whole?

For instance, a remote view of DNA might reveal influences from inherited patterns or external stressors affecting gene expression.

Step 5: Document and Reflect for Follow-Up (5 minutes)
Record all impressions, sketches, and notes from the session. Reflect on your findings and any new questions that emerged. Plan a follow-up session to build on what you've observed. For example:

- If you focused on the **energy of a tissue**, revisit to assess its healing potential.
- If you remote-viewed **DNA**, explore how specific sequences interact with their environment.

Repeating the session allows you to refine your perceptions and deepen your understanding.

Remote viewing biological samples enables a profound exploration of the microcosm of life. This practice not only offers insights into health and biology but also fosters a deeper connection to the intricate systems that sustain living beings. By revisiting targets and expanding your focus, you can uncover hidden dynamics and contribute to a greater understanding of life's mysteries.

Book

Remote viewing a book allows you to tap into its essence, message, and knowledge without physically accessing it. This practice can reveal insights about its content, themes, or even the emotions and intentions of the author. Whether you're seeking inspiration, understanding, or validation of its relevance, these steps guide your exploration.

Five Steps to Remote View a Book

Step 1: Define the Book and Your Intention (3–5 minutes)
Begin by clearly identifying the book you wish to remote view. This could be a specific title or a genre you're drawn to. Set your intention for the session:

- Are you seeking to understand the book's main themes?
- Do you want to determine if it aligns with your current interests or needs?

- Are you curious about the author's perspective or creative energy?

Maintain neutrality, setting aside preconceptions about the book.

Step 2: Establish an Energetic Connection (5–7 minutes)
Visualise the book in your mind's eye, focusing on its energy, physical appearance, or even its title.

- Imagine holding the book, feeling its weight, and sensing its energy.
- Envision its pages opening and inviting you to explore.

Allow your mind to connect with the essence of the book, observing any impressions or symbols that arise.

Step 3: Perceive Content and Themes (7–10 minutes)
Shift your focus to the book's content and themes.

- Are there specific ideas, images, or phrases that emerge?
- What emotions or energies are tied to the book's message?
- Can you sense the author's intent or the tone of the writing?

For example, if you're remote viewing a novel, you might perceive elements of its plot or characters. If it's a self-help book, you might sense its guidance and practical takeaways.

Step 4: Explore Context and Relevance (10–12 minutes)
Dive deeper into the broader context and significance of the book:

- How does the book's energy align with your current needs or goals?
- Does it feel like a source of wisdom, inspiration, or entertainment?
- Is there a specific chapter, topic, or idea that seems most relevant to you?

Consider whether this book resonates with your personal growth, professional development, or spiritual journey.

Step 5: Document and Plan a Follow-Up Session (5 minutes)
Summarize your findings, noting any key impressions, symbols, or insights. Reflect on the clarity of your perceptions and whether the book feels meaningful to you. Plan a follow-up session to dive deeper into areas of interest. For example:

- Revisit specific chapters or sections that seemed significant.
- Explore the author's energy or perspective in greater detail.
- Use the book's themes as a springboard for your own creative or intellectual projects.

Remote viewing a book bridges the gap between intuition and knowledge, offering a unique way to connect with written works. By repeating sessions and focusing on different aspects, you can deepen your understanding and uncover layers of meaning. Whether you're exploring literature, seeking personal alignment, or tapping into an author's wisdom, remote viewing a book is a profound tool for discovery

Bridge Structures

Remote viewing bridge structures provides insights into their design, history, and the energy they represent as connections between places, people, or ideas. By focusing on a specific bridge, you can explore its physical characteristics, symbolic meanings, and its interaction with the surrounding environment.

Five Steps to Remote View Bridge Structures

Step 1: Define the Bridge and Set Intentions (3–5 minutes)
Identify the specific bridge structure you wish to remote view, such as the Golden Gate Bridge, a local landmark, or even a symbolic bridge from the past. Set your intention for the session:

- Are you examining its architectural features or historical significance?
- Do you want to explore its energy as a connector of two spaces?
- Are you investigating its current condition or its emotional impact on those who cross it?

Stay neutral and open to whatever impressions arise.

Step 2: Establish an Energetic Connection (5–7 minutes)
Visualise the bridge and its surrounding environment.

- Imagine standing at one end of the bridge and feeling its energy.
- Sense its size, materials, and the flow of energy from one side to the other.

Allow yourself to connect with the bridge's purpose—whether it's practical, symbolic, or both. Observe any immediate impressions, such as its appearance, the weather around it, or its atmosphere.

Step 3: Explore Physical and Structural Details (7–10 minutes)
Focus on the bridge's physical characteristics and structure:

- What materials are used in its construction (metal, wood, stone)?
- How does the bridge integrate with its surroundings—rivers, valleys, or urban landscapes?
- Are there areas that feel strong or weak, harmonious or out of balance?

Sketch or describe the impressions you receive, noting specific details like the shape of the arches, the texture of the cables, or the flow of traffic or water below.

Step 4: Sense Historical and Energetic Context (10–12 minutes)
Shift your attention to the bridge's history and energetic significance:

- Who built the bridge, and for what purpose?
- Does the bridge carry the energy of its builders, users, or events it has witnessed?
- How does the bridge feel energetically—does it carry a sense of pride, weariness, or timeless endurance?

For example, a historical bridge might reveal glimpses of its era, while a modern structure could resonate with innovation and connectivity.

Step 5: Document and Reflect for a Follow-Up Session (5 minutes)
Write down your impressions, including any sketches or symbolic messages. Reflect on your findings:
- Did the bridge reveal any unexpected details or emotions?
- Are there areas or aspects you want to explore further, such as hidden structural elements or its symbolic significance?

Plan a follow-up session to build on your observations. For instance, you could delve deeper into its interaction with the environment or revisit its historical context.

Remote viewing bridge structures can provide profound insights into their physical and symbolic roles as connectors. Each bridge carries a unique story and energy, whether it's linking two places or serving as a metaphor for unity. By repeating sessions and refining your focus, you can uncover layers of meaning that deepen your understanding of these architectural marvels and their impact on human and environmental connections.

Business Deals
Remote viewing business deals offers a unique way to assess opportunities, risks, and alignments with your goals. By intuitively exploring the energy and potential outcomes of a deal, you can gain clarity and make informed decisions.

Five Steps to Remote View Business Deals

Step 1: Define the Business Deal and Your Intentions (3–5 minutes)
Clearly identify the business deal you wish to remote view. This could be a negotiation, partnership, investment, or contract. Set your intention for the session:
- Are you assessing the deal's alignment with your values and goals?

- Do you want to understand the motivations and energy of other parties involved?
- Are you seeking insight into potential outcomes or risks?

Stay neutral and avoid forming preconceived judgments about the deal.

Step 2: Connect to the Deal's Energy (5–7 minutes)
Visualise the business deal as an energetic entity. Imagine it as a table with all parties present or as a flow of resources and intentions.

- Focus on the energy dynamics between you and other stakeholders.
- Sense whether the deal feels balanced, harmonious, or tense.
- Observe any symbols, emotions, or impressions that arise related to the deal.

Step 3: Explore Details and Dynamics (7–10 minutes)
Shift your focus to specific aspects of the deal:

- Who are the key players, and what energy do they bring?
- What are the terms, and do they feel fair or skewed?
- Are there hidden opportunities or risks that might not be immediately apparent?

Pay attention to any intuitive nudges about areas requiring closer scrutiny or aspects that feel particularly promising.

Step 4: Assess Alignment and Outcomes (10–12 minutes)
Explore how the deal aligns with your personal or organizational goals and values:

- Does it resonate with your vision and purpose?
- What potential outcomes, both short- and long-term, do you perceive?
- Are there any red flags or areas of concern that stand out?

Consider the ripple effects of the deal, including financial, reputational, and relational impacts.

Step 5: Document Insights and Plan a Follow-Up Session (5 minutes)

Summarize your impressions, noting any key details, symbols, or feelings that emerged during the session. Reflect on your findings:

- Are you confident in pursuing or declining the deal?
- Did any areas require further exploration or clarification?

Plan a follow-up session to revisit specific aspects of the deal, such as its terms, the energy of other stakeholders, or potential risks. Use insights gained in the first session as a foundation for deeper exploration.

Remote viewing business deals allows you to tap into the intuitive aspects of decision-making, revealing insights that may not be visible through conventional analysis. By repeating sessions and refining your focus, you can make well-rounded decisions that align with your values, goals, and long-term success.

Cities

Remote viewing cities allows you to explore their energy, dynamics, and characteristics, helping you decide if the city's energy aligns with yours and if it's a good place for you to visit. This practice reveals how the city's atmosphere, human activity, and environment interact, giving you valuable insights into its essence and whether it resonates with your own energy.

Five Steps to Remote View Cities

Step 1: Define the City and Set Intentions (3–5 minutes)

Identify the city you want to remote view. This could be a historical metropolis like Rome, a bustling hub like New York, or a quiet town with personal significance. Clarify your purpose: are you examining its atmosphere, energy flow, or specific areas like landmarks, neighbourhoods, or social dynamics?

Step 2: Connect to the City's Energy (5–7 minutes)
Visualise the city from a high vantage point, observing its layout, colours, and activity. Sense the collective energy of its inhabitants, the rhythm of daily life, and the relationship between the natural and built environments. Tune into the city's unique personality—does it feel vibrant, calm, chaotic, or something else?

Step 3: Explore Specific Features and Dynamics (7–10 minutes)
Focus on key features such as landmarks, streets, or neighbourhoods. Observe architectural styles, transportation systems, or areas of energy concentration. Pay attention to the interactions of people and their activities. For example, explore the bustling energy of a market or the serene flow of a park. Notice how the city interacts with its surroundings, such as rivers, mountains, or coastlines.

Step 4: Sense Historical and Cultural Layers (10–12 minutes)
Tune into the city's history and cultural significance. What stories, traditions, or events shape its identity? Imagine the layers of time and the energy of past generations that still linger. Consider how the city feels as a living entity—how it has evolved and how it connects with its people and visitors.

Step 5: Document Impressions and Plan Follow-Up Sessions (5 minutes)
Record your impressions of the city's energy, including any feelings or insights about specific areas. Reflect on whether the city's overall energy aligns with yours—would you feel comfortable or energized visiting? Decide whether this city is a good fit for you, based on how its energy interacts with yours. If you're uncertain, plan a follow-up session to explore certain areas in more detail.

By following these steps, you can assess if the city's energy aligns with your own and if it's a place that would benefit your well-being to visit.

Coastal Areas

Coastal areas are often chosen for remote viewing due to their unique blend of natural beauty, energy flow, and the connection between land and sea. Whether for relaxation, exploration, or understanding environmental dynamics, remote viewing these areas can offer insights into their ecological balance, energy patterns, and even potential health benefits. By connecting with the energy of coastal environments, you can assess whether these areas are beneficial to your well-being and understand their impact on the surrounding ecosystem.

Five Steps to Remote View Coastal Areas

Step 1: Set Your Intentions and Identify the Coastal Area (3–5 minutes)
Begin by clearly identifying the coastal area you wish to explore. Coastal regions may include beaches, cliffs, shorelines, and bays—each with unique energy. Set your intention: Are you looking to explore the environmental health of the area, the energy it emits, or its suitability for your personal visit or retreat? This will help guide the focus of your session.

Step 2: Connect with the Energy of the Coastline (5–7 minutes)
Visualise the coastal area from above, sensing the energy of the land meeting the sea. Pay attention to the ebb and flow of the tides and the natural elements around you. Coastal areas are often places of high energetic exchange, where the natural rhythms of water, wind, and land create a dynamic energy. Tune into whether this energy feels calming, invigorating, or neutral—how does it resonate with you?

Step 3: Focus on the Ecological and Environmental Balance (7–10 minutes)
Explore the environmental features of the coastal area, including the health of the ecosystem, beaches, and wildlife. Observe how the sea and land interact—do they seem in harmony, or are there signs of

imbalance, such as pollution or disruption? This step can give you insight into how well the area is cared for and whether it's a safe or nurturing place to visit.

Step 4: Investigate the Impact of the Coastal Energy on Well-Being (10–12 minutes)
Pay attention to how the coastal area's energy might affect your personal well-being. Many people are drawn to coastal regions for their calming effects and rejuvenating energy. Observe if the area has a soothing impact on the mind, body, and spirit. Does the energy feel healing, energizing, or too overwhelming? Is it an ideal place for rest, rejuvenation, or spiritual growth?

Step 5: Document Impressions and Consider Future Exploration (5 minutes)
Record the energy you've perceived, any impressions of the environment, and how the coastal area might resonate with you personally. Reflect on whether the area feels like a good match for a visit or longer-term stay. You can also decide if you want to conduct further remote viewing sessions to explore different coastal zones, specific beaches, or local communities.

By using these steps, you can assess the energy and environmental health of coastal areas, and understand how the unique energy of land and sea might benefit your physical, emotional, and spiritual well-being. This can help you make more informed decisions about where to visit, live, or invest in coastal regions.

Communication Systems

Communication systems, such as global networks, telecommunication infrastructure, or satellite systems, play a vital role in modern life. Remote viewing these systems allows you to assess their functionality, security, and how well they align with your personal or professional needs. Whether you're interested in understanding the efficiency, reliability, or potential risks associated with a communication system, remote viewing provides a deeper insight. It can also help you decide if a particular system suits your requirements, whether for personal use, business, or technological exploration.

Five Steps to Remote View Communication Systems

Step 1: Define the Communication System and Set Your Intentions (3–5 minutes)

Start by specifying the communication system you want to view, such as internet networks, cellular systems, or satellite communication. Clearly state your intention: Are you investigating the system's general efficiency, potential security issues, or its alignment with your goals and needs? For instance, if you're looking into using a particular communication network for your business or personal use, decide whether you're assessing its suitability for your work or lifestyle.

Step 2: Connect to the Energy and Flow of the System (5–7 minutes)

Visualise the system in operation. For global networks, you might see the flow of data traveling through cables and servers. For satellite communication, visualise the signals passing through space and connecting to Earth. Tune into how the energy feels—whether it flows smoothly, energetically vibrant, or feels slow, blocked, or overloaded. Assess whether the system's energy aligns with your personal or professional needs. Does it feel like a good fit for your goals or way of working?

Step 3: Analyse the System's Structure and Weaknesses (7–10 minutes)

Focus on the infrastructure of the communication system—whether it's the cables, satellites, or data centres. Look for any signs of inefficiency, potential disruptions, or weak points in the system's design. Does it feel like it's built for longevity and reliability, or are there areas where the system might fail or require improvements? Evaluate if the structure aligns with your requirements. For example, if you need a highly reliable system for your business, does it appear robust and secure?

Step 4: Investigate Potential Interferences and External Impacts (10–12 minutes)
Examine any external factors that may impact the communication system, such as weather conditions, electromagnetic disturbances, or cybersecurity risks. Are there any signs of interference that might disrupt the system's functionality? Look for any vulnerabilities that could affect the system's overall performance and consider whether these potential risks would be a concern for you personally or professionally.

Step 5: Document Findings and Evaluate the System's Fit for You (5 minutes)
Write down your impressions and insights gained from the session. Reflect on whether the communication system's energy, structure, and security align with your needs. Does it feel like a good match for your work, lifestyle, or personal use? Consider if the system will provide the support or functionality you desire, or if adjustments might be necessary. You can repeat the session on a different day to refine your insights or explore areas that require further attention.

By using these steps, you can gain a deeper understanding of the communication system's overall performance and its suitability for your needs. Whether you're evaluating the reliability of a satellite system, assessing the efficiency of an internet network, or understanding the risks associated with a telecommunication infrastructure, remote viewing provides clarity on how well a system meets your personal or professional requirements.

Construction Projects

People often choose to remote view construction projects because these sites are dynamic and ever-changing, offering valuable insights into their progress, challenges, and potential outcomes. Remote viewing can help individuals assess the current state of a project, foresee potential delays or issues, and understand the energy and harmony of the construction site. It's a useful tool for project managers, investors, or anyone seeking to gain a deeper intuitive understanding of how a construction project is unfolding.

Five Steps to Remote View Construction Projects

1. **Preparation (5 minutes)**
   Find a quiet, undisturbed space and relax your mind. Close your eyes, breathe deeply, and set your intention to focus on the construction project. Imagine connecting with the energy of the site, holding a clear and neutral mindset.
2. **Create a Mental Connection (5 minutes)**
   Visualise the construction project as vividly as you can. If you have a specific location or description in mind, focus on that. Allow yourself to mentally "step into" the site, sensing its energy and observing its details.
3. **Explore the Project (10 minutes)**
   Observe the construction project in its current state. Look for elements such as the layout, ongoing work, machinery, and the presence of workers. Let your mind guide you to areas that stand out, whether they are fully formed structures or unfinished sections.
4. **Identify Challenges (10 minutes)**
   Tune into areas where the energy feels tense or out of sync. These may represent issues such as delays, material shortages, or design flaws. Note any impressions or solutions that come to mind, and focus on how these challenges might be addressed.
5. **Document Your Observations (5 minutes)**
   After completing the session, write down everything you experienced, including specific details, sensory impressions, or emotions tied to the site. This will serve as a record for analysing and revisiting the project.

To refine and deepen your understanding, revisit the project in a second session the next day. Use the notes and insights from your first attempt to focus on areas that need more clarity or detail. This iterative approach allows you to uncover new perspectives and form a more complete picture of the construction project.

Controversial Events

People often choose to remote view controversial events to gain clarity, uncover hidden truths, or understand multiple perspectives surrounding the situation. These events are often clouded by conflicting narratives, emotions, and agendas, making them challenging to analyse through conventional means. Remote viewing provides an intuitive way to explore the deeper layers of the event, helping to reveal insights about its causes, dynamics, and potential outcomes.

Five Steps to Remote View Controversial Events

1. **Set Your Intention and Ground Yourself (5 minutes)**
   Begin in a quiet space where you feel grounded and focused. Take deep breaths and centre yourself. Set a clear intention to approach the event with neutrality and curiosity, free from personal biases or preconceived ideas.
2. **Visualise the Event's Timeline (10 minutes)**
   Picture the event unfolding in its entirety, starting from its origins to the aftermath. Focus on identifying key moments or turning points. Allow yourself to "step into" the timeline and observe what stands out—whether it's specific individuals, actions, or emotions present during the event.
3. **Shift Perspectives (10 minutes)**
   Explore the event from different angles. Mentally place yourself in the position of various participants, observers, or even the environment itself. Ask yourself what each perspective reveals about motivations, decisions, and reactions surrounding the controversy.

4. **Sense Underlying Energies (10 minutes)**
   Focus on the emotional and energetic layers of the event. Does the energy feel chaotic, harmonious, fearful, or hopeful? Pay attention to patterns or symbols that might offer clues about deeper truths or hidden influences driving the event.
5. **Capture Your Insights (5 minutes)**
   Once you complete the session, write down your impressions in detail. Include key observations, recurring symbols, or emotions you encountered. Reflect on what the session revealed about the event's deeper meaning and its potential lessons.

To build on your understanding, revisit the controversial event in a follow-up session. Use your initial notes to focus on unresolved aspects or areas that need more exploration. Each session can uncover new dimensions, helping to piece together a fuller, more nuanced view of the event.

Crime Investigations

People often choose to remote view crime investigations to gain deeper insights into unresolved cases, uncover hidden details, or better understand the sequence of events and the motives of those involved. For law enforcement, remote viewing can complement traditional investigative methods. Families of victims may seek clarity or closure, while individuals with intuitive abilities might want to use their skills to assist in bringing justice or understanding to a case. Remote viewing offers a unique perspective, providing details that may not be immediately accessible through conventional means.

Note: This subject may not be suitable for everyone to remote view. The energy of the victim and their experiences can deeply affect the viewer during the process. It is essential to assess your emotional strength and balance before engaging in this type of remote viewing. Ensure you are adequately prepared to handle any emotional impact that may arise, and practice self-care after completing your session.

Remote viewing in this context requires neutrality, sensitivity, and a strong focus to maintain emotional balance.

Five Steps to Remote View Crime Investigations

1. **Prepare and Shield Yourself (10 minutes)**
   Start by grounding yourself through meditation or breathing exercises. Visualise a protective shield of light around you to guard against any heavy or negative energies. Set your intention to observe the crime neutrally, without becoming emotionally entangled.

2. **Focus on the Scene (10 minutes)**
   Bring your attention to the crime scene. Visualise its details—such as the location, objects, and any significant elements present. Allow impressions of the environment, the people involved, or the timeline of events to emerge naturally.

3. **Trace the Events (15 minutes)**
   Mentally follow the sequence of events leading up to, during, and after the crime. Pay attention to significant moments or changes in energy. Look for details about the actions, movements, or emotional states of those involved.

4. **Sense Emotional and Energetic Imprints (10 minutes)**
   Tune into the emotional and energetic residue left behind by the crime. What emotions dominate the scene—fear, anger, confusion? Be mindful of any symbols, colours, or sensations that might represent deeper truths or key elements of the case.

5. **Document Observations with Care (10 minutes)**
   Record your impressions in detail, including physical, emotional, and energetic observations. Write down any symbols, events, or patterns that stood out. Be sensitive to the weight of the subject matter as you organize your findings.

Remote viewing crime investigations requires great care and emotional resilience. After completing your session, give yourself time to process the experience and reflect on its impact. If you feel unsettled, take a break and ground yourself before considering further exploration. Revisiting the session on another day can help clarify and deepen your understanding of the case.

Crime Scenes

Refer to the steps outlined for viewing crime investigations (above); the process remains the same.

Cultural Festivals

People often choose to remote view cultural festivals to explore the vibrancy, traditions, and emotions that define these unique events. This can help them connect to different cultures, gain a deeper understanding of rituals and celebrations, or simply experience the joy and energy of a gathering they cannot attend in person. Remote viewing allows for a rich, immersive experience, offering insights into the festival's deeper meanings, its participants, and the collective atmosphere.

Five Steps to Remote View Cultural Festivals

1. **Set an Intention and Focus (5 minutes)**
   Begin by choosing a specific cultural festival you want to explore. Take a moment to research or reflect on its location, theme, or unique aspects. Set a clear intention to observe the festival neutrally and respectfully, allowing insights to flow naturally.
2. **Visualise the Environment (10 minutes)**
   Picture the festival's setting, whether it's in a city square, a rural village, or a sacred site. Focus on the details—colours, decorations, sounds, and the layout of the space. Imagine yourself entering this vibrant environment and absorbing its energy.
3. **Observe the Participants (10 minutes)**
   Shift your attention to the people attending the festival. Notice their clothing, interactions, and emotions. Are they

joyful, excited, or reflective? Pay attention to rituals or performances, and let impressions of their cultural significance come to you.

4. **Sense the Energy and Symbolism (10 minutes)**
   Tune into the collective energy of the event. What does it feel like—celebratory, sacred, or communal? Observe symbols, movements, or sounds that stand out. Reflect on how these elements might represent deeper cultural or spiritual meanings.

5. **Document Your Observations (5 minutes)**
   After the session, write down your impressions, focusing on sensory details, emotions, and key moments. Include any symbols or insights about the festival's purpose or cultural significance. Use these notes to deepen your understanding of the event.

Cultural festivals are rich with meaning, energy, and connection, making them an inspiring object for remote viewing. To gain a more complete perspective, revisit the festival in a follow-up session the next day. Focus on specific aspects you want to explore further, such as the energy of a particular ritual or the atmosphere of the crowd. This iterative process can help you form a clearer, more profound connection to the cultural celebration.

Dangerous Locations

People often choose to remote view dangerous locations to assess the risks, understand the energy present, or explore the conditions of a place that may be difficult or unsafe to approach physically. Whether it's a hazardous terrain, a war zone, or an area affected by natural disasters, remote viewing allows individuals to gather information without putting themselves at risk. This can be useful for personal safety, for research, or to gain a deeper understanding of dangerous environments that could impact people's lives or the surrounding area.

Note: Remote viewing dangerous locations can be emotionally intense and potentially unsettling. The energy of these places may include fear, trauma, or other negative emotions that could affect the viewer during the process. It's important to assess your emotional readiness and ensure you are well-grounded before engaging in this type of remote viewing. Always protect yourself with a grounding or shielding technique before beginning your session.

Five Steps to Remote View Dangerous Locations

1. **Set Clear Intentions and Protect Yourself (5 minutes)**
   Begin by grounding yourself through deep breathing or meditation. Set a clear intention to observe the location neutrally and without judgment. Visualise a protective shield around you to ensure you are not affected by any negative energies present in the environment.
2. **Visualise the Location's Boundaries (10 minutes)**
   Focus on the physical boundaries of the dangerous location—whether it's a hazardous area, a disaster site, or an unstable environment. Allow your awareness to expand and explore the details of the terrain, structure, or surroundings. Notice any signs of instability or danger.
3. **Explore the Energy of the Location (10 minutes)**
   Shift your focus to the energy present in the area. What does the environment feel like? Is there tension, fear, chaos, or danger? Pay attention to any sensations or emotions that arise as you explore the energy of the location. This can give you a sense of the risks involved.
4. **Identify Key Elements of the Danger (10 minutes)**
   Look for specific elements or aspects of the location that contribute to its danger—whether it's unstable terrain, the presence of hazardous materials, or social/political tensions. These details can help you understand the potential threats and provide insight into how to navigate or avoid them.

5. **Record Your Findings and Reflect (5 minutes)**
   Write down your observations, focusing on the physical and energetic aspects of the location. Reflect on any insights about the dangers, such as emotional patterns or warning signs. Pay attention to how the energy of the location might affect you, and note any actions you can take for safety or awareness.

By following these steps, you can gain valuable insights into dangerous locations without physically engaging with them. After your session, review your notes and consider revisiting the location in a follow-up session. Focus on deeper layers of the environment, and continue to refine your understanding of the risks and energies involved.

Data Centres

People often choose to remote view data centres to understand the technological infrastructure, assess the energy flow, and gather information on the operations within these highly secure, often inaccessible facilities. Data centres are the backbone of modern digital systems, hosting critical data for organizations worldwide. Examples of data centres include those operated by tech giants like Google, Amazon, and Microsoft, which store vast amounts of information, from cloud data to financial records. Remote viewing these centres can provide insights into their physical and technological workings, uncover potential vulnerabilities, or reveal inefficiencies in their operations.

Five Steps to Remote View Data Centres
1. **Set an Intention and Ground Yourself (5 minutes)**
   Start by grounding yourself through deep breathing or meditation. Set a clear intention to observe the data centre with neutrality, focusing on the structure and energy without judgment. Visualise a protective shield around yourself to block any overwhelming energy or distractions.

2. **Visualise the External Environment (10 minutes)**
   Picture the exterior of the data centre. Focus on the physical building, its surroundings, and its security measures, such as fences, cameras, or guard stations. Notice any environmental factors such as location, access points, and the overall layout.
3. **Enter the Interior Energetically (10 minutes)**
   Mentally step inside the data centre. Pay attention to the layout, the energy flow, and the arrangement of equipment. Are there large server racks, cooling systems, or security mechanisms? Notice any patterns or organization within the space.
4. **Sense the Energy Flow and Technology (10 minutes)**
   Tune into the energy flow within the facility. What is the atmosphere like—efficient, organized, or chaotic? Observe how the technology operates energetically. Are there any areas of concern, such as overworked systems, cooling issues, or weak points in security?
5. **Document and Reflect on Your Findings (5 minutes)**
   Write down all the impressions, observations, and insights you've gathered from the session. Focus on physical, technological, and energetic aspects of the data centre. Reflect on any areas of interest, vulnerabilities, or areas for improvement that you may have perceived.

After completing your remote viewing session, it is useful to revisit the data centre the next day to explore specific details further. You can refine your observations, check for any overlooked aspects, and deepen your understanding of how the systems work or any potential issues that need attention. Regular practice will help you enhance your skills and refine your ability to remote view complex locations like data centres.

Energy Sources

People often choose to remote view energy sources to better understand how different types of energy are generated, distributed, and consumed. This can include natural energy sources like solar, wind, or geothermal, as well as conventional sources like fossil fuels or nuclear power. Remote viewing energy sources can help uncover inefficiencies, environmental impacts, or the flow of energy in specific locations. For example, individuals might want to explore wind farms to observe how they generate power, or investigate oil rigs to understand their operation and potential risks. It can also provide insight into energy consumption patterns and ways to promote more sustainable energy use.

Five Steps to Remote View Energy Sources
1. **Set a Clear Intention and Ground Yourself (5 minutes)**
Start by grounding yourself with deep breaths or meditation. Set a clear intention to observe the energy source without judgment, focusing on its process, structure, and flow. Visualise a protective shield around you to ensure neutrality and avoid being affected by strong or overwhelming energies.
2. **Visualise the Location of the Energy Source (10 minutes)**
Picture the geographical location of the energy source, whether it's a solar farm, a wind turbine installation, an oil refinery, or a geothermal plant. Pay attention to the terrain, surrounding environment, and any infrastructure related to energy generation.
3. **Observe the Energy Generation Process (10 minutes)**
Focus on the method of energy generation at the site. For example, with solar, observe the solar panels and how they capture sunlight; with wind, focus on the movement of turbines. Tune into the energy flow, noticing how it is created, stored, and possibly distributed.
4. **Assess the Environmental Impact (10 minutes)**
Tune into the broader environmental effects of the energy source. Are there signs of pollution, depletion of resources, or harm to local ecosystems? Consider how the energy source interacts with its surroundings and whether it contributes to sustainability or poses risks.

5. **Document Your Insights and Reflect (5 minutes)**
   Write down your observations, focusing on both the technical and energetic aspects of the energy source. Reflect on any insights regarding efficiency, sustainability, or potential improvements. Pay attention to any concerns or suggestions that may have come up during the session.

After completing your remote viewing session, consider revisiting the energy source the next day to explore more details or investigate any aspects you may have missed. This will allow you to refine your understanding and continue gathering insights for further reflection or action.

Environmental Changes

People often choose to remote view environmental changes to understand the impact of human activities, natural events, or climate changes on ecosystems, landscapes, and the atmosphere. Environmental changes can include deforestation, pollution, shifts in weather patterns, or the consequences of natural disasters like floods or wildfires. Remote viewing these changes allows individuals to gain insights into areas that are hard to access or observe directly, offering a unique perspective on the current state and future implications. For example, someone might remote view a region affected by drought to see the impact on water sources or remote view an area undergoing deforestation to understand the ecological shifts.

Five Steps to Remote View Environmental Changes
1. **Set Your Intention and Ground Yourself (5 minutes)**
   Begin by grounding yourself with deep breathing or meditation. Set a clear intention to observe the environmental changes with a neutral, open mind. Visualise a protective shield around you to block any overwhelming energy or negative influences while you explore the location.

2. **Focus on the Geographic Area Affected by the Change (10 minutes)**
   Visualise the specific geographic area that is undergoing environmental change. Picture the landscape, weather conditions, and any significant features such as forests, rivers, or cities. Focus on the region where the changes are most noticeable.
3. **Observe the Impact of the Environmental Change (10 minutes)**
   Tune into the effects of the environmental change. Is it a desertification process, an area suffering from flooding, or an ecosystem disrupted by pollution? Pay attention to physical signs of change, such as shifts in vegetation, soil quality, or water availability.
4. **Examine the Energy Flow and Consequences (10 minutes)**
   Tune into the energy flow within the affected environment. How is the change impacting the overall balance? Notice any disruption in the natural harmony, whether it's an imbalance in ecosystems, energy shifts in the environment, or distress in animal or plant life.
5. **Document Your Observations and Reflect (5 minutes)**
   Write down all the details you've observed, focusing on the physical and energetic aspects of the environmental change. Reflect on any insights you received about the causes, consequences, and possible solutions or improvements for the environment.

By following these steps, you can gain deeper insights into the ongoing environmental changes. After completing your session, it is useful to revisit the area the next day to further explore and refine your observations. This repeated approach can help you gather more information about the broader impact and any long-term effects on the environment.

Fashion Trends

People often choose to remote view fashion trends to gain insight into the direction of style, fabric innovation, consumer preferences, or emerging influences in the fashion industry. Remote viewing fashion trends can help identify future design concepts, popular colour schemes, and the societal factors shaping clothing choices. By observing the evolution of fashion, individuals can learn about upcoming shifts in styles or anticipate what may be trending in the next season. For example, remote viewing fashion shows or popular fashion hubs like Paris or New York could reveal the creative energy behind upcoming collections, materials, and patterns.

Five Steps to Remote View Fashion Trends

1. **Set an Intention and Ground Yourself (5 minutes)**
   Start by grounding yourself through breathing exercises or meditation. Set a clear intention to observe the current and emerging fashion trends with neutrality and an open mind. Visualise a protective shield around you to stay neutral and objective during your session.
2. **Focus on the Fashion Scene or Location (10 minutes)**
   Visualise the fashion scene you wish to observe, whether it's a specific fashion show, a designer's studio, or a global fashion hub. Focus on the energy and atmosphere of the location, considering the creativity, innovation, and ambiance surrounding the fashion environment.
3. **Observe Clothing Styles, Fabrics, and Designs (10 minutes)**
   Tune into the styles, fabrics, and designs that are most prominent in the current or future collections. Pay attention to trends in silhouette, colour, texture, and material usage. Notice if there are any new or emerging trends in the fashion industry, such as sustainable fashion, gender-neutral designs, or futuristic elements.

4. **Examine the Energy of Consumer Influence (10 minutes)**
   Observe the energy of consumer preferences and how they are influencing fashion. Are there global shifts, such as a growing interest in sustainable or ethical fashion? Look for patterns in how consumers are responding to certain styles or movements, and observe if there are significant influences from pop culture, politics, or social movements.
5. **Document Your Observations and Reflect (5 minutes)**
   Write down all the details you've observed, focusing on the key trends, designs, and the energy surrounding the fashion scene. Reflect on what resonates most with you and any insights you've gained about the future of fashion.

After completing your remote viewing session, it's useful to revisit the fashion trends the next day for further exploration. This allows you to deepen your understanding of the trends and observe any shifts or emerging details that you may have missed initially. Repeated sessions will help you refine your ability to tune into the nuances of the fashion industry.

Food Products

People often choose to remote view food products to understand trends in consumer preferences, the origins of certain foods, or even the energy and ingredients behind a product. Remote viewing food products can provide insights into the nutritional value, sourcing practices, or potential health impacts of what is being produced or consumed. Additionally, observing food products allows individuals to sense how the energy of a particular food resonates with their own energy. This can reveal how certain foods might influence personal well-being, mood, or physical health. For example, remote viewing a popular snack or beverage might not only uncover its composition and production process but also how it aligns or contrasts with your own energetic needs or preferences.

Five Steps to Remote View Food Products

1. **Set Your Intention and Ground Yourself (5 minutes)**
   Begin by grounding yourself through deep breathing or meditation. Set a clear intention to observe the food product with neutrality, focusing on its energy, ingredients, and impact on the consumer. Visualise a protective shield around you to maintain objectivity during your session.

2. **Visualise the Food Product and Its Origins (10 minutes)**
   Picture the food product you want to explore. Visualise its appearance, texture, and packaging. Then, focus on its origins—where and how it is produced, and what ingredients are involved. Tune into the energy of the product and its production process, from farm to factory to shelf.

3. **Examine the Ingredients and Composition (10 minutes)**
   Focus on the individual ingredients within the food product. Tune into the energy of each ingredient, how they come together, and any potential health effects they may have. Observe the quality of the ingredients and how they contribute to the overall impact or appeal of the product.

4. **Assess the Consumer Energy and Reception (10 minutes)**
   Shift your focus to the energy surrounding consumers' interaction with the product. How do people respond to it emotionally and physically? Are there certain characteristics, such as taste, convenience, or health benefits, that attract them? Consider how the product fits into broader cultural or dietary trends.

5. **Document Your Insights and Reflect (5 minutes)**
   Write down your observations, paying attention to the ingredients, the energy of the product, and its reception. Reflect on any new insights you've gained regarding the food product, its market impact, and its potential effects on consumers.

After completing your remote viewing session, it's helpful to revisit the food product the next day to further explore any details you may have missed. This allows you to deepen your understanding of the product and refine your ability to detect underlying factors that influence its development and consumer popularity.

Geographic Features

People often choose to remote view geographic features to gain insights into the energy, history, and environmental conditions of specific locations. Geographic features such as mountains, rivers, forests, deserts, or coastal areas hold unique energies that can influence human activity, wildlife, and ecosystems. Remote viewing these areas allows individuals to explore their natural beauty, environmental significance, and the unseen forces at play. For example, one might remote view a mountain range to understand the energy it holds, how it shapes the surrounding environment, or its cultural and spiritual significance. This kind of remote viewing helps people connect with the land, uncover hidden patterns, and gain a deeper understanding of natural formations.

Five Steps to Remote View Geographic Features

1. **Set Your Intention and Ground Yourself (5 minutes)**
   Begin by grounding yourself through breathing exercises or meditation. Set the intention to observe the geographic feature with an open and neutral mind, allowing the energy of the location to come through. Visualise a protective shield around you to stay balanced and focused throughout the session.
2. **Visualise the Geographic Feature and Its Surroundings (10 minutes)**
   Focus on the specific geographic feature you wish to explore, such as a mountain, river, or forest. Visualise its appearance, scale, and shape. Expand your focus to include the surrounding environment—forests, valleys, or bodies of water that may influence or be influenced by this geographic feature.

3. **Tune into the Energy and Natural Forces (10 minutes)**
   Observe the energy of the location, whether it is peaceful, powerful, turbulent, or serene. Notice any natural forces such as water flow, wind patterns, or geological activity (e.g., tectonic shifts). Pay attention to how these forces interact with the environment and influence life around them.
4. **Examine the Human Interaction with the Location (10 minutes)**
   Shift your focus to how humans interact with the geographic feature. Is the location used for tourism, agriculture, or cultural practices? Are there any impacts from human activity, such as pollution or development? Observe the balance between the natural and human-made energies in the area.
5. **Document Your Insights and Reflect (5 minutes)**
   Write down all the details you've observed, focusing on the energy, physical features, and human interaction with the location. Reflect on the significance of the geographic feature and how it fits into the larger environmental context.

Revisit the geographic feature the next day to further explore any new details that may arise. This allows you to gain deeper insights into the energy of the location and refine your understanding of its role in the surrounding environment.

Government Facilities

People often choose to remote view government facilities to gain insight into the operations, energy, and influences of these important institutions. Government facilities, such as embassies, military bases, or administrative buildings, play a crucial role in shaping policies, security, and societal structures. Remote viewing these locations can reveal the inner workings, the energy surrounding them, and any hidden patterns or dynamics at play. For example, remote viewing a government facility might uncover how decisions are made, the atmosphere in the building, or even the intentions of the individuals working there. By observing these spaces, one can gain a broader understanding of political or administrative power, security concerns, and the energy that drives governance.

Five Steps to Remote View Government Facilities

1. **Set Your Intention and Ground Yourself (5 minutes)**
   Begin by grounding yourself through deep breathing or meditation. Set the intention to observe the government facility with neutrality and focus, allowing you to remain objective and non-judgmental. Visualise a protective shield around you to maintain a balanced and clear mind throughout the session.

2. **Focus on the Exterior and Energy of the Facility (10 minutes)**
   Visualise the government facility, whether it is an embassy, military base, or administrative building. Focus on its exterior appearance, the energy it radiates, and the atmosphere surrounding it. Pay attention to any patterns or symbols that may be present, which could represent the facility's purpose or significance.

3. **Explore the Interior and Key Areas (10 minutes)**
   Shift your attention to the interior of the facility. Observe the layout, key areas of activity, and any rooms or spaces where decisions are made or important interactions occur. Pay attention to the energy of each area—whether it is calm, tense, or focused—and notice any interactions between people or between people and the space itself.

4. **Tune into the Energy of the People Inside (10 minutes)**
   Focus on the individuals working within the facility. Observe their energy, actions, and how they interact with one another. Are there any signs of tension, collaboration, or power dynamics? Notice how the energy of the people reflects the purpose of the facility and its role in governance or security.

5. **Document Your Observations and Reflect (5 minutes)**
   Write down your insights, focusing on the facility's energy, structure, and the people within it. Reflect on the dynamics you observed and any patterns or themes that stood out. Consider how these elements might influence the decisions or outcomes associated with the facility.

After your remote viewing session, it's useful to revisit the government facility the next day by doing another remote viewing session. This allows you to deepen your understanding of its operations, the energy within it, and how it interacts with its external environment. Repeated sessions can provide more clarity and refine your observations.

Historical Landmarks

People often choose to remote view historical landmarks to explore the energy, significance, and history behind these iconic locations. Historical landmarks are often deeply tied to cultural, political, or spiritual events that have shaped the course of history. Remote viewing these sites allows individuals to connect with the past, uncover hidden stories, and sense the energetic imprint of events that occurred there. By observing a landmark, one can gain insights into its historical importance, the energy it has accumulated over time, and how it continues to impact the surrounding community or culture. For example, remote viewing the Great Wall of China might reveal not only its physical structure but also the centuries of history, wars, and rituals associated with it.

Five Steps to Remote View Historical Landmarks
1. **Set Your Intention and Ground Yourself (5 minutes)**
   Begin by grounding yourself through deep breathing or meditation. Set the intention to observe the historical landmark with an open mind, focusing on its energy, history, and significance. Visualise a protective shield around you to remain neutral and centred throughout the session.

2. **Visualise the Landmark and Its Location (10 minutes)**
   Focus on the historical landmark you wish to explore. Visualise its physical appearance and location. Pay attention to its size, structure, and how it fits within the surrounding landscape. Consider how the landmark interacts with the natural environment and any cultural or spiritual elements nearby.
3. **Tune into the Energy of the Landmark (10 minutes)**
   Focus on the energy of the landmark itself. Does it feel peaceful, powerful, or charged with intense history? Observe any impressions or sensations that arise, such as the weight of historical events, the energy of past generations, or the feelings of those who visited or lived near the landmark.
4. **Examine the Historical Context and Events (10 minutes)**
   Shift your focus to the events and history associated with the landmark. Visualise any key moments, people, or actions that occurred there. Observe how these historical events have influenced the energy and significance of the location. Tune into the stories and impressions left by these events.
5. **Document Your Observations and Reflect (5 minutes)**
   Write down all the details you've observed, focusing on the energy, physical features, and historical significance of the landmark. Reflect on how these elements come together to shape the overall importance of the site and how it continues to resonate with people today.

After completing your remote viewing session, revisit the historical landmark the following day to explore any additional layers of history or energy you may have missed. This repeated investigation allows for a deeper understanding of the landmark's enduring influence and the ongoing connections it holds with the past.

Hidden Treasures

People are often drawn to remote viewing hidden treasures because of the intrigue and mystery surrounding valuable or rare objects lost to history or hidden away for centuries. These treasures may be physical items, such as priceless artifacts, or they could be symbolic, like knowledge or secrets waiting to be discovered. Remote viewing hidden treasures allows individuals to tap into the energies and mysteries of these lost objects and uncover what has been concealed, sometimes revealing stories of their origins, the people who hid them, and the secrets they hold. The allure of treasure hunting goes beyond the object itself—it's about the journey, the connection with past eras, and the uncovering of ancient mysteries. For example, remote viewing a long-lost shipwreck could provide visions not only of gold and jewels but also the energies surrounding the sailors who perished with it, the storms that sank it, and the currents that carried its secrets away.

Five Steps to Remote View Hidden Treasures

1. **Set the Mood and Ground Yourself (5 minutes)**
   Begin by creating an atmosphere of mystery. Dim the lights, light a candle, or use incense to help shift your consciousness into a state of curiosity and openness. Ground yourself by breathing deeply, and set the intention to explore the unknown, allowing the energy of the hidden treasure to reveal itself to you. Visualise a protective barrier around you, ensuring that only the energy of the treasure and its story can reach you.
2. **Connect to the Energy of the Treasure (10 minutes)**
   Focus on the concept of the hidden treasure. Let the mystery of it unfold before you. What does it look like, and where is it concealed? Allow your intuition to guide you to the treasure's energetic signature. Does it feel buried under earth, water, or perhaps hidden in a secret chamber? Tap into the energy of the object itself—does it feel precious, dangerous, or powerful?
3. **Follow the Trail of the Treasure's Story (10 minutes)**
   Instead of focusing solely on the treasure, follow the trail of its story. Where did it come from, and who hid it? Let images

or emotions come to you that reveal the circumstances surrounding the treasure's concealment. Were there individuals or events tied to its hiding? Did something significant happen to it? Allow the path leading to the treasure to reveal itself, piece by piece, as if solving a puzzle.
4. **Explore the Surroundings and Hidden Guard (10 minutes)**
Once you have connected with the treasure, explore its surroundings. What is it hidden inside, behind, or under? Is there a physical or energetic barrier guarding it? Pay attention to any obstacles or protections that may have been set up around it. These could be physical elements like walls or natural forces like water or earth, or they could be energetic blocks tied to the treasure's energy.
5. **Document Your Impressions and Reflect (5 minutes)**
Write down the impressions, images, and sensations you've experienced. What did you see, feel, or sense about the hidden treasure and the path that led to it? Reflect on the significance of the treasure and why it was hidden in the first place. What lessons or stories does it hold, and why is it calling to you now?

To unravel the deeper mysteries, return to the hidden treasure the following day. As you repeat the process, new fragments of its history, location, or energetic essence may reveal themselves—secrets that once lay shrouded in darkness, now calling you closer to the truth. With each visit, the treasure's story unfolds, piece by elusive piece, guiding you through the veils of time and secrecy that have kept it concealed for so long.

Hotels

People often choose to remote view hotels to assess whether the energy of the space aligns with their own. Hotels, as dynamic spaces filled with a variety of people and experiences, can carry unique energies that either resonate with or repel an individual. Remote viewing a hotel allows you to connect with its atmosphere, helping you determine if it's a place where you will feel comfortable and at ease, or if it carries energy that may affect you negatively. Whether you're seeking a peaceful retreat or a vibrant, bustling environment, remote viewing can give you insights into the hotel's energetic signature, helping you decide if it's the right place for you to stay.

Five Steps to Remote View Hotels
1. **Set the Intention and Ground Yourself (5 minutes)**
   Begin by centring yourself with deep breaths. Set the intention to connect with the hotel's energy in a neutral and open-minded way. Visualise a protective shield around you to ensure that only the energy of the hotel and its surroundings can reach you, keeping you grounded throughout the session.
2. **Visualise the Hotel and Its External Energy (10 minutes)**
   Focus on the exterior of the hotel. Picture its architecture, its location, and the overall energy it radiates. Is it a bustling, modern hotel or an older, more secluded building? Pay attention to any sensations you receive about the energy around the hotel, whether it's filled with movement and excitement or quiet and still.
3. **Explore the Interior and Common Spaces (10 minutes)**
   Shift your attention to the interior of the hotel. Visualise the common spaces—lobbies, hallways, restaurants, or lounges—and the energy within them. Do these spaces feel welcoming or tense? Is there an underlying story in these areas, perhaps linked to past events or the types of guests who stay there? Notice how the space feels and what emotions come to the surface.
4. **Tune Into the Energy of Guests and Staff (10 minutes)**
   Focus on the people within the hotel. Observe the guests and staff and the emotions or interactions that surround them. Do the guests appear relaxed, stressed, or filled with anticipation? What is the energy of the hotel staff, and how do they interact with the space and guests? Are there any lingering energies tied to past stays or events?

5. **Document Your Impressions and Reflect (5 minutes)**
   Write down the details you've observed—the physical features, the energy of the building, and the emotions tied to the people inside. Reflect on how these elements combine to form the atmosphere of the hotel. Does it feel like a space of healing, excitement, or relaxation, or is there an underlying tension that lingers in the air?

To know if this hotel aligns with your energy, revisit it the following day. The repeated experience will allow you to uncover any additional layers of its energy and atmosphere, helping you determine whether the space is suitable for you to stay and resonate with your personal energy.

Houses

People often choose to remote view houses to assess whether the energy of the home aligns with their own. A house is more than just a physical space; it carries the energy of those who have lived there, the land it stands on, and the events that have taken place within its walls. Remote viewing allows you to tap into the energetic signature of the house, helping you determine if the atmosphere supports your well-being and resonates with your own energy. Whether you're considering moving in or simply curious, remote viewing can provide valuable insights into whether the house is a harmonious match for you, or if it carries energies that might feel discordant or uncomfortable.

Five Steps to Remote View Houses
1. **Set Your Intention and Ground Yourself (5 minutes)**
   Begin by taking a few deep breaths to centre yourself. Set the intention to connect with the house's energy in a neutral and open way. Visualise a protective energy shield around you to ensure you remain grounded and shielded from any unintended energies as you explore the house's atmosphere.

2. **Visualise the Exterior and Surrounding Energy (10 minutes)**
   Focus on the outside of the house, including its surroundings. Is it located in a quiet neighbourhood or a busy area? What is the energy like around it—calm and serene, or chaotic and tense? Pay attention to the land and how it feels—are there any specific areas that feel either inviting or unsettling?
3. **Explore the Interior of the House (10 minutes)**
   Shift your attention to the interior of the house. Visualise walking through the rooms, hallways, and common spaces. What kind of energy do the rooms carry? Is the atmosphere light and welcoming, or does it feel heavy or tense? Are there any areas in the house that feel particularly positive or negative? Take note of your emotional and physical reactions to different spaces.
4. **Tune Into the Energy of the Previous Inhabitants (10 minutes)**
   Reflect on the energy of those who have lived in the house before. What emotions or patterns remain within the space? Are there unresolved energies, such as sadness, conflict, or joy, that have been left behind? Pay attention to how these energies might affect your experience in the house.
5. **Assess Compatibility with Your Energy (5 minutes)**
   Now, tune into your own energy and how it resonates with the house. Does the energy of the house feel aligned with yours? Do you feel relaxed and comfortable, or do you sense tension and unease? Pay attention to how your body and mind respond to the space—this can give you a clear indication of whether the house is a good match for you.

By revisiting the house the following day, you can deepen your understanding of its energy. This will help you gain more clarity on whether it is truly compatible with your own energy and if the space will support your well-being over time. The process of repeated exploration allows you to uncover more subtle details that may not have been immediately apparent, giving you a fuller picture of whether this house is the right place for you.

Industrial Facilities

People often choose to remote view industrial facilities to gain insight into their energy dynamics, operational flow, and potential environmental impact. Industrial facilities, whether factories, warehouses, or production plants, can carry powerful and sometimes heavy energy due to the nature of their work. Remote viewing allows you to tap into the atmosphere of these facilities, helping you understand if the energy aligns with your personal values or if there are any concerns related to their operations. Whether you're assessing the potential for environmental impact, the well-being of employees, or the overall energy of the space, remote viewing can offer valuable information to help determine how compatible the facility is with your own energy and perspective.

Five Steps to Remote View Industrial Facilities

1. **Set Clear Intentions and Protect Your Energy (5 minutes)**
   Begin by grounding yourself and setting the intention to observe the energy of the industrial facility with neutrality and clarity. Create a protective shield around yourself to ensure that only the facility's energy can connect with you while maintaining your personal energy intact and undisturbed.
2. **Focus on the Facility's Exterior and Environment (10 minutes)**
   Visualise the outside of the industrial facility. Observe its size, structure, and surrounding environment. Is it situated in an isolated area, or is it part of a larger industrial complex? What is the energy of the land around it? Pay attention to whether the area feels clean, chaotic, or polluted. Take note of any energetic imbalances or areas that feel particularly stagnant or vibrant.

3. **Explore the Interior and Operational Energy (10 minutes)**
   Shift your focus to the interior of the facility. Visualise the layout, machinery, production lines, and the general flow of work. What is the energy like inside—busy and active, or tense and stressful? How do the workers feel, and what is the energy of the equipment and machinery? Is there a sense of harmony in the way things are operating, or do you sense something off-balance in the production process?
4. **Observe the Impact on People and the Environment (10 minutes)**
   Tune into the energy surrounding the workers and the facility's impact on the environment. How do the employees interact with the space and each other? Are they focused and motivated, or is there an underlying sense of stress or fatigue? Pay attention to how the facility's operations might affect the surrounding area, including any environmental or energetic changes.
5. **Evaluate the Energy and Your Personal Reaction (5 minutes)**
   Finally, reflect on your own energy in relation to the industrial facility. Does the facility feel in alignment with your personal values, or does it carry energy that feels uncomfortable or out of balance? How does it resonate with your emotional and physical state? Do you feel inspired and positive, or do you sense resistance or negativity in the energy of the space?

If you feel uncertain or if there is any lingering discomfort, it may be helpful to revisit the facility the next day to gather more detailed insights. This repeated exploration can provide deeper clarity about how the facility's energy aligns with your own and if it poses any concerns for your personal or professional well-being.

Information Networks

It is important to remote view information networks because they play a pivotal role in how data is shared, processed, and stored across the globe. Whether it's communication, financial, social, or energy networks, understanding how they function and their potential impact can provide valuable insights for personal or professional decisions. By remote viewing these networks, you can uncover hidden details about their structure, security, energy flow, and their overall alignment with your values and goals. Additionally, understanding whether a particular network is compatible with your energy can help you determine if it's the right choice for you to engage with.

Five Steps to Remote View Information Networks

1. **Set Your Intentions and Protect Your Energy (5 minutes)**
   Before you begin, ground yourself and establish clear intentions for your remote viewing session. Focus on the specific type of network you want to explore, whether it's a communication network, financial network, or any other. Visualise a protective shield around your energy to ensure you stay centred and unaffected by the network's energy during the session.

2. **Visualise the Network's Structure and Components (10 minutes)**
   Picture the network's layout—how it is connected, how data or information flows, and the different entities or systems involved. Is the network a web of interconnected nodes, or does it have distinct pathways that form its structure? Take note of whether it feels organized and efficient, or fragmented and disjointed.

3. **Tune into the Energy of the Network (10 minutes)**
   Connect with the network's energetic frequency. Pay attention to how the network feels energetically. Does it feel harmonious, balanced, and supportive, or does it feel dissonant and chaotic? Trust your intuition to understand the overall vibrational quality of the network and whether it aligns with your personal energy.

4. **Assess the Network's Purpose and Impact (10 minutes)**
   Examine the purpose of the network and its effect on the people or entities using it. Does the network serve a positive purpose, such as facilitating communication, financial transactions, or energy distribution? Or does it have potential negative effects, such as spreading misinformation, creating imbalance, or contributing to harm? Notice how the energy of the network aligns with your ethical beliefs and personal values.
5. **Evaluate Its Compatibility with Your Energy (10 minutes)**
   Now, assess how the network aligns with your personal energy or goals. Does the network resonate with your vibration, or does it create a sense of discomfort or misalignment? For example, if it's a social network, does it enhance your connection with others, or does it create stress and negativity? If it's a business-related network, does it support your goals, or does it feel draining? This step will help you determine whether the network is a good fit for you.

By following these steps, you will have a clearer understanding of the energy, structure, and purpose of the information network you are viewing. To know whether the network is good for you and aligns with your energy, trust your intuition and the feelings that arise during your session. If you feel unsettled or unsure, it may be a sign that the network isn't in harmony with you. Consider revisiting the network the next day to gather more insights or clarify your impressions. This process can deepen your understanding of the network's compatibility with your energy and needs.

International Borders

Remote viewing international borders can be a powerful way to understand the energetic and geopolitical dynamics that shape global boundaries. People often choose to remote view international borders to gain insight into the movement of people, goods, and information, and to understand the broader social, cultural, and environmental impacts of these borders. By exploring these areas, remote viewers can uncover hidden tensions, historical significance, and the energetic flow between countries or regions. This can help in understanding how borders influence political relations, migration patterns, and even environmental conditions, and whether a particular border resonates with one's energy or values.

Five Steps to Remote View International Borders

1. **Set Intentions and Ground Yourself (5 minutes)**
   Begin by grounding yourself and clarifying your intention. Focus on the specific international border you wish to explore. This could be the physical boundary between two countries, or the more energetic, less visible boundaries that exist in the social or political realm. Visualise a protective shield around you to ensure that you are grounded and protected as you delve into this sensitive subject.

2. **Visualise the Border's Physical and Energetic Structure (10 minutes)**
   Picture the boundary line and its physical features—mountains, rivers, fences, or other markers that define the border. Observe how these features divide the land or people. Then, focus on the energetic structure of the border. Does it feel like a clear line, or is it blurred and shifting? What type of energy is contained within the border, and does it feel restrictive, protective, or porous?

3. **Tune Into the Energy Flow at the Border (10 minutes)**
   Connect with the flow of energy that passes through the border. Does the energy feel smooth and harmonious, or are there blockages or disruptions? Pay attention to any tension, unresolved conflicts, or sense of separation. If the border has a history of conflict, it may feel tense or unbalanced. If it's a peaceful border, it may feel open and free-flowing.

4. **Assess the Emotional and Social Dynamics (10 minutes)**
   Explore the emotional energy associated with the border. How do the people living near or around this border feel? Is there a sense of unity or division? What emotions are tied to this border—fear, hope, sadness, pride, or something else? Consider the impact the border has on the communities, their relationships, and their sense of identity.
5. **Evaluate Its Compatibility with Your Energy and Intentions (10 minutes)**
   Finally, assess how this border aligns with your energy and intentions. Does it resonate with your values, or do you feel discomfort or dissonance? If you are exploring a border related to migration, for example, do you feel openness or restriction in the energy? Consider how the border might affect you personally, emotionally, or even professionally, and determine whether it aligns with your goals or needs.

Remote viewing international borders allows you to gain insight into the complex web of physical, social, and political forces that shape our world. To know if a particular border aligns with your energy, trust the feelings and impressions that arise during the session. If the energy feels restrictive or misaligned with your values, it may be a sign that the border is not a good fit for you. Revisit the border on another day to deepen your understanding and clarify your impressions, allowing you to gain more clarity on its energy and significance.

Island Locations

Remote viewing island locations can reveal their unique energy, history, and natural beauty. People often choose to remote view islands to explore their isolation, biodiversity, or cultural significance. Islands can also carry unique energies due to their separation from mainland influences, making them intriguing for personal exploration or future travel plans. By remote viewing, you can assess if the island's energy resonates with you and whether it aligns with your goals, such as finding a peaceful retreat or a vibrant adventure.

Five Steps to Remote View Island Locations

1. **Set Your Intentions and Focus (5 minutes)**
   Begin by deciding on the specific island you want to view. It could be a famous tropical paradise, a remote and mysterious landmass, or a historical island with cultural significance. Ground yourself and set a clear intention to connect with the island's essence and energy while maintaining a calm, neutral mindset.

2. **Visualise the Island's Physical Characteristics (10 minutes)**
   Picture the island from above, observing its size, shape, and natural features such as mountains, beaches, forests, or lagoons. Imagine its surrounding waters—calm and inviting, or rough and turbulent. Take note of how the island feels physically and how its environment interacts with the sea and sky.

3. **Sense the Island's Energy (10 minutes)**
   Tune into the island's energetic frequency. Does it feel tranquil, vibrant, mysterious, or heavy? Explore its core energy—is it welcoming, isolating, or full of life? Islands often carry unique energies due to their separation and self-contained ecosystems. Determine if the energy feels aligned with your personal vibration or goals.

4. **Explore the Island's History and Vibrations (10 minutes)**
   Delve into the past energy of the island. Are there impressions of historical events, cultural activities, or spiritual practices? Sense any imprints left behind by its inhabitants or natural forces. Explore whether the island feels ancient and wise, bustling with modern energy, or untouched and primal.

5. **Evaluate Its Compatibility with Your Energy (10 minutes)**
   Finally, assess if this island aligns with your intentions or personal energy. Would visiting or connecting with this location

bring peace, excitement, or clarity? Or does it feel misaligned or unsettling? Imagine yourself physically being there—does the energy support your well-being and goals?

Remote viewing island locations can be a fascinating way to connect with their natural beauty, unique energy, and history. If an island feels resonant and compatible with your energy, it could signify a place worth exploring physically or energetically. Revisit the island in another session to gather additional insights, allowing its mysteries and energies to unfold further with each viewing.

Language Translations

Remote viewing language translations can help you connect with the energy of communication and understanding across different languages. People often choose to remote view translations to sense the deeper meaning behind words, the emotions they convey, and the cultural nuances embedded in language. This can be especially useful for understanding the essence of foreign texts, determining the accuracy of a translation, or exploring the energy of a language and how it resonates with you personally.

Five Steps to Remote View Language Translations

1. **Set Your Intention and Focus on the Source Material (5 minutes)**
   Begin by choosing a specific piece of text, phrase, or conversation to explore. Set your intention to connect with its essence and the energy of the language. Calm your mind and visualise the original text or sound as an energetic field.
2. **Visualise the Process of Translation (10 minutes)**
   Imagine the original text transforming into the target language. Focus on the flow of meaning, considering how each word or phrase might carry emotional or cultural weight. Visualise the translation as an energetic exchange between the source and the target languages.

3. **Sense the Energy of the Translation (10 minutes)**
   Tune into the translated text's energy. Does it feel faithful to the original or diluted? Explore how the meaning, tone, and emotion resonate in the target language. Pay attention to any areas where the energy feels blocked, distorted, or misaligned.
4. **Explore Cultural and Emotional Context (10 minutes)**
   Reflect on the cultural and emotional nuances of the translation. Does it capture the essence of the original, or does it miss key subtleties? Sense if the translation carries the same vibrational impact, or if cultural differences influence its interpretation.
5. **Evaluate Alignment with Your Understanding and Intentions (10 minutes)**
   Finally, assess whether the translation aligns with your understanding of the original and your intentions. Does the energy resonate with you, or do certain phrases or words feel off? Imagine how the translation might impact its intended audience or purpose.

Remote viewing language translations provides an opportunity to delve into the energetic and cultural layers of communication. If the translation feels harmonious and aligned, it may signify accuracy and resonance with the original meaning. Revisit the text or phrase in subsequent sessions to uncover deeper insights, ensuring a more profound understanding of its essence and how it connects with your energy and intentions.

Laboratory Findings

Remote viewing laboratory findings can offer insights into the energy and clarity of scientific results, their implications, and their alignment with truth or objectivity. People often choose to remote view laboratory findings to assess their accuracy, explore hidden details, or gain a deeper intuitive understanding of the data. This process can also help determine whether the findings resonate with personal or professional goals, aiding in decisions about research directions or applications.

Five Steps to Remote View Laboratory Findings
1. **Set Your Intentions and Focus on the Laboratory Findings (5 minutes)**
   Begin by identifying the specific laboratory findings you want to explore—these could be medical test results, research data, or experimental outcomes. Calm your mind, set your intention to connect with the findings, and visualise their essence as energy or information.
2. **Visualise the Findings and Their Source (10 minutes)**
   Picture the laboratory setup or process that produced the findings. Imagine the environment, instruments, and researchers involved. Sense whether the energy around the findings feels clean and precise, or if there is any interference, bias, or uncertainty.
3. **Tune Into the Energy of the Results (10 minutes)**
   Focus on the findings themselves—do they feel clear and truthful, or clouded and ambiguous? Observe any sensations, emotions, or symbolic images that arise as you connect with the energy of the data. Sense whether the findings align with their intended purpose or reveal unexpected insights.
4. **Explore the Implications and Hidden Details (10 minutes)**
   Delve deeper into what the findings mean. Do they suggest clear next steps or raise unanswered questions? Explore whether there are hidden layers of meaning or potential consequences that may not be immediately obvious.
5. **Assess Alignment with Your Energy and Goals (10 minutes)**
   Finally, evaluate whether the findings resonate with your personal or professional objectives. Do they feel aligned with truth and integrity? Imagine how they might impact decisions, outcomes, or broader research, and whether their energy supports or hinders your intentions.

Remote viewing laboratory findings allows for an intuitive exploration of their energy, implications, and potential biases. By engaging in this process, you can gain clarity and confidence in how to interpret and apply the results. Revisit the findings in subsequent sessions to uncover deeper layers of understanding and ensure alignment with your goals and energy.

Landmarks

Remote viewing landmarks can provide a deeper understanding of their history, energy, and significance. Landmarks—whether natural wonders like mountains, man-made structures like the Eiffel Tower, or sacred sites like Stonehenge—often carry rich cultural and spiritual vibrations. People choose to remote view landmarks to explore their historical context, uncover their energetic imprint, or determine whether visiting them aligns with their personal energy or spiritual journey. This process can help you feel connected to a place and decide if it resonates with your intentions.

Five Steps to Remote View Landmarks

1. **Set Your Intention and Focus on the Landmark (5 minutes)**
   Begin by choosing a specific landmark to view. Calm your mind and set an intention to connect with its energy and essence. Visualise its physical form, whether it's a towering monument, a quiet historical site, or a natural feature of the earth.

2. **Visualise the Landmark and Its Surroundings (10 minutes)**
   Imagine the landmark in detail—its shape, size, materials, and environment. Explore its surroundings, such as bustling cities, serene landscapes, or rugged terrain. Observe how the landmark integrates into its setting and how it interacts with the energies around it.

3. **Sense the Landmark's Energy and Imprint (10 minutes)**
   Tune into the energetic vibration of the landmark. Does it feel ancient and wise, lively and inspiring, or heavy with past

events? Explore the emotional or spiritual impact it might have. Pay attention to any feelings, images, or impressions that arise as you connect with its energy.

4. **Explore the Landmark's History and Significance (10 minutes)**
   Delve into the landmark's past. Sense the events, people, or natural forces that shaped it. Reflect on its significance—why was it created or preserved, and what does it symbolize? Feel the layers of history embedded in the site and how they influence its energy today.

5. **Assess Resonance with Your Energy (10 minutes)**
   Finally, determine if the landmark's energy aligns with your own. Imagine yourself physically visiting the site—does it feel uplifting, grounding, or calming? Or does it feel unsettling or overwhelming? Consider whether connecting with this landmark supports your personal or spiritual growth.

Remote viewing landmarks can reveal fascinating details about their energy and significance, allowing you to form a deeper connection with them. If a landmark resonates with your energy, it could signal a meaningful destination or point of exploration. Revisit the site in another session to uncover additional layers of its essence and further clarify your connection to it.

Military Bases

Remote viewing military bases is a fascinating application of this skill that draws interest from individuals curious about security, historical significance, or strategic operations. While remote viewing these highly secure locations, it's essential to maintain neutrality and a non-invasive approach. People engage in this practice to explore their remote viewing abilities, understand military structures from a neutral perspective, or satisfy curiosity about the energy dynamics of such spaces.

Expectations from remote viewing military bases include encountering strong protective energies, structured environments, and a sense of purpose or discipline. Ethical considerations are paramount, ensuring the practice is done with kind intentions and respect for the boundaries of sensitive spaces.

Five Steps to Remote View Military Bases

1. **Prepare Your Mind and Set Intentions**
   - Begin with a calming meditation to quiet your thoughts and establish neutrality.
   - Set an intention to explore the military base without preconceived judgments or emotional attachment.
   - Affirm that your goal is to observe rather than influence or interfere.
2. **Focus on the Target**
   - Use coordinates, a mental image, or the name of the military base to focus your attention.
   - Visualise the base from an aerial perspective to gain an overall sense of its layout, surroundings, and structural design.
3. **Sense the Energy Dynamics**
   - Pay attention to the energy within and around the base.
   - Notice feelings of order, protection, and purpose, as these are often prevalent in military environments.
   - Be open to subtle shifts in energy, indicating areas of heightened activity or importance.
4. **Observe Key Structures and Activities**
   - Focus on significant elements such as buildings, vehicles, or open spaces.
   - Mentally explore specific areas within the base, such as command centres, training grounds, or storage facilities, while remaining detached from any emotional response.
   - Use a layered approach, starting with general impressions and refining your observations as details emerge.
5. **Record and Reflect**
   - Document your impressions, including physical details, energy patterns, and any notable sensations.

- Reflect on your findings to identify patterns or insights about the base's operation and purpose.
- Compare your observations with publicly available information, if applicable, to validate your practice.

Conclusion

Remote viewing military bases is an intriguing and challenging exercise that allows practitioners to hone their skills while exploring the intricate energy and structure of these strategic locations. It requires neutrality, respect, and a detached curiosity to ensure the process is ethical and insightful. By following these steps, you can deepen your remote viewing practice and expand your understanding of complex environments while maintaining integrity and professionalism.

Mysterious Locations

Mysterious locations, such as ancient ruins, underwater cities, or enigmatic landscapes like the Bermuda Triangle, have always intrigued humanity. Remote viewing offers a unique opportunity to explore these places from the comfort of your mind, providing insights into their history, energy, and purpose. People are drawn to remote viewing mysterious locations to uncover secrets, connect with the past, or simply satisfy their curiosity about the unknown.

When remote viewing such places, expect to encounter unusual energy signatures, a sense of awe or wonder, and sometimes surprising details that challenge conventional knowledge. These locations often hold layers of meaning, making them an exciting target for exploration.

Five Steps to Remote View Mysterious Locations
1. **Set Your Intentions and Prepare Your Space**
   - Begin with a grounding meditation to centre your mind and body.

- Set a clear intention to explore the target location with curiosity, respect, and neutrality.
- Create a quiet, distraction-free environment to enhance focus.

2. Establish a Connection to the Target
- Use a name, image, or coordinates of the mysterious location to focus your attention.
- Visualise the place as vividly as possible, either as it appears today or as it might have looked in the past.
- Allow your intuitive mind to connect with the location's essence.

3. Sense the Energy and Atmosphere
- Tune into the energy field of the location. Does it feel ancient, peaceful, charged, or heavy?
- Observe any emotions or impressions the place evokes, such as mystery, reverence, or even foreboding.
- Be open to unexpected sensations or images, as mysterious places often have multi-layered energy signatures.

4. Explore the Details
- Mentally move through the location, observing its physical features and surroundings.
- Focus on key areas of interest, such as structures, natural formations, or unusual objects.
- Pay attention to symbols, patterns, or phenomena that stand out, as they may hold clues about the location's significance.

5. Record Your Observations
- Write down everything you perceive, including visual details, feelings, and any symbolic or intuitive impressions.
- Reflect on how the place's energy or history might connect to broader themes, such as human evolution, ancient civilizations, or universal mysteries.
- If possible, compare your findings with known information about the site.

Conclusion

Remote viewing mysterious locations opens a doorway to uncovering the secrets of enigmatic places while expanding your understanding of time, space, and consciousness. These journeys offer not only insights into the unknown but also a deeper connection to the vast tapestry of existence. By practicing respect, neutrality, and open-mindedness, you can explore the mysteries of the world and beyond, one remote viewing session at a time.

Natural Disasters

Remote viewing natural disasters—such as hurricanes, earthquakes, or volcanic eruptions—can provide a deeper understanding of the immense forces shaping our planet. However, this practice is not for everyone. The intense energy, chaos, and emotional residue associated with such events can be overwhelming, especially for sensitive individuals.

People may choose to remote view natural disasters to study the mechanics of the event, gain insights for preparedness, or connect with the Earth's energy. However, it is crucial to approach these targets with caution, detachment, and respect, as the negative energy of these events can deeply affect an unprepared mind.

Five Steps to Remote View Natural Disasters
1. **Assess Your Readiness and Set Boundaries**
   - Before attempting to remote view a natural disaster, evaluate your emotional and mental resilience.
   - Set a strong intention to remain neutral and detached from the event's energy.
   - Visualise a protective shield around yourself to prevent absorbing negative or chaotic energies.
2. **Focus on the Target**
   - Use specific details, such as the time, location, or type of disaster, to connect with the event.

- Visualise the disaster from a high-level perspective, such as viewing a storm from above or observing the movement of tectonic plates.
- Avoid immersing yourself in the event's emotional or human impact to maintain a calm state of mind.

3. **Observe the Energy Dynamics**
   - Tune into the energy of the natural forces at play. What does the energy feel like—raw, destructive, or transformative?
   - Notice patterns, movements, or other details that provide insights into the mechanics of the event.
   - Acknowledge the immense power of nature without judgment or fear.

4. **Explore the Broader Context**
   - Look for connections to the Earth's energy systems, such as fault lines, weather patterns, or volcanic activity.
   - Consider how the event may impact the surrounding environment or ecosystems.
   - Be mindful of any intuitive impressions, such as the event's role in the planet's natural balance or cycles.

5. **Ground Yourself and Reflect**
   - After completing the session, ground yourself with deep breaths, physical movement, or spending time in nature.
   - Record your observations, focusing on the objective details of the disaster rather than emotional aspects.
   - Reflect on the experience and evaluate how it aligns with your intentions and abilities.

Remote viewing natural disasters can be a profound and humbling experience, but it is not a suitable target for everyone. The intense energy of these events demands emotional resilience, strong boundaries, and a neutral mindset. If approached thoughtfully, this practice can deepen your understanding of Earth's natural processes while reinforcing the importance of respect and care for our planet. Always prioritize your emotional well-being and approach these targets with caution and reverence.

Natural Resources

Remote viewing natural resources—such as water, minerals, forests, or fossil fuels—can be an enlightening practice for understanding the Earth's abundance and how it sustains life. People may choose to explore natural resources through remote viewing to gain insight into their location, quality, and role in the planet's ecosystem.

However, it is important to approach this practice with a respectful and ethical mindset. Natural resources are essential to life and often tied to delicate environmental and social balances. Remote viewing them can reveal their energetic significance and potential, but it should be done with an awareness of the responsibility we hold as stewards of the Earth.

Five Steps to Remote View Natural Resources

1. **Set an Ethical Intention and Prepare Your Space**
   - Begin by meditating and grounding yourself to establish a calm, neutral mindset.
   - Set a clear intention to explore natural resources with respect for the environment and its balance.
   - Affirm that your purpose is observation and understanding, not exploitation or harm.

2. **Focus on the Target Resource**
   - Choose a specific type of natural resource (e.g., groundwater, oil, or a mineral deposit) and identify its general location or characteristics.
   - Visualise the resource and its surrounding environment, imagining both its physical and energetic presence.
   - Use coordinates, maps, or general impressions to guide your focus.

3. **Sense the Energy of the Resource**
   - Tune into the energy field of the resource. Is it abundant, depleted, or balanced?
   - Observe how it interacts with the surrounding environment, such as supporting ecosystems or human activity.

- Pay attention to the emotions or impressions that arise, as they may provide clues about the resource's significance.
4. **Explore the Surrounding Environment**
   - Mentally examine the area where the resource is located, noting any physical features like terrain, water sources, or vegetation.
   - Consider the resource's accessibility and how it might influence human activity or ecological balance.
   - Reflect on any symbolic impressions you receive, such as the role of the resource in the Earth's cycles.
5. **Document and Reflect**
   - Record your observations in detail, noting any visual, energetic, or intuitive insights.
   - Reflect on the ethical and ecological implications of what you've perceived.
   - Consider how the resource might be sustainably managed or protected based on your findings.

Remote viewing natural resources provides a unique way to connect with the Earth's wealth and understand its role in supporting life. This practice can uncover hidden insights about the energy and balance of resources, emphasizing the importance of stewardship and sustainability. By approaching this with a neutral and ethical mindset, you can use remote viewing to foster a deeper appreciation for the planet and its interconnected systems. Always respect the environment and align your exploration with intentions of care and preservation.

Night Skies

The night sky has fascinated humanity for millennia. Whether it's the vast expanse of stars, the phases of the moon, or distant planets, the night sky is a gateway to exploration, wonder, and discovery. Remote viewing the night skies allows practitioners to connect with celestial bodies, cosmic phenomena, and even the energetic influences of space.

People might choose to remote view the night skies to gain insight into astronomical events, uncover cosmic mysteries, or simply feel a deeper connection to the universe. However, remote viewing celestial targets is unique in that it requires a deep sense of expansiveness and openness to the unknown. Expect to experience a sense of vastness and wonder as you tune into the energy of the stars and planets.

Five Steps to Remote View the Night Skies
1. **Set Your Intention and Ground Yourself**
    - Begin by calming your mind through meditation, breathing deeply, and grounding yourself into the present moment.
    - Set a clear intention to connect with the night skies and explore without preconceived notions.
    - Visualise yourself opening to the vastness of the universe, allowing your consciousness to expand beyond earthly limitations.
2. **Focus on a Celestial Target**
    - Choose a specific celestial body or event, such as a star, constellation, planet, or the moon, and establish your focus.
    - If observing a particular astronomical event (like a comet or eclipse), set the intention to tune into its energetic impact.
    - Let your mind freely flow toward the energy of the chosen target, without forcing the connection.
3. **Tune into the Energy of the Cosmos**
    - As you focus, notice the energy of the night sky. Does it feel expansive, silent, peaceful, or filled with movement?
    - Pay attention to any sensations that arise—such as a feeling of deep stillness, awe, or connection to something larger than yourself.
    - Observe the way light and dark interact in the sky and how the stars or planets convey information.

4. **Observe Celestial Patterns and Interactions**
    - Mentally explore the sky's patterns: the movement of stars, the orbit of planets, the phases of the moon.
    - Notice any changes in energy, such as shifts in brightness, color, or intensity.
    - Be open to the possibility of receiving intuitive impressions or messages related to the celestial body or event you are viewing.
5. **Reflect and Record Your Observations**
    - Write down everything you perceive during the session, including visual impressions, energetic shifts, and intuitive insights.
    - Reflect on how the energy of the sky felt in relation to your own energy and awareness.
    - Consider what this exploration reveals about the universe or your connection to it, and how it fits into your broader understanding of reality.

Remote viewing the night skies is a transformative practice that allows you to connect with the vast, mysterious universe beyond Earth. Whether you're exploring stars, planets, or cosmic events, this practice invites a deeper understanding of the energy and consciousness of the cosmos. By maintaining openness, neutrality, and a sense of awe, you can experience the night sky in a new and profound way, expanding your awareness of both the universe and your place within it.

Ocean Depths

The ocean depths are one of the most mysterious and unexplored areas of our planet. Beneath the surface lies a world full of secrets, unknown creatures, and powerful energy. Remote viewing the ocean depths can offer profound insights into marine life, underwater geography, and even the hidden energetic forces at play beneath the waves.

People may be drawn to remote view the ocean depths to explore marine ecosystems, study underwater phenomena, or tap into the mysterious energy of the ocean. However, it's important to approach this practice with caution, as the dark, heavy energy of the deep ocean can be intense and difficult to navigate for those unprepared. Expect to encounter a sense of vastness, isolation, and sometimes unsettling sensations during your session.

Five Steps to Remote View the Ocean Depths

1. **Set Your Intention and Protect Your Energy**
   - Begin with grounding meditation to clear your mind and centre your body.
   - Set a strong, clear intention to explore the ocean depths with respect, neutrality, and curiosity.
   - Visualise a protective shield around you, ensuring that no heavy or negative energies from the ocean will affect your personal energy.

2. **Choose Your Focus and Visualise the Target**
   - Select a specific part of the ocean or a particular area of interest, such as a coral reef, the ocean floor, or a deep-sea trench.
   - Visualise the location and the environment around it, allowing yourself to feel the immense scale of the ocean.
   - Be open to perceiving the energy of the place, whether it's calm and serene or turbulent and mysterious.

3. **Sense the Energy and Atmosphere**
   - Tune into the energy of the ocean at various depths. How does the water feel—dense, light, cold, or heavy?
   - Pay attention to any emotional sensations that arise—such as a sense of isolation, awe, or a feeling of mystery.
   - Observe any physical elements in the ocean, like waves, currents, or underwater formations, and notice how they interact energetically.

4. Explore the Ocean Environment
- Move deeper into the target location, observing the creatures, plant life, or geographical features.
- Pay attention to the colors, shapes, and movement of the ocean. Notice how light plays a role in the environment, especially as you descend into darker areas.
- Explore the connection between the ocean and the environment surrounding it, including the energy of the earth, air, and water as they interact in this ecosystem.

5. Record Your Observations and Reflect
- After completing your session, document everything you perceived, including visual impressions, physical sensations, and intuitive insights.
- Reflect on how the experience felt—did it feel expansive and peaceful, or overwhelming and tense?
- Consider any deeper messages you may have received from the ocean depths, and how they relate to the larger environment or your personal energy.

Remote viewing the ocean depths is a powerful way to connect with one of Earth's most mysterious and vital realms. Whether you're exploring the marine life, the physical landscape, or the energetic forces of the ocean, this practice offers insights into the hidden dynamics of our planet. Due to the intense and often heavy energy found in deep waters, it's important to approach this practice with mindfulness and respect. By maintaining neutrality and protection, you can explore the ocean depths safely, expanding your awareness of both the Earth's mysteries and your connection to them.

Organizations

Remote viewing organizations—whether governmental, corporate, non-profit, or other types—can offer intriguing insights into the inner workings, energy, and structures of various entities. People may remote view organizations to understand their influence, internal dynamics, or how they operate on both conscious and subconscious levels. This could include everything from a company's strategic decisions to the energetic patterns that guide its operations.

Remote viewing organizations is a highly sensitive practice. These entities often carry collective energy, with intricate webs of relationships and intentions influencing their outcomes. While exploring an organization through remote viewing can provide valuable insights, it is essential to remain neutral, detached, and ethical throughout the process.

Five Steps to Remote View Organizations

1. **Define Your Intention and Establish Boundaries**
   - Begin by meditating and grounding yourself to achieve a calm, centred state.
   - Set a clear intention for your remote viewing, focusing on understanding the organization in a neutral, non-judgmental way.
   - Establish boundaries to protect your energy from absorbing any chaotic or unbalanced energy that may be present within the organization.

2. **Focus on the Organization's Energy and Structure**
   - Visualise the organization's physical and energetic structure. This could include its headquarters, key leadership, or internal systems.
   - Consider the organization's purpose, its goals, and how it interacts with the external world.
   - Tune into the organizational energy—how does it feel? Is it cohesive or fragmented? Does it seem balanced or chaotic?

3. **Explore the Inner Dynamics of the Organization**
   - Observe the relationships within the organization, including leadership dynamics, employee interactions, and the flow of information.
   - Pay attention to any patterns, such as power structures, decision-making processes, or underlying emotional currents within the team.

- Be mindful of intuitive insights that may reveal the organization's purpose beyond its surface activities.

4. **Investigate the Impact of External Forces**
   - Remote view the organization's interactions with external factors, such as societal trends, market forces, or political influence.
   - Notice how these external influences affect the organization's energy, growth, or potential.
   - Observe how the organization responds to challenges, opportunities, and changes in its environment.

5. **Reflect and Document Your Findings**
   - Record your observations, including impressions about the organization's energy, relationships, and any intuitive insights gained during the session.
   - Reflect on how the organization's energy resonates with your own, and whether any patterns or messages arose that are significant.
   - Consider the ethical implications of your remote viewing, ensuring you are not overstepping boundaries or accessing sensitive information without permission.

Remote viewing organizations can provide valuable insights into the dynamics and energy that shape how they function. This practice allows you to tap into the larger consciousness of the group, revealing internal systems, power structures, and external influences. However, it is important to approach these sessions with integrity, neutrality, and respect for privacy. By maintaining clear intentions and boundaries, you can explore the hidden aspects of organizations in a way that benefits both your understanding and your ethical standards.

Political Figures

From my experience with remote viewing, people often choose to view political figures due to the intense emotions and diverse opinions these individuals evoke. Political figures can embody power, influence, and controversy, making them a subject of fascination. Remote viewing political figures allows one to gain insights into their motivations, mental state, and energetic dynamics. People may seek to understand their leadership style, decision-making processes, or even their future actions.

However, remote viewing political figures requires a high level of responsibility and ethical mindfulness. These figures are often surrounded by complex energy fields, including collective societal emotions, and viewing them can stir personal biases or judgments. It's essential to approach this practice with a neutral mindset and avoid engaging with negative emotions or perceptions.

Five Steps to Remote View Political Figures
1. **Clarify Your Intention and Ground Yourself**
   - Start with grounding exercises to centre yourself and clear your mind.
   - Set a clear, focused intention for your session: whether you want to understand the political figure's motivations, actions, or energy dynamics.
   - Affirm that your goal is to observe and gain insights, not to judge, criticize, or manipulate the person being viewed.
2. **Choose the Political Figure and Set the Focus**
   - Select the political figure you want to explore. This could be someone you know or a prominent public figure.
   - Tune into the energy of the person, allowing your consciousness to connect with theirs.
   - Use their name, image, or known public actions to guide your focus, but ensure that you do not over-identify with the individual or become emotionally entangled.
3. **Observe Their Energy and Emotional State**
   - Pay attention to the emotional energy surrounding the political figure. Are they calm, anxious, or determined?

- Observe how they carry themselves energetically. Do they feel confident, fearful, or perhaps conflicted?
- Notice any energetic patterns, such as an aura of power, insecurity, or stress. Be aware of any sensations or impressions that emerge, but avoid attaching judgment to them.

4. **Explore the Figure's Motivations and Intentions**
   - Tune into the motivations that drive the political figure. What are they trying to achieve or protect?
   - Observe how their intentions align with their actions or public image. Are they genuinely invested in their cause, or are there hidden agendas or influences?
   - Explore the deeper layers of their psyche to understand what is influencing their decisions or the way they interact with others.

5. **Document Your Insights and Reflect on Ethics**
   - Record your observations, including emotional patterns, impressions, and any intuitive insights you received.
   - Reflect on whether your session was neutral and ethical, ensuring that you were not swayed by personal biases or external influences.
   - Consider how this remote viewing experience contributes to your own understanding of the political figure and whether any personal lessons arose from the session.

Remote viewing political figures can offer fascinating insights into the complexities of leadership and human behaviour. It provides an opportunity to understand the energetic patterns and emotional states that guide their decisions and actions. However, it's vital to approach this practice with neutrality, respect, and ethical consideration. By remaining detached and focusing on observation, remote viewing can deepen your understanding of political dynamics and help you cultivate a more balanced, compassionate perspective on those in positions of power.

Private Residences

From my experience with remote viewing, people often choose to explore private residences to gain insights into the lives of others, understand the energy of a home, or even assist with personal decisions regarding spaces. A private residence, whether a family home or a personal retreat, carries its own unique energy and emotional imprint, reflecting the personalities, experiences, and history of its occupants. Remote viewing can offer a way to understand the dynamics within a space—its atmosphere, history, or the energy patterns that reside there.

However, remote viewing private residences must be approached with extreme care and respect. A home is a deeply personal and private space. The energy within can be influenced by the thoughts, emotions, and experiences of those who live there. Remote viewing these spaces requires an ethical commitment to neutrality, consent, and mindfulness, as entering someone's private domain can be intrusive if not done with respect.

Five Steps to Remote View Private Residences

1. **Establish Your Intention and Protect Your Energy**
   - Begin with grounding techniques, focusing on clearing your mind and centring your energy.
   - Set a clear intention for your remote viewing: are you exploring the energy of the space, its history, or the well-being of the people who live there?
   - Visualise a protective shield surrounding you to ensure that only the information meant for you comes through, and that you are not absorbing any negative or invasive energy from the space.
2. **Focus on the Residence and Its Energy**
   - Visualise the private residence, or focus on the address or location you wish to explore.
   - Tune into the energy of the space itself, paying attention to the overall atmosphere: Is it warm, inviting, cold, oppressive, or light?

- Notice if there are any imbalances or stagnant energies present. Homes often carry the imprints of past emotions, so be sensitive to any areas where energy may feel heavy or unresolved.

3. **Explore the Rooms and Their Energy Signatures**
   - Begin by mentally moving through the rooms of the home, starting with the entryway or most prominent spaces.
   - Observe the energy in each room. Is it different in each area? For example, living rooms may feel more social and welcoming, while bedrooms might carry a more intimate or private energy.
   - Pay attention to any emotional imprints that linger in the space—are there unresolved conflicts, moments of joy, or sadness that the environment holds onto?

4. **Observe the Residents' Energy and Emotional State**
   - Tune into the energy of the people who live in the space, if you feel comfortable doing so. How do their individual energies affect the home?
   - Observe any emotional patterns that may be present in the home, such as stress, harmony, or tension between individuals. How does the space feel in terms of the emotional state of the residents?
   - Be mindful of not overstepping personal boundaries. Focus on the energetic aspects rather than detailed personal information, as this is a sensitive area.

5. **Document Your Observations and Reflect on Ethics**
   - Record everything you observed during your session: impressions of the space, the energy, and any intuitive insights you received.
   - Reflect on whether you maintained neutrality and respect during the process. Did you avoid judgment or interference with the space or its residents?
   - Consider the ethical implications of your exploration and how the information gathered may be used. Always be mindful that remote viewing a private residence should be

done for the highest good, with respect for privacy and personal boundaries.

Remote viewing private residences can provide valuable insights into the energetic dynamics of a home and the lives of those who inhabit it. By understanding the energy within a space, you can help address emotional imbalances or enhance well-being. However, it is crucial to approach this practice with integrity, respect, and a non-intrusive mindset. By maintaining a clear intention, protecting your energy, and reflecting on ethical boundaries, you can navigate the energy of private spaces safely and responsibly.

Research Labs

From my experience with remote viewing, people may choose to view research labs to gain insights into the ongoing projects, innovations, or scientific energy present within these spaces. Research labs are environments where cutting-edge discoveries, experiments, and breakthroughs take place, and they carry unique energy based on the work being done. Remote viewing these spaces can help uncover hidden dynamics, understand the energy behind specific projects, or even reveal the emotional states of the scientists and researchers involved.

However, remote viewing research labs comes with significant ethical considerations. These environments are often highly sensitive and involve intellectual property, confidential experiments, and sometimes even high-risk research. It is crucial to approach such sessions with neutrality, respect for privacy, and an understanding of the potential impact that your findings could have.

Five Steps to Remote View Research Labs
1. **Set Clear Intentions and Prepare Mentally**
   - Start by grounding yourself and clearing your mind to ensure a calm and neutral state.
   - Set a clear intention for your remote viewing: Are you trying to understand the purpose of the research being

conducted? Are you focused on the energy of the lab itself or the impact of the research?
- Mentally prepare yourself by asking for clarity and protection, ensuring that only the necessary and ethically appropriate information is received.

2. **Focus on the Research Lab's Energy and Purpose**
   - Visualise the location of the research lab, or use any available details such as the name of the institution or the specific project being conducted.
   - Tune into the overall energy of the lab. Does the space feel charged with intellectual excitement, urgency, or curiosity?
   - Observe any high-energy activities or areas of focus within the lab—are there any specific experiments or projects that seem particularly significant or active?

3. **Explore the Key Areas and Activities**
   - Move mentally through the research lab, exploring different sections. You may focus on the laboratory benches, equipment, or any places where research is taking place.
   - Observe the type of work being conducted in the lab: Is it biological, technological, or theoretical?
   - Pay attention to the energy of the researchers and their interactions with each other, the equipment, and the subject of their research. Are they collaborative, intense, or isolated? Do any specific objects or experiments seem to hold significant energy?

4. **Observe the Emotional and Mental States of the Researchers**
   - Tune into the researchers' emotional and mental states. What emotions are they experiencing as they conduct their work? Are there any signs of stress, excitement, or frustration?
   - Notice how their energy influences the research process. Are they focused and clear, or is there confusion or uncertainty present?

- Be mindful of the collective energy in the lab: How do the energy and emotions of the researchers align with the lab's overall goals and experiments?

5. **Reflect and Document Your Findings, Maintain Ethical Standards**
   - Write down everything you observed, including the energy of the space, the experiments, and the emotional states of the individuals involved.
   - Reflect on whether you maintained a neutral, non-judgmental approach during your remote viewing. Ensure that you did not access any sensitive or confidential information beyond what is ethically permissible.
   - Consider the potential implications of your findings. Could the information you've gathered be used to influence or assist the lab's work in a constructive way? Always respect intellectual property and confidentiality.

Remote viewing research labs can offer valuable insights into the work being done and the energy that drives scientific discovery. By understanding the emotional and energetic states of the researchers and the environment, you can uncover the underlying dynamics that influence their work. However, remote viewing these spaces should be approached with the utmost respect for privacy, confidentiality, and ethical boundaries. By remaining neutral, protecting your energy, and reflecting on the impact of your findings, you can explore research labs responsibly and in alignment with the highest ethical standards.

Rescue Operations

From my experience with remote viewing, people often choose to explore rescue operations to gain insight into the dynamics of ongoing rescue missions, such as those responding to natural disasters, accidents, or emergencies. These operations involve a high level of urgency, collaboration, and often life-and-death situations. Remote viewing these operations can provide valuable information about the location of victims, the state of the environment, or the overall energy and emotional state of the team involved. However, rescue operations are also highly sensitive and require careful consideration when approaching them.

The ethical considerations when remote viewing rescue operations are significant. These situations are charged with high emotional energy, and any insights gained can have a profound impact on the teams involved or the individuals they are trying to save. Therefore, it is essential to approach such sessions with neutrality, respect, and caution, ensuring that the information gathered is used in a constructive and ethical manner.

Five Steps to Remote View Rescue Operations
1. **Set Your Intention and Prepare for Clarity**
   - Begin by grounding yourself and clearing your mind to achieve a calm and focused state.
   - Set a clear intention for your remote viewing session: Are you attempting to gather information about the location of people in danger, the progress of the rescue mission, or the energy surrounding the team's efforts?
   - Ask for protection during the session and ensure that you are focused only on the information that will help with the mission, while avoiding any unnecessary interference or emotional entanglement.
2. **Focus on the Rescue Operation's Location and Context**
   - Visualise the area of the rescue operation. This could be a disaster zone, an accident site, or an emergency location where help is being provided.
   - Tune into the immediate energy of the area. Is the environment chaotic, calm, or tense? Are there specific locations where energy feels more concentrated, such as areas where people might be trapped or in danger?

- Take note of any physical features or environmental conditions that stand out, such as terrain, weather conditions, or obstacles the rescuers might face.
3. **Observe the Rescue Teams and Their Actions**
   - Move your focus to the rescue team members. What are they doing? Are they calm and efficient, or are they facing challenges and emotional stress?
   - Pay attention to their energy levels. Are there areas of the operation where the energy is high, such as during rescue efforts, or where the team may be feeling fatigued or overwhelmed?
   - Notice if there are any team members that stand out in terms of leadership, anxiety, or other emotional influences.
4. **Locate Victims and Assess the Situation**
   - Once you've tuned into the general environment, focus on locating any individuals who may be trapped or in danger.
   - Observe the energy surrounding these people. Are they conscious or unconscious? Are they panicked, calm, or injured?
   - Be mindful of the ethical responsibility in this step. Your goal should be to provide helpful insights without overstepping boundaries or interfering with the emotional process of the individuals involved. Respect the privacy and dignity of those you are viewing.
5. **Reflect, Document, and Maintain Neutrality**
   - After the session, write down everything you observed, including the location, energy, actions of the rescue team, and status of the victims.
   - Reflect on whether you maintained a neutral, detached perspective. Did you approach the session with kindness and the intention to help, rather than interfering emotionally with the situation?

- Ensure that the information you have gathered can be used in a responsible and ethical manner, especially if it could be shared with the rescue teams or other individuals involved.

Remote viewing rescue operations can provide critical insights that help guide emergency responders, identify the locations of victims, or understand the emotional and energetic dynamics at play. However, these operations are often high-pressure and emotionally intense, and it is essential to approach them with deep respect, neutrality, and caution. The information you gather should be used to support the safety and success of the mission, and always with the highest ethical standards in mind. By maintaining an impersonal and compassionate approach, remote viewing can contribute positively to the effectiveness of rescue operations.

Rivers

From my experience with remote viewing, people often choose to explore rivers for various reasons, such as understanding their natural flow, uncovering hidden ecological patterns, or assessing environmental changes. Rivers are dynamic environments that connect and nourish landscapes, playing a significant role in the local ecosystem and human activities. Remote viewing rivers can help reveal the flow of energy within a river system, detect imbalances, or observe how the surrounding environment interacts with the water. It can also provide insights into the health of the ecosystem or how human actions may have impacted the river.

However, rivers are powerful and often unpredictable forces of nature, and remote viewing them requires a careful and respectful approach. The energy surrounding rivers can be both calming and overwhelming, and understanding their balance and flow is key. It is important to approach these sessions with respect for the river's natural processes and the surrounding environment, considering the ecological, cultural, and spiritual significance of the water.

Five Steps to Remote View Rivers

1. **Set Your Intention and Clear Your Mind**
   - Begin by grounding yourself and centring your energy to ensure a calm, clear, and focused state.
   - Set a clear intention for your remote viewing: Are you exploring the overall health of the river, its energy flow, or changes due to human impact? Are you interested in understanding its role in the local ecosystem or its spiritual significance?
   - Protect your energy by visualizing a shield of light around you, ensuring that you are only receiving information that is necessary and beneficial.

2. **Focus on the River's Energy and Flow**
   - Visualise the river in its entirety, or use any available information to tune into its specific location.
   - Observe the river's flow—does the water move swiftly, gently, or stagnantly? Is the current strong, or are there areas where the flow is disrupted or blocked?
   - Pay attention to the surrounding environment. Is the water clear or murky? Are there any signs of pollution, stagnation, or ecological imbalance? Rivers often carry energy in their flow, and you may pick up on this energy as you observe them.

3. **Explore Key Features of the River**
   - Mentally navigate through the different areas of the river, focusing on significant features such as bends, tributaries, dams, or natural obstacles.
   - Notice how the energy changes in different parts of the river. Are there areas of harmony, or are there disturbances in the flow of water?
   - Pay attention to any signs of environmental stress, such as areas with reduced flow, increased sedimentation, or signs of human interference, such as nearby constructions or pollution.

4. **Tune Into the Surrounding Ecosystem**
   - Expand your awareness to include the ecosystem around the river, observing how the river interacts with the land, plants, animals, and human activities.
   - Is the river nourishing the land and wildlife, or are there signs of imbalance or degradation?
   - Observe the emotional or energetic states of the living beings around the river—do the plants, animals, or people seem to thrive from the river's presence, or are they affected by negative energy, such as contamination or water scarcity?
5. **Reflect, Document, and Maintain Neutrality**
   - After the session, write down all your observations, including the flow, energy, and any ecological or environmental details you noticed about the river and its surroundings.
   - Reflect on whether you maintained a neutral and non-judgmental perspective during your session. Ensure that you did not impose any preconceived notions about the river's condition but allowed the energy to reveal itself authentically.
   - Consider any ethical implications. Rivers are sacred to many cultures and vital to ecosystems; always approach them with reverence and ensure your findings are used with respect for the environment and its interconnected systems.

Remote viewing rivers can provide valuable insights into the health, energy, and flow of these vital natural resources. By understanding the river's role in the ecosystem and the surrounding environment, you can uncover potential imbalances or gain deeper knowledge about its connection to the land and people. However, it is important to approach these sessions with sensitivity and respect for the river's natural energy and significance. Rivers carry both physical and spiritual importance, and maintaining neutrality, respect, and ethical mindfulness will help ensure that your remote viewing experience supports the highest good of the environment and all beings connected to it.

Ruins

From my experience with remote viewing, people often choose to explore ruins to uncover hidden historical or energetic information about ancient structures or civilizations. Ruins are the remnants of once-thriving places, carrying with them the stories, energies, and memories of past inhabitants. These spaces can hold powerful emotional or spiritual vibrations, offering insights into what once existed and what was lost. Remote viewing ruins allows individuals to connect with the energies of ancient cultures, uncover secrets hidden in the architecture, or even explore the remnants of rituals or events that shaped the course of history.

However, ruins are not always just physical remnants; they can be charged with the collective memories of their past. Remote viewing ruins can sometimes bring up strong emotional or unsettling energies, so it is important to approach these sessions with caution, respect, and neutrality. Understanding the context of these ruins is key to interpreting what you may encounter, as some sites carry powerful or sacred energies that require a balanced and careful approach.

Five Steps to Remote View Ruins

1. **Set Your Intention and Ground Yourself**
   - Begin by grounding yourself to ensure a calm and neutral energy state. Clear any distractions from your mind and focus solely on the task at hand.
   - Set a clear and specific intention for your remote viewing: Are you seeking to understand the history of the ruins, uncover hidden energies or symbols, or explore the emotions of those who once inhabited the space?
   - Visualise a protective shield of light surrounding you to prevent any overwhelming or negative energy from affecting your session. Make sure to approach the ruins with reverence and respect.

2. **Tune Into the Energy of the Ruins**
   - Visualise the ruins, focusing on their location, size, and any details that stand out in your mind. Pay attention to the overall energy of the space—does it feel abandoned, sacred, or filled with energy from past events?
   - Take note of the ruins' condition. Are they well-preserved, crumbled, or overtaken by nature? This may reveal clues about the history or significance of the site.
   - Observe any strong emotional or energetic impressions. Are there feelings of sorrow, peace, power, or decay connected to the space?
3. **Explore the Specific Structures and Areas**
   - Focus on individual structures or parts of the ruins, such as walls, temples, statues, or chambers. Explore what is present in the physical and energetic sense.
   - What stories or energies do these structures hold? Are there specific symbols, carvings, or architectural features that stand out? These may provide insights into the beliefs, practices, or priorities of the people who once inhabited the space.
   - Notice if any areas of the ruins feel more charged or significant than others. These places may be linked to particular events, rituals, or energetic focal points.
4. **Connect with the Past Inhabitants**
   - Tune into the emotional or energetic residues left by those who once lived in or visited the ruins. What are the emotions or states of mind that linger in the space?
   - Are there any individuals or groups of people whose presence you sense? What are they doing—are they engaged in daily activities, rituals, or moments of significance?
   - Observe how the inhabitants interact with their environment. Do they feel connected to the space, or are they haunted by past events or trauma? Understanding the emotional or spiritual connection between the people and the space can provide insight into the meaning of the ruins.

5. **Reflect, Document, and Stay Neutral**
    - After the session, take time to reflect and document your observations. Write down everything you sensed, including the condition of the ruins, any significant areas or features, and the emotional and energetic impressions you encountered.
    - Review whether you were able to maintain a neutral, non-judgmental perspective during your session. Avoid projecting personal biases or preconceived ideas onto the ruins; instead, let the energy and information unfold naturally.
    - Consider the ethical implications of your remote viewing. Ruins are often sacred, and it's important to treat them with respect. Ensure that any information you gather is shared thoughtfully and responsibly, especially if it involves sensitive cultural or historical knowledge.

Remote viewing ruins provides a unique opportunity to connect with the energies, histories, and memories of ancient places. These spaces hold deep emotional and spiritual significance, offering profound insights into the past. However, ruins can also carry complex and sometimes intense energies that must be approached with care and respect. By maintaining neutrality, protecting your energy, and grounding yourself before and after your session, you can safely explore these ancient spaces and uncover the wisdom and stories that lie hidden within. Always remember to approach ruins with reverence, and use the information you gather responsibly, keeping in mind the sacredness of these spaces.

Satellites

From my experience with remote viewing, people often choose to explore satellites to gather information about their purpose, functionality, and the broader impact they may have on Earth and space. Satellites are powerful tools that help in communication, weather forecasting, navigation, scientific research, and military operations. Remote viewing satellites can provide insight into their design, operations, and their interactions with the environment, both in space and on Earth. This type of remote viewing may offer valuable knowledge about how satellites impact our daily lives, how they contribute to global monitoring systems, or even their potential influence on geopolitical or technological developments.

Satellites are typically highly engineered and contain advanced technologies that are often classified or not fully accessible to the public. When engaging in remote viewing of satellites, it's important to approach the task with caution, neutrality, and respect for privacy and security. It's crucial to remember that satellites, especially military or intelligence satellites, are not only highly sensitive but also bound by ethical considerations regarding their observation and use.

Five Steps to Remote View Satellites

1. **Set Your Intention and Ground Yourself**
   - Start by grounding yourself and clearing your mind, ensuring that you enter the session with a calm and neutral energy.
   - Clearly define your intention for the session. Are you exploring the satellite's design, function, or impact on the Earth? Are you interested in understanding its role in communication, surveillance, or weather forecasting? Setting a specific goal will help you focus your energies and prevent unnecessary distractions.
   - Visualise a protective shield around you to prevent any energy interference and to keep your mind clear during the remote viewing session.
2. **Tune Into the Satellite's Energy and Purpose**
   - Visualise the satellite and its position in space, focusing on its shape, size, and energy. What purpose does the satellite serve? Does it appear to be actively working, or is it inactive or malfunctioning?

- Observe the satellite's interaction with its environment. How does it move through space, and how does its energy interact with the Earth or other satellites?
- Pay attention to any energetic or emotional impressions that may come through. Some satellites, particularly those related to military or surveillance operations, may have a more covert or charged energy, while others, like scientific satellites, may feel more neutral or exploratory.

3. **Explore the Satellite's Systems and Functionality**
   - Focus on specific components of the satellite, such as its sensors, antennas, solar panels, or communication systems. How do these parts interact with each other?
   - Observe the technology used in the satellite and its function. Is it focused on collecting data, transmitting signals, or monitoring specific locations?
   - You may also sense whether there are any operational challenges or issues affecting the satellite, such as damage, energy loss, or a malfunctioning part. This can provide valuable information about the satellite's overall health and performance.

4. **Understand the Satellite's Impact and Connections**
   - Expand your awareness to explore how the satellite connects to Earth and interacts with various systems or entities. Does it monitor weather patterns, assist with communications, or track specific geographic locations?
   - If the satellite is linked to a particular organization, military force, or government, try to understand how it fits into their broader operations. Does the satellite serve an intelligence, surveillance, or scientific purpose?
   - Pay attention to the satellite's role in the larger context of global communication, environmental monitoring, or technological advancement. How does its operation influence the way people live, work, and communicate?

5. Reflect, Document, and Stay Neutral
- After the session, take time to reflect on the information you've received. Write down your observations about the satellite's purpose, functionality, and impact, noting any details about its technology, energy, and interactions with the Earth or space.
- Review whether you were able to maintain neutrality during the session. Avoid projecting personal opinions or judgments onto the satellite; instead, focus on receiving pure, objective data.
- Be mindful of any ethical considerations involved. Satellites, especially those involved in security or intelligence work, are subject to privacy and national security regulations. Ensure that any information gathered is used responsibly and within the appropriate context.

Remote viewing satellites offers an intriguing opportunity to understand the technological, scientific, and geopolitical significance of these space-based devices. By observing their design, purpose, and impact, you can gain valuable insights into how satellites contribute to our modern world, from communication networks to weather systems. However, remote viewing satellites requires a careful, neutral approach due to the sensitive nature of the data they collect and the ethical considerations involved. By grounding yourself, maintaining neutrality, and respecting the boundaries of privacy and security, you can successfully explore these advanced technologies and understand their place in the world.

Scientific Experiments

From my experience with remote viewing, people often choose to explore scientific experiments to uncover information about research methodologies, findings, or the deeper implications of scientific work. Scientific experiments are designed to test hypotheses, explore new theories, and discover unknown truths. Remote viewing scientific experiments can offer valuable insights into how experiments are conducted, what results are being obtained, and the potential impact of these findings on society, technology, or health.

However, it is important to recognize that scientific experiments—especially those in sensitive areas such as genetics, medicine, or defence—may involve complex, proprietary, or classified information. When remote viewing scientific experiments, the goal is not to interfere but to observe and understand. It's important to approach such sessions with respect, neutrality, and integrity to ensure that the information accessed is used responsibly and ethically.

Five Steps to Remote View Scientific Experiments
1. **Set Your Intention and Ground Yourself**
   - Begin by grounding yourself, clearing your mind, and ensuring you are in a neutral state. Remote viewing requires a calm, open mind to receive accurate and unbiased information.
   - Clearly set your intention for the session: What specific scientific experiment are you exploring? Are you interested in the process, the results, or the potential applications of the experiment?
   - Visualise a protective shield of light around you to prevent any interference from external energies and maintain a focused, clear connection.
2. **Tune Into the Energy of the Experiment**
   - Visualise the experiment, its setting, and the environment where it is being conducted. Are you in a laboratory, a field station, or a controlled testing environment? Observe the energy of the space—is it sterile and clinical, or more chaotic and exploratory?
   - Focus on the experiment itself. What materials, equipment, or tools are involved? Pay attention to any unique or specialized instruments used in the experiment.
   - Tune into the energy of the experiment's process—are the scientists or researchers calm and methodical, or

is there a sense of urgency or excitement around the experiment?
3. **Observe the Methodology and Procedures**
    - Zoom in on the specific steps of the experiment. What procedures are being followed? What variables are being manipulated or controlled?
    - Pay attention to any data being collected—whether through instruments, observations, or participant responses. What measurements are being taken, and how are they recorded?
    - Observe whether there are any challenges or setbacks occurring during the experiment. Are there any issues with the equipment, results, or procedure that are impacting the outcome?
4. **Investigate the Results and Implications**
    - Focus on the outcomes of the experiment. What data or results have been produced, and what do they reveal?
    - Consider the broader implications of the findings. Are the results confirming or contradicting a hypothesis? Are they leading to new scientific discoveries or theories?
    - Observe whether there are any unexpected or unexplored outcomes that could have a significant impact on future research or applications.
5. **Reflect, Document, and Stay Neutral**
    - After the session, take time to reflect on the information you've received and write down your observations. Record the details of the experiment, including its process, results, and potential implications.
    - Review whether you maintained neutrality throughout the session. Remote viewing requires you to set aside personal beliefs or biases and simply observe what is happening.
    - Consider the ethical responsibility of accessing information about scientific experiments. Experiments, especially

those involving human subjects or sensitive topics, require careful consideration. Ensure that any information gathered is handled responsibly and with integrity.

Remote viewing scientific experiments can provide valuable insights into the methodologies, findings, and broader implications of scientific work. Whether exploring new technologies, medical advancements, or environmental studies, remote viewing allows you to observe the processes that drive human discovery. However, it is essential to approach scientific experiments with caution, respect, and neutrality. By grounding yourself, staying focused, and maintaining a sense of ethical responsibility, you can gain deeper understanding while ensuring that the information gathered is used for constructive and responsible purposes.

Secret Meetings

From my experience with remote viewing, people often choose to explore secret meetings to gain insights into hidden decisions, strategic plans, or confidential discussions that could have significant societal or geopolitical implications. Secret meetings may involve key players in politics, business, military, or other sectors, and they are often shrouded in secrecy to maintain privacy, security, or competitive advantage. Remote viewing these meetings can provide valuable information about ongoing negotiations, strategies, and outcomes that could affect the course of future events.

However, it's important to acknowledge that accessing information about secret meetings raises ethical concerns. These meetings are intentionally private for reasons of confidentiality, security, and sensitive matters. Remote viewing them requires a high level of respect for privacy and neutrality. The goal should not be to invade personal or organizational privacy but to explore the dynamics and purpose of these gatherings while remaining impartial.

Five Steps to Remote View Secret Meetings

1. **Set Your Intention and Ground Yourself**
   - Start by grounding yourself and centring your energy. It is crucial to be in a calm, neutral state to ensure that the information you receive is unbiased and objective.
   - Clearly define your intention for the session. Are you focusing on the dynamics of the meeting, the key players involved, or the subject of discussion?
   - Visualise a protective shield around you, maintaining clear boundaries to avoid interference and to ensure that your energy remains impartial throughout the session.

2. **Tune Into the Meeting's Energy**
   - Visualise the space where the secret meeting is taking place. Is it in a private office, a secluded room, or a remote location? Pay attention to the setting's atmosphere and energy.
   - Focus on the general tone and purpose of the meeting. Does it feel tense, cooperative, or highly strategic? Tune into the underlying intention of the gathering—why is it happening, and what are the participants hoping to achieve?
   - Observe the emotional energy in the room. Are there underlying tensions, alliances, or conflicts among the attendees? Pay attention to any shifts in the atmosphere that might indicate key moments of decision-making or disagreement.

3. **Observe the Key Players and Their Roles**
   - Focus on the individuals involved in the meeting. Who are they? What roles do they play within the meeting—leaders, advisors, negotiators, or mediators?
   - Pay attention to the dynamics between participants. Are there any power struggles, alliances, or subtle influences at play? How do the participants communicate with each other—verbally, nonverbally, or through energy exchanges?
   - You may also notice whether certain individuals are more dominant, passive, or emotionally charged during the

discussion. Their body language and energy can reveal important clues about the meeting's outcomes.
4. **Explore the Subject Matter and Discussions**
    - Tune into the topics being discussed in the meeting. What issues are at the forefront—political decisions, business strategies, security concerns, or personal matters?
    - Observe the flow of conversation. Is there agreement on key points, or are there disagreements that could affect the outcome? Pay attention to any specific decisions being made, proposals being presented, or plans being set into motion.
    - Focus on any underlying motivations that may not be openly expressed. Are there hidden agendas or unspoken goals that could influence the direction of the meeting?
5. **Reflect, Document, and Stay Neutral**
    - After the session, take time to reflect on the information you've gathered. Write down the key details of the meeting—such as the energy, the roles of participants, the main discussion points, and any decisions or plans that were made.
    - Be sure to evaluate whether you maintained a neutral, detached perspective throughout the session. Remote viewing secret meetings requires objectivity and impartiality, so avoid judgment or personal opinions.
    - Consider the ethical implications of your findings. Secret meetings are private for a reason, and accessing this type of information requires responsibility. Ensure that any insights gathered are used appropriately and without violating privacy or trust.

Remote viewing secret meetings can provide valuable insights into decision-making processes, strategic plans, and the motivations of key players. By observing the dynamics of these meetings, you can gain a deeper understanding of the forces shaping important decisions. However, it is essential to approach these sessions with respect for privacy and confidentiality. Maintaining a neutral, objective mindset and considering the ethical implications of your work are crucial to ensuring that remote viewing is used responsibly and constructively.

Shipwrecks

From my experience with remote viewing, people often choose to explore shipwrecks to uncover lost histories, locate hidden treasures, or understand the circumstances surrounding the sinking of a ship. Shipwrecks are not only fascinating from a historical perspective but can also reveal valuable clues about past maritime disasters, the lives of those aboard, and the ships' journeys. Remote viewing shipwrecks can offer insights into the conditions of the wreck, the location, and even the fate of the crew.

However, it is important to approach shipwrecks with respect, particularly because many of these sites are also gravesites. Some wrecks contain human remains, and many are considered protected or sacred by various organizations or cultures. Remote viewing these sites should always be conducted with sensitivity, neutrality, and respect for the lives lost and the historical significance of the wreck.

Five Steps to Remote View Shipwrecks
1. **Set Your Intention and Ground Yourself**
   - Begin by grounding yourself and achieving a neutral, centred state. Make sure your mind is calm and clear to receive accurate, unbiased impressions.
   - Define the intention of your remote viewing session. Are you interested in exploring the shipwreck's location, the cause of the wreck, the condition of the wreck, or the events leading up to it?
   - Visualise a protective energy field around you, ensuring that you remain detached and respectful of the sensitive

nature of the site. Make sure your energy remains open to observation, not interference.
2. **Tune Into the Shipwreck's Location and Environment**
   - Begin by visualizing the location of the wreck. Is it near the shore, in deep water, or in a more remote part of the ocean? Pay attention to the physical environment surrounding the wreck—water conditions, the seabed, and any notable features nearby (such as reefs or underwater caves).
   - Focus on the ship itself. What type of vessel was it? What size is it? Is it intact or scattered across the seabed? Are there signs of erosion, corrosion, or disintegration? Observe the general energy of the wreck site—is it peaceful, turbulent, or does it hold an unsettling energy?
   - Tune into the conditions surrounding the wreck—was it calm weather, or were there rough seas at the time of the sinking? What was the water like when the ship went down? This can help you understand the broader context of the disaster.
3. **Explore the Events Leading to the Shipwreck**
   - Focus on the events that led to the shipwreck. Was it a sudden storm, navigational error, a collision, or sabotage? What were the factors contributing to the ship's fate?
   - Observe the moment the ship sank or was destroyed. How did the crew react? What was the emotional energy at that moment? Were there survivors? What happened to them after the wreck?
   - If the ship was carrying cargo, you may also receive information about what was being transported. This could be useful in understanding the broader context of the ship's mission or its significance at the time.
4. **Observe the Condition of the Wreck**
   - Focus on the current condition of the shipwreck. Is it well-preserved, deteriorated, or scattered? Are any parts of the

ship still identifiable, such as the hull, the stern, or specific machinery?
- Pay attention to any notable features around the wreck—debris, artifacts, or remnants of cargo. What remains of the ship, and what has been lost to time?
- Tune into any energy related to the wreck itself. Does it feel like the site is calm, or is there a lingering unrest or sadness? Remember, many shipwrecks are the final resting places for those who perished, and the energy at the site may reflect that.

5. **Reflect, Document, and Stay Neutral**
   - After your session, take time to reflect on the impressions you've gathered. Write down details about the location, the ship's condition, and any specific events related to the wreck.
   - Review your observations to ensure neutrality. Remote viewing shipwrecks requires respect for both the history and the people involved, so it is important to approach the site with sensitivity and detachment.
   - Consider the ethical aspects of exploring shipwrecks. Many wreck sites are considered burial grounds or protected heritage sites. It's essential to use the information gathered responsibly and avoid interfering with efforts to preserve or protect these locations.

Remote viewing shipwrecks can be an incredibly enlightening and respectful way to uncover lost histories, understand the events that led to maritime disasters, and discover the condition of wreck sites. These experiences allow us to connect with the past, explore the mysteries of the deep, and sometimes find valuable insights into human history. However, it is essential to approach these sites with the utmost respect for the lives lost, the protection of cultural heritage, and the privacy of those involved. By maintaining a neutral, ethical stance and focusing on observation, we can explore shipwrecks while honouring their significance.

Shopping Malls

From my experience with remote viewing, shopping malls are often explored to gain insights into consumer behaviour, the dynamics of retail spaces, or the energy flow of a particular location. People may choose to remote view shopping malls to understand the atmosphere of the mall, observe interactions between shoppers and employees, or detect subtle energies in commercial spaces. These locations are often bustling with activity, creating a unique environment where social dynamics, marketing strategies, and energy flow can be observed. Remote viewing can provide insights into how malls operate, how shoppers move through the space, and even how certain stores or areas affect the mood and behaviour of visitors.

However, it's important to approach shopping malls with an awareness of the ethical considerations. These spaces are not only commercial hubs but also public gathering places where personal privacy and individual experiences are important. Remote viewing these locations should be done with respect for the people in the space, avoiding intrusive or judgmental thoughts, and maintaining a focus on the energy and dynamics of the environment rather than individuals.

Five Steps to Remote View Shopping Malls
1. **Set Your Intention and Ground Yourself**
    - Start by grounding yourself and achieving a neutral, centred state. This ensures you are in the right mindset to receive clear and unbiased information.
    - Clarify your intention before beginning the session. Are you observing the overall atmosphere of the mall, the movement of shoppers, the store layouts, or the energy flow within the space?
    - Visualise a protective energy shield around yourself to maintain neutrality and focus solely on the environment. This will prevent interference from the personal energies of others in the space.

2. **Tune Into the Energy of the Mall**
   - Begin by focusing on the energy of the mall as a whole. Is the space busy, chaotic, relaxed, or organized? Pay attention to the general feeling of the atmosphere—does it feel welcoming, overwhelming, or sterile?
   - Observe how the space is laid out—how are the different areas of the mall connected? How do people move through the space? Are certain areas more crowded or energetic than others?
   - Tune into the sensory experience of the space. What does it feel like energetically—warm, cold, bright, or dim? Does the mall have a certain mood or vibe that influences shoppers and their behaviour?
3. **Observe the Flow of Shoppers and Interactions**
   - Focus on the movement of people through the mall. How do shoppers navigate the space? Are they in a hurry, casually strolling, or gathering in certain sections?
   - Observe interactions between shoppers and store employees. Are there any noticeable patterns in how people engage with products, promotions, or each other?
   - You may also notice the influence of advertisements, music, or lighting on shopper behaviour. Does the environment evoke specific emotions—like excitement, stress, or calmness? How do these external factors affect the energy of the space?
4. **Examine Specific Stores or Areas**
   - Direct your attention to specific stores or areas within the mall that may have unique energy or purpose. For example, is there a store that draws a lot of people, or a section that feels abandoned or less energetic?
   - Observe the layout of the stores and the interactions within them. How do they create energy or influence shopping behaviour? Are there certain stores that draw more attention, and why?

- You may also explore how certain items or displays in stores attract customers or create a certain ambiance. Pay attention to any subtle energy shifts as you examine the spaces inside individual shops.
5. **Reflect, Document, and Stay Neutral**
    - After your session, take time to reflect on the observations you've made. Write down the key impressions about the mall's overall atmosphere, the behavior of shoppers, and the energy dynamics within different areas.
    - Evaluate whether you maintained a neutral and impartial perspective. Remote viewing shopping malls requires staying detached and respectful of the public and private nature of the space.
    - Consider how the insights gained can be used responsibly. Shopping malls are public spaces, and the information you collect should be treated with care and respect for the individuals and businesses within the space.

Remote viewing shopping malls can offer valuable insights into the energy flow, consumer behaviours, and dynamics of retail environments. It allows you to observe how people interact with the space and each other, and how the design and layout of the mall influence shopping patterns. However, it's important to approach this practice with respect for the people within the mall, maintaining neutrality and avoiding intrusive thoughts. By focusing on the energy and atmosphere of the space, remote viewing can provide a deeper understanding of how malls function and the subtle influences at play.

Space Stations

From my experience with remote viewing, space stations are often explored by those interested in understanding the dynamics of life in space, the operational aspects of these advanced environments, or the scientific experiments conducted onboard. Remote viewing space stations can provide insights into the behaviour of astronauts, the functionality of the station, and the energy present in such a unique and isolated location. Space stations, particularly those orbiting Earth, are isolated environments where the human body is affected by zero gravity, and where a mix of science, technology, and human resilience come together.

However, remote viewing space stations requires careful consideration of ethical principles. Space stations are places of work, research, and collaboration, where privacy, safety, and confidentiality are crucial. Remote viewing should be conducted with respect for the individuals aboard and the sensitive nature of the work being done. Also, as these environments are often high-tech and strategic, it's important to maintain a neutral and ethical perspective throughout the process.

Five Steps to Remote View Space Stations
1. **Set Your Intention and Ground Yourself**
   - Begin by grounding yourself in the present moment and achieving a calm, centred state. This allows you to detach from distractions and focus solely on the remote viewing process.
   - Clarify your intention: Are you interested in the internal environment of the space station, the energy and dynamics among astronauts, or the scientific research being conducted?
   - Visualise a protective energy bubble around you to ensure your focus remains neutral and that you are not unduly influenced by the thoughts or intentions of others. This helps you maintain clarity in your observations.
2. **Tune Into the Energy of the Space Station**
   - Focus on the overall energy of the space station. Is the environment sterile and controlled, or is there a sense of openness and calm among the crew?
   - Tune into the station's structure and function. How are the different modules or areas arranged? What is the overall

atmosphere within the space station? Does it feel dynamic and busy, or quiet and isolated?
- Observe the external environment—what is the view like from the space station? Can you sense the Earth below or the vastness of space around it? What does the environment feel like energetically, considering the weightlessness of space and the sophisticated technology aboard?

3. **Observe the Astronauts' Activities and Interactions**
   - Focus on the astronauts and their activities. What are they working on, and how do they move through the space station? Is there a sense of routine or high-stakes urgency in their actions?
   - Observe the emotional and psychological energy of the crew. Are they working together harmoniously, or are there signs of stress, tension, or fatigue due to the isolation of space?
   - Pay attention to how astronauts interact with the technology on the station. How do they interact with the equipment and systems that keep the station running? Are there any malfunctions or challenges being faced in maintaining the station's operations?

4. **Explore the Scientific Research and Experiments**
   - If you are interested in the scientific aspect of the space station, focus on the types of research and experiments being conducted. What is the purpose of the ongoing research?
   - Tune into the energy and flow of the scientific work. Is there a sense of excitement, focus, or experimentation among the astronauts? What are they trying to achieve through their research—whether in biology, physics, or materials science?
   - Look for any unusual findings or experiments that stand out. Is there new technology or groundbreaking research occurring on the space station that could have a significant impact on Earth or space exploration?

5. **Reflect, Document, and Stay Neutral**
   - After completing the remote viewing session, take time to reflect on the impressions and insights you've gathered. Write down key observations about the energy of the space station, the activities of the crew, and any specific research or experiments being conducted.
   - Ensure that you maintained neutrality throughout the session. Space stations are highly controlled environments, and it's crucial to avoid influencing or misinterpreting the energy or information you receive.
   - Consider the privacy and confidentiality involved in the activities aboard the space station. Any sensitive information should be treated with care and respect, especially in the context of ongoing experiments or strategic operations.

Remote viewing space stations can provide valuable insights into the unique dynamics of life in space, the scientific work being conducted, and the operational aspects of space exploration. It allows for an understanding of how astronauts interact with their environment and how they maintain the functionality of these high-tech, isolated stations. However, remote viewing space stations requires respect for the privacy of the astronauts and the sensitive nature of their work. By maintaining neutrality, focusing on the environment, and respecting ethical considerations, remote viewing can offer a deeper understanding of the complexity and challenges of living and working in space.

Special Events

From my experience with remote viewing, people often choose to explore special events to gain insights into the atmosphere, dynamics, and underlying energies that shape these significant moments. Special events, such as large celebrations, political gatherings, concerts, or ceremonies, carry unique energies that reflect the emotions, intentions, and interactions of those involved. These events are often charged with collective emotions—excitement, tension, joy, or anticipation—that influence not only the participants but also the surroundings.

While remote viewing special events can provide a rich understanding of the energy and dynamics at play, it is crucial to approach these sessions with care. Special events are often public, emotionally charged, and may involve private moments that require respect for privacy. It is important to avoid intrusive thoughts or judgments and maintain neutrality throughout the process.

Five Steps to Remote View Special Events

1. **Set Your Intention and Ground Yourself**
   - Start by grounding yourself and centring your energy. This ensures that you are able to connect clearly with the event without being distracted by outside influences.
   - Clearly define your intention: Are you interested in observing the overall energy of the event, the emotions of participants, or the flow of interactions? Make sure you understand the purpose of your viewing.
   - Visualise a protective energy shield around you to ensure you stay focused on the event itself and prevent any personal or emotional influence from interfering with your observations.

2. **Tune Into the Energy of the Event**
   - Focus on the collective energy of the event. Is there excitement, tension, calm, or joy in the air? How do the people involved feel? What kind of emotional charge does the event carry?
   - Observe the overall atmosphere—what is the environment like? Are there decorations, sounds, or visual cues that contribute to the energy? What does the space feel like in terms of light, sound, and movement?
   - Pay attention to the timing of the event. Are people in anticipation, reacting to something in real-time, or reflecting on a past moment? Can you sense any shifts in the energy as the event progresses?

3. **Observe Key Interactions and Moments**
   - Focus on the main participants and their energy. Are there key individuals whose actions or presence seem to influence the event more than others? Observe how they interact with each other and the audience.
   - Look for any significant moments or turning points in the event. Are there moments of high emotion, conflict, resolution, or celebration? What emotional tones accompany these moments?
   - Pay attention to the flow of energy—are there moments of calm, intensity, or rapid change in the energy of the participants or the event itself? How do people react, and how do their emotions shift throughout the event?
4. **Explore the Subtle Energies and Unseen Factors**
   - Tune into any subtle, unseen energies at play. For example, are there hidden tensions, unspoken agreements, or energetic connections that influence the event?
   - Explore how the space or environment itself may be affecting the event. For example, does the layout of the venue, the acoustics, or the physical presence of objects or symbols contribute to the energy or emotional tone?
   - You may also observe the collective energy of the crowd. How do the emotions and intentions of the people involved influence the outcome or direction of the event?
5. **Reflect, Document, and Stay Neutral**
   - After completing your remote viewing session, take time to reflect on your observations and document the key insights. Record the emotional energy, significant moments, and overall atmosphere you experienced.
   - Review your session to ensure you remained neutral throughout. Special events can stir strong emotions, and it's important to observe without judgment or bias.
   - Consider the privacy and personal nature of some events. While public events are more open to external

observation, private events or personal moments should be respected, and any information gained should be handled responsibly.

Remote viewing special events can offer profound insights into the emotional and energetic dynamics of significant moments in time. Whether observing large celebrations, political gatherings, or intimate ceremonies, remote viewing allows you to explore the subtle energies, interactions, and underlying emotional currents that shape the event. However, it is essential to approach these sessions with care and respect for the participants involved, maintaining neutrality and avoiding intrusive or judgmental thoughts. By staying grounded and focused, you can gain a deeper understanding of how energy flows within these unique and often transformative occasions.

Sports Events

From my experience with remote viewing, sports events are a popular area of interest for those looking to understand the energy dynamics of competition, team interactions, and the mental and emotional states of athletes and audiences. These events, filled with high energy, excitement, and sometimes tension, offer a unique glimpse into the human spirit, perseverance, and emotions under pressure. Remote viewing a sports event can help you observe the flow of competition, the strategies being used, and the emotional dynamics of the individuals involved.

However, it's essential to approach remote viewing sports events with respect for the privacy and integrity of the participants. These events are public but often involve intense personal and team experiences. Viewing sports events should be done with the intention of gaining insights into the energy of the game or match, without crossing ethical boundaries or influencing the outcome with personal biases.

Five Steps to Remote View Sports Events

1. Set Your Intention and Ground Yourself
- Begin by grounding yourself and centring your energy. It's essential to be calm and clear-headed before beginning a remote viewing session, especially when observing the high-energy environment of a sports event.
- Clarify your intention: Are you interested in the overall energy of the event, the dynamics between teams or players, the emotional states of the athletes, or the strategies being used?
- Visualise a protective shield around you to ensure that you remain neutral and detached from any personal biases or emotional involvement with the game.

2. Tune Into the Energy of the Event
- Focus on the overall energy of the sports event. How does the environment feel? Is there an intense, competitive energy or a more relaxed, playful vibe?
- Observe the crowd: What emotions are they expressing? Are they excited, tense, or hopeful? How do their reactions influence the overall energy of the event?
- Pay attention to the flow of the game or match. Is there a sense of momentum shifting, a high point of energy, or moments where the atmosphere changes—such as after a goal or a critical play?

3. Observe the Players and Team Dynamics
- Tune into the individual players and their emotional states. Are they focused, tense, excited, or fatigued? How do they respond to pressure or setbacks during the event?
- Pay attention to how the team members interact with each other. Is there a strong sense of collaboration and support, or are there moments of tension or miscommunication?
- Look for any psychological strategies being used. Are players confident, doubting, or pushing themselves beyond their limits? How do they handle victory or defeat in the moment?

4. **Explore Key Moments and Turning Points**
   - Focus on the pivotal moments of the event—critical plays, goals, or shifts in strategy. What is the energy around these moments? How do they impact the players, the teams, and the crowd?
   - Observe the emotional reactions to these key moments. Do players feel empowered, deflated, or reinvigorated after a significant play or turn of events?
   - Look for underlying motivations. Are certain players or teams more motivated by winning, proving themselves, or responding to previous actions during the game? Pay attention to the mental states that drive decisions and plays.

5. **Reflect, Document, and Stay Neutral**
   - After your session, take time to reflect and document your observations. Write down the key moments, emotional energy, and interactions you observed, as well as any insights into the strategies or psychological states of the athletes.
   - Review the session to ensure you maintained neutrality and did not project your personal emotions or biases onto the event. Remember, sports events are charged with intense energy, and it's easy to become emotionally involved, so maintaining detachment is crucial.
   - Consider the privacy and personal aspects of the players involved. While public events are more accessible, it's important to remember the athletes' emotional states and experiences are private, and any information gained should be handled with respect.

Remote viewing sports events provides an exciting opportunity to observe the emotional and energetic dynamics that unfold during high-stakes competition. From the mental states of athletes to the strategies used and the emotional flow of the game, remote viewing can give you a deeper understanding of what makes these events so powerful. However, it's important to approach remote viewing of sports events with respect and neutrality. By focusing on the overall energy, maintaining a detached perspective, and observing the dynamics of the game without personal bias, you can gain valuable insights into the unfolding drama of the sport while respecting the integrity of the participants and the event itself.

Storage Facilities

From my experience with remote viewing, storage facilities are a unique area of interest for those seeking insights into the organization, flow, and hidden elements within large storage or warehouse spaces. These facilities, which may include everything from climate-controlled storage units to vast industrial warehouses, are often designed for efficiency and security. People may choose to remote view storage facilities to understand the layout, the contents, or to identify any energetic imbalances or hidden factors that may influence the operation of these spaces.

Storage facilities are not always heavily monitored by individuals, and thus, they can harbor forgotten items, unused potential, or hidden energies. While remote viewing these locations, it's important to approach with care and respect for privacy and security, especially since these spaces may house personal or sensitive materials. The purpose of remote viewing storage facilities should focus on obtaining useful insights about the energy of the space, its organizational structure, or identifying any areas that might require attention or improvement.

Five Steps to Remote View Storage Facilities
1. **Set Your Intention and Ground Yourself**
    - Before beginning your remote viewing session, ground yourself and ensure your energy is centred and calm. Remote viewing large, impersonal spaces like storage facilities can require a sense of detachment and neutrality.
    - Define your specific intention: Are you looking to understand the organizational structure of the space, uncover

hidden or forgotten items, identify energy blockages, or assess the general atmosphere of the facility? Be clear about what you wish to observe.
- Visualise a protective energy field around you to ensure your focus remains purely on the space and the energy of the facility, without any interference from external influences or distractions.

2. **Tune Into the Layout and Energy Flow of the Facility**
   - Focus on the overall layout of the storage facility. How is the space organized? Is it cluttered, neat, chaotic, or systematically arranged? What does the energy of the space feel like—calm, busy, stagnant, or energetic?
   - Notice the flow of energy within the space. Do certain areas feel more energized than others? Are there parts of the facility that feel abandoned, congested, or disorganized? Pay attention to the path the energy takes within the space.
   - Is there a clear sense of order in the facility, or is there disarray? Look for any blockages or disruptions in the flow of energy. These could indicate areas where improvements are needed or where there might be hidden items or untapped resources.

3. **Observe the Contents and Emotional Imprints**
   - Tune into the types of items stored within the facility. What objects or materials are present, and how do they feel energetically? Do certain items seem to hold more energy, importance, or emotional charge?
   - Look for hidden or forgotten items. Sometimes, objects stored away in storage facilities can carry emotional imprints, memories, or unresolved energies. Are there any items that stand out or have an unusual energy around them?
   - Take note of the emotional atmosphere tied to the stored items. Are there any feelings of neglect, disuse, or abandonment? Conversely, are there areas of the storage facility

that seem to hold more sentimental or valuable items, generating a different emotional energy?

4. **Investigate the People or Entities Connected to the Facility**
   - Pay attention to any individuals or entities that may have interacted with or contributed to the current state of the storage facility. Are there lingering energies from people who used the space in the past?
   - Are there signs of human activity within the facility—such as recent visits, routine maintenance, or unresolved issues that could impact the overall energy? Consider how the emotions or actions of past users might still resonate within the facility.
   - If the storage facility is linked to a specific organization or business, observe any energy tied to the company's practices, leadership, or overall management. Are there energetic imbalances that may stem from the way the facility is being used or maintained?

5. **Reflect, Document, and Stay Neutral**
   - After completing your remote viewing session, take time to reflect on the energy and information you have gathered. Document your observations, including the layout, energy flow, key contents, emotional imprints, and any insights about the people or practices tied to the facility.
   - Review your session to ensure that you remained neutral and detached. Avoid judgmental thoughts or projections. A storage facility may hold vast amounts of energy or hidden information, and your goal is to observe and document, not to alter or influence the space with personal opinions.
   - Remember that remote viewing storage facilities, especially private or sensitive ones, should be approached with respect for privacy. Any findings should be handled ethically, ensuring that they are not shared inappropriately or used for personal gain.

Remote viewing storage facilities can provide valuable insights into the hidden energies, organizational patterns, and emotional imprints that reside in these often-overlooked spaces. Whether exploring the flow of energy, uncovering forgotten items, or identifying areas that require improvement, remote viewing these facilities allows you to see beyond the physical structure and understand the deeper dynamics at play. However, as with any remote viewing session, it is essential to approach these spaces with neutrality, respect, and ethical consideration. By staying grounded and focused, you can uncover insights that help optimize the space, clarify hidden factors, and bring greater awareness to its use and energy.

Subterranean Spaces

From my experience with remote viewing, subterranean spaces—such as caves, underground bunkers, tunnels, and mines—present a unique challenge and opportunity for exploration. These spaces, often hidden below the surface, are rich in mystery, energy, and history. People choose to remote view subterranean spaces for a variety of reasons: to understand the flow of energy within these spaces, uncover hidden elements, or to gain insights into their purpose, origins, or contents. However, it is important to note that subterranean environments often carry dense, heavy energies due to their isolation and the natural forces at play. Therefore, it's crucial to approach these locations with care, neutrality, and respect.

While remote viewing subterranean spaces can offer fascinating insights, the energy present in these environments may be more intense or challenging than above-ground locations. There may be feelings of isolation, secrecy, or even tension. Understanding the nuances of these energies will allow you to gain a deeper connection and a more meaningful exploration.

Five Steps to Remote View Subterranean Spaces
1. **Set Your Intention and Ground Yourself**
   - Begin by grounding yourself thoroughly before attempting to remote view a subterranean space. These spaces, often

disconnected from the natural flow of light and air, can hold intense or stagnant energies that may feel heavy. A strong connection to the Earth and a clear focus will help you navigate the environment.
- Define your intention: Are you seeking to explore the structure of the space, uncover hidden objects or areas, or simply sense the general energy of the environment?
- Visualise a protective shield around you, as subterranean spaces can sometimes harbor residual energies that may affect your well-being or cloud your perceptions. Ensure that you maintain emotional neutrality throughout the session.

2. **Tune Into the Energy of the Space**
   - Focus first on the overall energy of the subterranean environment. Is it dense and heavy, or does it feel more open and expansive? The energy of these spaces can vary depending on their purpose and history.
   - Pay attention to the atmosphere: Do you sense any lingering emotional imprints, such as fear, isolation, or mystery? Many subterranean spaces have been used for specific functions—such as storage, shelter, or protection—and these energies may persist within the structure.
   - Notice the temperature, air quality, and sensations in your body. Subterranean spaces can often feel cooler and more closed in, and these physical sensations may be indicative of the overall energetic makeup of the space.

3. **Explore the Structure and Layout**
   - Begin to explore the structure and layout of the subterranean space. Is it a natural cave or a man-made construction? How is it organized—linear or complex, with multiple tunnels, chambers, or rooms?
   - Focus on the flow of energy within the space. Are there any areas that feel particularly stagnant or obstructed? Are there any places that feel more open or energized?

- If you're exploring a mine or tunnel system, pay attention to whether there are abandoned sections, hidden areas, or objects that may not be immediately visible. Consider how human activity in the past may have altered the flow or structure of the space.

4. **Investigate Hidden or Abandoned Areas**
   - Subterranean spaces often contain hidden or abandoned sections that may not be obvious. Pay special attention to any feelings or impressions related to these areas. Are there places that feel more secluded, forgotten, or untouched?
   - Look for objects, remnants, or artifacts that may have been left behind. These could carry emotional or historical imprints that offer additional insights into the function or past use of the space.
   - If you sense the presence of others—whether human or energetic entities—take note of how they relate to the space. Are there any specific imprints of activity that feel recent or distant? Be mindful that these energies can range from residual emotional patterns to more active, energetic presences.

5. **Reflect, Document, and Stay Neutral**
   - After your session, reflect on the information you gathered about the subterranean space. Write down your observations, including the energy of the space, the layout, and any hidden elements you uncovered.
   - Review your experience to ensure you maintained neutrality throughout the session. Be cautious not to project your own thoughts or judgments onto the space. Keep in mind that subterranean spaces can hold heavy or unresolved energies, so maintaining a calm and detached perspective is important.
   - Consider the ethical implications of your findings. Some subterranean spaces may be private, sacred, or sensitive. Be respectful of any boundaries, whether physical or energetic, and ensure that you handle the information you receive responsibly.

Remote viewing subterranean spaces offers a fascinating opportunity to explore hidden or isolated environments that are often shrouded in mystery. Whether exploring the physical layout, uncovering forgotten objects, or sensing the emotional and energetic imprints left behind, these spaces can provide deep insights into their history and purpose. However, as with any remote viewing session, it is essential to approach subterranean spaces with care and respect. The dense, isolated energy of these locations can be challenging, but with grounding, neutrality, and ethical considerations, you can gain valuable insights while maintaining a safe and detached perspective.

Technology Innovations

From my experience with remote viewing, technology innovations are a fascinating and dynamic area to explore. These innovations represent the cutting edge of human progress, often hidden within labs, private projects, or high-security facilities. People may choose to remote view technology innovations to gain insights into new developments, understand how emerging technologies might shape the future, or even to uncover hidden breakthroughs that are not yet made public. As with all remote viewing, it is essential to approach this area with neutrality, as the potential impacts of new technologies can be both inspiring and controversial.

Technology innovations often come with layers of secrecy, competition, and strategic interests, so it's important to respect the boundaries of privacy and intellectual property. Remote viewing in this context offers a unique perspective, allowing the viewer to gain knowledge about the energy, purpose, and potential effects of new technologies, while also being mindful of the ethical considerations surrounding them.

Five Steps to Remote View Technology Innovations
1. **Set Your Intention and Ground Yourself**
   - Before beginning your session, take time to ground yourself and create a neutral, calm state of mind.

Technology innovations can have both physical and energetic elements, and being grounded helps you avoid becoming overwhelmed by the intensity of what you may perceive.
- Define your intention: Are you focusing on a specific technology, company, or innovation? Are you trying to understand its purpose, how it works, or its potential impact on society or the environment? Be specific in your focus to avoid confusion or distraction during the session.
- Create a protective energy shield around yourself to keep your energy clean and focused. This will help maintain neutrality and avoid any unnecessary energetic attachments or influences during your exploration.

2. **Tune Into the Energy of the Innovation**
   - Focus on the energy surrounding the technology innovation. How does it feel energetically? Does the technology itself radiate energy that is calm, neutral, or charged with excitement?
   - Pay attention to the emotional and psychological imprint of the innovation. Does it feel like something that could have a transformative or disruptive impact? Alternatively, does it feel hidden or shielded, possibly due to concerns or unknown consequences?
   - Note any energetic patterns related to the development of the innovation. Are there patterns of resistance or enthusiasm within the people involved in its creation or application? Is the technology in its nascent, testing, or ready-to-deploy phase?

3. **Investigate the Function and Purpose of the Innovation**
   - Once you have tuned into the energy of the innovation, begin to explore its function and purpose. How is this technology designed to work? What is it meant to accomplish or solve, and who will benefit from it?
   - Consider how the innovation fits into the broader technological landscape. Does it represent a leap forward in its

field, or is it more of a refinement or enhancement of existing technologies?
- Look for any subtle or hidden features that may not be immediately obvious but could have significant long-term implications. Are there ethical considerations, unintended consequences, or potential misuses of the technology that may not be fully recognized yet?

4. **Explore the People and Entities Involved**
   - Investigate the individuals or organizations behind the technology innovation. What is their role in the development or promotion of this technology? Are there any dominant energy imprints from specific people or entities involved, such as corporate interests, private investors, or scientific leaders?
   - Pay attention to the emotional and ethical energy of those involved. Is there a sense of excitement, pressure, or ethical concern surrounding the creation or deployment of the technology? Are the people involved approaching this innovation with openness, or is there a feeling of secrecy, competition, or hidden motives?
   - If the technology is being kept under wraps or protected, be mindful of the energetic barriers that may exist to prevent full transparency. Understand the reasons behind this and avoid trying to force access to information that may be restricted for a valid purpose.

5. **Reflect, Document, and Maintain Neutrality**
   - After completing your session, reflect on your findings and document everything you observed. Record the energy, purpose, function, and potential implications of the technology, as well as any ethical concerns or hidden features that emerged.
   - Review your notes to ensure that you have remained neutral and objective throughout the session. Avoid projecting your own beliefs or assumptions onto the technology.

Instead, let the data speak for itself, focusing on factual observations rather than emotional reactions.
- Recognize the power and influence that technology innovations can have on individuals and society. Be mindful of how this information is used, ensuring that it aligns with ethical practices and respects privacy, security, and intellectual property.

Remote viewing technology innovations allows you to explore the future of human progress and understand the unseen forces shaping our world. Whether examining the energy, function, or impact of a particular technology, this type of remote viewing offers a deeper perspective on how new inventions are conceived, developed, and deployed. However, it is crucial to approach these sessions with a strong sense of neutrality, respect for privacy, and an awareness of the ethical implications surrounding technological advancements. By maintaining calmness, grounding yourself, and focusing on the broader implications, you can gain insights that are valuable, objective, and ethically sound.

Traffic Patterns

From my experience with remote viewing, traffic patterns are an interesting and practical area to explore. People may choose to remote view traffic patterns for various reasons, such as understanding the flow of movement in a particular area, predicting congestion, or exploring how human behaviour and energy influence the movement of vehicles. It can be useful for urban planning, forecasting, or even understanding the energy dynamics at busy intersections or highways.

Traffic patterns often reflect a mix of human behaviour, infrastructure design, and external factors such as weather or events. While remote viewing traffic can seem simple, the energetic flow of vehicles and people can be intricate, influenced by both the physical environment and the collective human energy of drivers, pedestrians, and cyclists. As with all remote viewing, neutrality and respect for privacy are key.

Five Steps to Remote View Traffic Patterns
1. Set Your Intention and Ground Yourself
- Begin by grounding yourself and establishing a calm, neutral mindset before diving into remote viewing. Traffic patterns can be influenced by both predictable factors, such as rush hour times, and unpredictable ones, like accidents or weather conditions. A strong connection to the present moment will help you remain objective and avoid being overwhelmed by unexpected events.
- Define your specific intention. Are you interested in viewing the traffic flow at a specific time of day, a particular location, or a specific event that may influence the traffic? Setting a clear intention will help you stay focused during your session.
- Protect your energy by imagining a shield or light surrounding you, ensuring that any energetic disturbances from the environment, such as congestion or chaotic traffic, do not affect your focus.

2. Tune Into the Energy of the Location
- Begin by tuning into the location where you want to view the traffic. Notice the energy of the area. Does the location feel busy, congested, or calm? Are there any noticeable shifts in energy depending on the time of day or specific circumstances (e.g., during a special event or roadwork)?
- Observe the underlying emotional energy. Are drivers feeling stressed or rushed, or is there a more relaxed flow? How does the environment contribute to the traffic patterns? For instance, are there many traffic signals that influence the flow, or is the area known for being prone to bottlenecks?
- Be open to noticing the energy shifts in the environment. Traffic patterns can be highly influenced by the emotional

energy of the people driving and walking, as well as the physical space itself (e.g., narrow roads, intersections, or construction sites).

3. **Observe the Flow of Movement**
   - Focus on the movement of vehicles and pedestrians. How do they interact with each other and the environment? Are vehicles moving smoothly or slowing down due to congestion? Pay attention to where traffic builds up and where it flows more freely.
   - Look for patterns: Is the traffic flow predictable, or does it feel erratic? Are there peaks in traffic at certain times of the day, or do traffic patterns change based on specific events or conditions?
   - Notice how energy moves throughout the traffic system. Does it feel like a harmonious flow, or do you observe disruptions or disruptions in the natural flow of traffic, such as accidents, roadblocks, or delays?

4. **Examine External Influences**
   - Look for any external factors influencing the traffic. Are there weather conditions, construction projects, or road closures impacting the flow? Pay attention to how these factors alter the normal patterns and how they affect the overall energy of the space.
   - Consider how people's behavior and decisions (e.g., impatience, road rage, or caution) affect the flow of traffic. Are there moments where collective human energy influences the entire traffic pattern, such as a sense of urgency or confusion that creates a bottleneck?
   - Note any subtle energies in the environment that could shift traffic patterns, such as new developments, changes in infrastructure, or even changes in local laws or regulations that might affect the flow.

5. **Reflect, Document, and Maintain Neutrality**
   - After your session, take a moment to reflect on your experience and document the insights you gathered. Write

- down your observations about the traffic flow, external influences, and any emotional energy you sensed in the area.
- Review your experience to ensure that you've remained neutral and objective. Avoid projecting personal feelings or assumptions onto the traffic patterns. Instead, focus on facts and impressions that you've gathered.
- Consider any ethical implications, especially if you're using the information for public or professional purposes. Make sure that you respect privacy and avoid infringing upon people's personal experiences or behavior. Use the insights gained to better understand and support the improvement of traffic systems or urban planning, where relevant.

Remote viewing traffic patterns offers a fascinating way to gain insights into the flow of human movement within a given space. By tuning into the emotional and energetic influences on the movement of vehicles and pedestrians, you can uncover patterns, predict congestion, or understand how external factors affect the traffic environment. Whether you are exploring specific traffic situations or simply observing the general flow, the key to successful remote viewing in this context is neutrality and grounding. Respect for privacy and a detached perspective will allow you to uncover valuable insights without being overwhelmed by the intensity of the energetic movement.

Transportation Systems

From my experience with remote viewing, transportation systems are a complex and interconnected area that many choose to explore for various reasons. People may choose to remote view transportation systems to understand how goods and people are moved across regions, how different modes of transportation (roads, rail, air, and sea) integrate with each other, or to observe the infrastructure, efficiency, and challenges of these systems.

Transportation systems are key to global economies, urban planning, and personal mobility, yet many aspects of them remain hidden or unexamined. Remote viewing can provide insights into how these systems operate, where inefficiencies or issues may arise, and how the flow of people and goods is influenced by both external and internal factors. As with any form of remote viewing, neutrality and ethics are vital when exploring such a dynamic and impactful subject.

Five Steps to Remote View Transportation Systems

1. **Set Your Intention and Ground Yourself**
   - Begin by grounding yourself and creating a calm, neutral state of mind. Transportation systems are complex and involve multiple layers, so it's essential to clear your mind of any distractions and focus solely on your intention.
   - Clearly define your intention before starting the session: Are you interested in a specific transportation system (e.g., roadways, public transit, air travel, or freight systems), or do you wish to understand how different modes of transportation interconnect within a specific region or city?
   - Visualise a protective shield of light or energy around you to maintain energetic neutrality and to avoid interference from the chaotic energies that can exist in busy transportation hubs.
2. **Tune Into the Energy of the Transportation System**
   - Focus your attention on the transportation system you intend to view. Tune into the overall energy of the system—whether it's roads, railways, airports, or seaports. How does the system feel energetically? Is it flowing smoothly, or is there tension, congestion, or stress associated with it?
   - Observe if the system feels harmonious or disrupted. Are there areas where energy seems stagnant or where traffic (whether human or vehicle) is blocked or slowed down? What external or internal factors are affecting the flow?

- Pay attention to the infrastructure itself—does it feel well-planned and efficient, or are there noticeable bottlenecks, broken connections, or points of friction in the system?

3. **Explore the Flow of Movement**
   - Once you have tuned into the system's overall energy, focus on the flow of movement within it. Observe how people and vehicles (or goods) are moving from one place to another. Do the transportation modes function in harmony, or are there disruptions that affect the overall flow?
   - Take note of any patterns in traffic, whether vehicles or people. Are there peak periods where the flow intensifies, or are there certain locations where delays or accidents are more likely?
   - Investigate how the different modes of transportation interact—how do vehicles, public transit, trains, and planes operate within the same transportation ecosystem? Is there integration or fragmentation between different systems, and how does this affect overall efficiency?

4. **Investigate External Influences on the System**
   - Observe the external factors influencing the transportation system. Are there weather conditions, special events, or socio-political factors (e.g., protests, strikes, or policy changes) affecting the smooth functioning of the system?
   - Pay attention to how the physical environment (such as construction, urban development, or geography) impacts the transportation system. Are there new developments or plans that might change the flow of movement in the near future?
   - Look for any changes in energy based on time of day or season. For example, are certain routes or systems busier during rush hour, holidays, or specific events? What shifts in energy can be detected at different times or in different seasons?

5. **Reflect, Document, and Maintain Neutrality**
    - After your session, reflect on the insights you've gained and document your observations. Write down your impressions about the flow of movement, external influences, and the overall energy of the system.
    - Review your findings to ensure you have remained neutral and objective throughout your exploration. Avoid injecting personal judgments or emotional reactions into your documentation.
    - Be mindful of the ethical considerations. If you intend to use the information gained through remote viewing for professional or public purposes, ensure that it is done in a way that respects privacy, security, and intellectual property. You must use the insights responsibly, particularly in areas with sensitive data related to transportation infrastructure.

Remote viewing transportation systems can offer valuable insights into how human mobility, goods transportation, and infrastructure interact on a global scale. Whether investigating the flow of traffic on highways, the efficiency of public transit, or the connectivity of air and sea travel, remote viewing can help you understand the underlying energy, patterns, and influences that shape these systems. It's essential to approach this area with a neutral, grounded perspective, recognizing the complexity and scale of the subject. By respecting the energetic flow and remaining detached from personal biases, you can uncover valuable information that can lead to a deeper understanding of how transportation systems impact individuals, communities, and economies.

Tourist Attractions

People often choose to remote view tourist attractions out of curiosity or to gain a deeper understanding of these locations without physically visiting them. Tourist attractions can range from famous landmarks, natural wonders, and cultural sites to hidden gems, all of which carry unique energy, history, and significance. Remote viewing these sites allows for an exploration of their ambiance, visitor experiences, and the influence these places have on the people who visit.

Remote viewing a tourist attraction can offer insights into the emotional and energetic connections people have with a place, the cultural or historical importance of the location, and even potential energetic shifts or changes that occur due to human presence. Understanding these elements can provide a more profound appreciation of the attraction, and help inform those planning to visit or manage these sites.

Five Steps to Remote View Tourist Attractions

1. Set Your Intention and Ground Yourself

- Before you begin remote viewing, take time to centre yourself and ground your energy. As tourist attractions often attract large numbers of people, the energetic vibrations can be intense and varied. You need to establish a calm and neutral mindset to avoid becoming overwhelmed by the collective energy.
- Clearly define your intention. Are you interested in the general energy of the location, the feelings it evokes in visitors, or perhaps specific events that take place there? You may also want to explore the impact of the attraction on the surrounding community or environment.
- Visualise yourself surrounded by a protective light to maintain energetic neutrality, ensuring that you do not absorb or become distracted by the excitement or emotions of the people at the attraction.

2. Tune Into the Energy of the Attraction

- Focus on the energy of the location itself. Does the attraction feel vibrant and welcoming, or does it carry a more sombre or historical energy? Consider the type of attraction you are viewing—whether it's a natural wonder, a cultural or historical site, or a modern tourist

hotspot—and notice how these different factors influence the overall atmosphere.
- Observe the emotional energy of the people who visit the attraction. Do they seem excited, peaceful, or reflective? Are there any particular emotions that dominate the energy of the space, such as awe, excitement, or even frustration from overcrowding or waiting in lines?
- Notice any shifts in energy at different times of the day or seasons. Some attractions may have distinct energetic patterns depending on the time of year, special events, or the weather, which might impact how visitors engage with the space.

3. **Observe the Interactions of Visitors**
   - Tune into how people interact with the environment and with each other. Are visitors connecting with the location in a meaningful way, or are they focused on more superficial experiences, such as taking photos or rushing through the site?
   - Look at the flow of people—how do they move through the attraction? Is there a sense of organized chaos, or do they seem to flow smoothly in a calm, almost meditative way?
   - Take note of any collective energetic shifts that may occur as visitors gather in certain areas. Are there parts of the attraction that seem to resonate more with people emotionally, or do certain locations hold special significance, drawing visitors in?

4. **Examine the Influence of the Surrounding Environment**
   - Explore how the surrounding environment—whether it's urban, rural, or natural—affects the energy of the attraction. Do external factors such as weather, local culture, or the natural landscape enhance or detract from the experience?
   - Observe how the attraction influences the surrounding community and environment. For example, does the tourism create positive economic effects, or does it

lead to overdevelopment, pollution, or other negative consequences?
- Investigate how the history of the location might impact its energetic signature. Is there a deeper, perhaps even spiritual, connection that visitors form with the place, especially in sites with rich historical or cultural significance?

5. **Reflect, Document, and Maintain Neutrality**
   - Once your session is complete, take time to reflect on your findings and document your observations. Write down the impressions you gathered about the energy of the attraction, the emotional energy of the visitors, and any significant interactions that occurred.
   - Review your session to ensure that you have remained neutral and detached from personal biases. Tourist attractions often carry a lot of cultural and personal significance, so it's essential to avoid projecting your own feelings or assumptions onto the experience.
   - Consider the ethical implications of your findings, especially if you plan to share your remote viewing results. Be mindful of respecting the privacy of the people involved, and use the information gained to deepen your understanding of the attraction, rather than exploit or sensationalize it.

Remote viewing tourist attractions provides a unique opportunity to explore the energetic dynamics of these sites without being physically present. By observing the interactions between visitors, the energy of the location itself, and the influence of the surrounding environment, you can gain valuable insights into the attraction's emotional and cultural significance. Maintaining neutrality and respect for the experiences of others is key to ensuring that your remote viewing session is ethical and objective. Whether for personal curiosity, professional purposes, or simply to gain a deeper connection to a place, remote viewing can offer an enriched perspective on the vibrant world of tourist attractions.

Unsolved Mysteries

People often choose to remote view unsolved mysteries because of the intrigue and desire to uncover hidden truths about unexplained phenomena, missing persons, mysterious events, or unresolved cases. Unsolved mysteries can range from historical enigmas and paranormal occurrences to unsolved crimes and missing persons investigations. By remote viewing these situations, individuals aim to gain insights that may help shed light on what happened, what remains unknown, or what could potentially be uncovered.

Remote viewing unsolved mysteries can be deeply engaging, but it also comes with ethical considerations. Because these cases can involve real people, sensitive topics, or unresolved pain, it's crucial to approach remote viewing in this area with care, neutrality, and a sense of respect. The information you receive may not always be conclusive or easy to interpret, but it can offer valuable perspectives on the unknown.

Five Steps to Remote View Unsolved Mysteries
1. **Set Your Intention and Ground Yourself**
   - Before beginning your remote viewing session, take time to ground and centre your energy. This step is crucial for any session, but especially when exploring unsolved mysteries, as the emotional and energetic impact can be intense.
   - Clearly define your intention. Are you exploring a specific unsolved mystery, such as a missing persons case, a cold crime, or a historical enigma? The intention should be specific to the mystery you wish to understand or unravel, as this focus will guide your session.
   - Calm your mind and visualise yourself surrounded by a protective shield of light to maintain energetic neutrality. This will help you stay detached from any emotional responses that may arise during your exploration.
2. **Tune Into the Energy of the Mystery**
   - Once grounded, direct your attention toward the energy of the mystery. Take a moment to understand the

emotional, historical, or spiritual weight of the case or situation.
- Ask yourself: What energy surrounds this unsolved mystery? Is there an air of confusion, sadness, tension, or unresolved conflict? Pay attention to any overwhelming feelings that arise, as they may reflect the emotional undercurrent of the mystery.
- Be mindful of your own emotions, as they can influence your remote viewing experience. Stay neutral and objective as you connect with the essence of the situation, whether it is an event, a missing person, or an unsolved crime.

3. **Investigate the Key Elements of the Mystery**
    - Focus on the core elements of the mystery. This may involve specific events, individuals, locations, or timeframes. As you tune into these elements, try to observe the facts, rather than make judgments or conclusions.
    - For example, if you are viewing a missing persons case, focus on the person's energy: What were they doing before their disappearance? Where did they last go? What is the energy of the place where they were last seen?
    - When investigating a historical mystery, consider what energy still lingers in the location or event. Is there something important that was overlooked or hidden? Look for new connections or hidden details that could offer additional clues or insights into the mystery.

4. **Explore the Unresolved Questions and Gaps**
    - Identify the gaps or unresolved aspects of the mystery and focus your attention on them. These may be areas where facts are unclear, or where contradictory information exists.
    - Explore what is missing or what is preventing the mystery from being solved. Are there overlooked details, unnoticed patterns, or hidden forces at play that have not been acknowledged?

- Keep an open mind to what emerges during this stage. Often, unsolved mysteries involve layers of complexity or information that is not immediately apparent. Allow your intuition to guide you through these gaps and listen to any impressions or messages that arise.

5. **Reflect, Document, and Maintain Neutrality**
   - Once your session is complete, reflect on your findings and document your observations. Write down all the details and impressions you received, even if they seem abstract or fragmented.
   - Review your session for any biases or emotional influences that may have affected your neutrality. It's essential to remain detached and objective, especially when dealing with emotionally charged or sensitive cases.
   - Consider the ethical implications of your findings. Be mindful of how the information may affect those involved in the mystery, especially if it pertains to real people or sensitive topics. Use your insights with care, and remember that remote viewing is a tool for discovery, not for making judgments or conclusions.

Remote viewing unsolved mysteries can provide fascinating insights into events, people, or circumstances that remain hidden or unresolved. It offers the potential to uncover new perspectives, find overlooked clues, and connect the dots that may have been missed. However, due to the emotional weight and complexity often involved in these mysteries, it's crucial to approach them with a neutral mindset and a deep sense of respect for the subject matter.

Unsolved mysteries are often multi-dimensional and deeply interwoven with human emotion, history, and circumstance. By maintaining an objective and ethical approach to remote viewing, you can offer valuable insights while ensuring that the process remains respectful, constructive, and helpful.

Virtual Environments

People often choose to remote view virtual environments, such as video games, online worlds, or simulated settings, to explore their energy, interactions, and dynamics. Virtual environments are crafted through digital means, yet they often contain rich, layered experiences that can affect participants emotionally and energetically. This makes them an intriguing subject for remote viewing, as they present an opportunity to understand how people interact with and perceive these artificial yet impactful spaces.

Remote viewing virtual environments offers a way to explore the intentions behind the creation of these spaces, the experiences of the people who engage with them, and the energy that is generated within these environments. However, it's important to approach this type of remote viewing with neutrality and awareness of the boundaries between virtual and physical realities. Understanding the energy in these spaces can provide valuable insights into human behaviour, societal trends, and the psychological impact of technology.

Five Steps to Remote View Virtual Environments
1. **Set Your Intention and Ground Yourself**
   - Begin by grounding yourself and clearing your mind. Virtual environments can often carry energetic patterns related to collective thought and behaviour, which can be intense or distracting. It's essential to remain grounded to stay connected to your higher self during the process.
   - Define your intention clearly. Are you exploring a specific virtual world, like a video game or online simulation? Or are you seeking to understand how people interact within these spaces or how the virtual environment itself affects the participants?
   - Visualise yourself surrounded by a protective shield of light to ensure that you remain unaffected by any external influences, such as the emotional or energetic responses of people within the virtual space.

2. **Tune Into the Energy of the Virtual Environment**
    - Focus on the energy that permeates the virtual environment. Virtual spaces may carry an energetic imprint based on their design, purpose, and the emotions of those interacting within them.
    - Observe how the design of the environment influences its energy. Does it feel welcoming, chaotic, artificial, or oppressive? Pay attention to the colours, sounds, and layout, as these can have an energetic effect on the participants.
    - Tune into the overall emotional energy of the space. Do people seem relaxed, immersed, anxious, or distracted? These emotional responses can influence the energy within the virtual environment.
3. **Observe the Interactions Between Participants**
    - Virtual environments often host interactions between users, so it's important to focus on how people engage with one another. Are the interactions positive, competitive, or collaborative?
    - Pay attention to the emotional and energetic exchanges between participants. Are there conflicts, alliances, or shared goals? These social dynamics can reveal much about the nature of the virtual environment and the motivations behind its design.
    - Also, observe the influence of avatars or representations of people. Do the avatars embody certain traits or behaviours that indicate the underlying energy of the person controlling them? How do these avatars interact with each other?
4. **Explore the Purpose and Creation of the Environment**
    - Consider the purpose behind the creation of the virtual space. What was the intention of its creators? Is it meant to entertain, inform, connect, or provide an escape? Understanding the purpose behind a virtual environment can offer deeper insights into its energy and how it affects participants.

- Observe if there are any unseen forces or designs shaping the environment. Some virtual spaces may have elements that influence the behavior or mindset of those within them, such as gamification techniques, persuasive designs, or subconscious cues embedded in the experience.
- Explore whether the environment carries a collective or personal energetic signature, shaped by the collective mindset of the participants or the developer's intention.

5. **Reflect, Document, and Maintain Neutrality**
   - Once your session is complete, reflect on what you've observed and document the insights you gained. Write down the emotional and energetic patterns you noticed, the interactions between participants, and any hidden dynamics that you sensed within the virtual space.
   - Revisit your session to ensure that you have remained neutral and objective. Virtual environments, like physical ones, can carry emotional weight, so it's essential to ensure you haven't been influenced by your own preferences or biases.
   - Consider the ethical implications of your findings. If you plan to share insights about virtual environments, ensure that you respect the privacy and experiences of those who may be interacting within these spaces. Keep your observations focused on the energy and dynamics of the environment rather than the individuals involved.

Remote viewing virtual environments offers a fascinating way to explore the energy, dynamics, and emotional undertones of digital spaces. By examining how these environments are structured, how participants interact within them, and the underlying intentions behind their creation, you can gain a deeper understanding of their impact and significance.

However, as with all remote viewing, it is essential to approach virtual environments with neutrality, respect, and mindfulness. These spaces, while virtual, still contain real emotional and energetic exchanges that can influence participants in profound ways. By remaining grounded and detached, you can explore these environments ethically, offering valuable insights into the ways we engage with technology and the digital world.

Water Sources

People often choose to remote view water sources because water is fundamental to life, carrying both physical and symbolic significance. Water sources—such as rivers, lakes, oceans, wells, and springs—are essential for survival and have long been linked to emotional healing, energy flow, and environmental balance. Remote viewing water sources can offer insights into the health of ecosystems, the vitality of communities that rely on them, and even uncover hidden or unknown water reserves that may be of great importance.

Water, in its many forms, is a conduit for energy. It's capable of storing and transmitting information, and it plays a role in shaping both physical environments and the emotional states of individuals. By remote viewing water sources, you may access information about the flow of energy within a geographical area or uncover hidden water sources that could be crucial for human or environmental health.

When remote viewing water sources, it's important to approach the practice with respect and neutrality. These natural elements carry energies that can be both healing and destructive, depending on their current state. Understanding the energy patterns in these locations can provide valuable information about their condition, but also about the broader environment they influence.

Five Steps to Remote View Water Sources
1. **Set Your Intention and Ground Yourself**
   - Begin by grounding your energy, as water sources often carry strong emotional and environmental imprints. This grounding helps you stay neutral and focused during the session.

- Define your intention clearly. Are you exploring a specific water source, like a river, spring, or ocean? Do you want to understand its quality, the energy surrounding it, or its potential impact on the local environment or community?
- Visualise yourself surrounded by a protective field of light to shield you from any negative or chaotic energies that may arise from the water source or surrounding area.

2. **Tune Into the Energy of the Water Source**
   - Focus on the energy of the water itself. Water can carry emotional and environmental imprints, such as the collective energy of those who have interacted with it over time or its current state (polluted, pure, stagnant, flowing).
   - Observe how the water feels energetically. Is it calm, flowing, clear, or murky? Are there any imbalances or disturbances within the water's energy? These impressions may reflect the physical state of the water or the emotional energy it carries from its surroundings.
   - Pay attention to any sensations you experience in your own body while connecting with the water. Water sources can influence people energetically, so any shifts you feel may give you insight into the state of the water and its connection to the environment.

3. **Observe the Surrounding Environment and Ecosystem**
   - Water sources don't exist in isolation—they are part of larger ecosystems. Take time to observe the land surrounding the water. Are there any plants, animals, or human activities that stand out? How do these elements interact with the water?
   - Explore the health of the ecosystem. Are the plants lush and thriving, or are there signs of degradation or imbalance? Do the animals in the area seem healthy and active, or are there signs of distress?
   - These observations can provide clues about the overall condition of the water source, including pollution, overuse, or the presence of beneficial energies.

4. **Look for Hidden or Overlooked Aspects**
   - Water sources can sometimes hide important or overlooked aspects, such as underground streams, hidden reservoirs, or areas that are impacted by human interference. Focus on uncovering these hidden details.
   - If you are exploring a river or stream, for example, look for areas where the water may be diverted or blocked. If you're observing a spring, notice whether there are energy blockages or unhealed aspects related to its flow.
   - Be aware of the water's history—has it been affected by human activity, pollution, or changes in the natural environment? This historical context can give you insights into its current state and future potential.
5. **Reflect, Document, and Maintain Neutrality**
   - Once the session is complete, reflect on the information you've gathered. Document all of the sensory impressions, emotions, and energy patterns you experienced during the remote viewing session. Even if some of the information seems unclear or incomplete, writing it down can provide insights upon later reflection.
   - Maintain neutrality and objectivity in your analysis. Be cautious not to interpret your findings through personal biases or preconceived notions. Water sources are highly sensitive to energy, and their energetic state can shift over time, so remain open to receiving evolving information.
   - Consider the ethical implications of your findings. If the water source you viewed is connected to a community, think about how the information you've gathered can be used in a responsible way. Ensure that your insights are respectful and don't cause unnecessary worry or fear.

Remote viewing water sources is an enlightening practice that connects you to the vital flow of life that sustains both natural ecosystems and human societies. By tuning into the energy of water, you can gain insight into its current state, the impact of surrounding environments, and uncover hidden aspects that may be of great importance. Whether you are exploring the purity of a river, understanding the vitality of an underground spring, or investigating the health of an ocean, remote viewing offers a powerful tool for accessing valuable information about the state of water.

However, this practice requires a high degree of sensitivity, neutrality, and ethical consideration. Water is an element that is deeply intertwined with life and emotion, and the information received through remote viewing should be handled with care and respect. By approaching water sources with mindfulness, you can gain deeper understanding and offer valuable insights that may promote the health and well-being of both people and the environment.

Wildlife Habitats

People often choose to remote view wildlife habitats in order to gain insights into the health, energy, and dynamics of ecosystems that support animal life. Wildlife habitats, ranging from forests and wetlands to grasslands and oceans, play a crucial role in the survival of countless species. By remote viewing these areas, you can gain a deeper understanding of how these habitats are functioning, how they are impacted by human activity, and how animals interact within them.

Remote viewing wildlife habitats provides an opportunity to explore the energetic and emotional states of the environment, uncover patterns of wildlife behaviour, and detect hidden ecological imbalances. These natural spaces are often full of unseen connections and energy flows, making them fascinating subjects for remote viewing. However, like all forms of remote viewing, approaching wildlife habitats requires respect, neutrality, and a deep sense of responsibility, as the balance of these habitats is essential for maintaining biodiversity.

Five Steps to Remote View Wildlife Habitats
1. **Set Your Intention and Ground Yourself**
   - Begin by grounding your energy and centring your mind. Wildlife habitats can carry a mix of natural energies, and grounding helps you stay connected to your higher self and avoid being overwhelmed by the emotional intensity of these environments.
   - Define your intention clearly: Are you exploring a specific wildlife habitat, like a forest, savannah, or ocean ecosystem? Are you seeking to understand the health of the environment, the behaviour of specific species, or any imbalances affecting the habitat?
   - Create a protective shield of light around you to ensure that you remain unaffected by any disruptive or negative energy from the habitat or the animals within it.
2. **Tune Into the Energy of the Habitat**
   - Focus on the energy of the habitat as a whole. Notice the overall vibrancy, health, and harmony of the ecosystem. Does the habitat feel lush and thriving, or does it carry signs of degradation or imbalance?
   - Observe how the environment feels. Are there areas of calm or serenity? Are there disturbances, like areas where the energy feels more chaotic or tense? Pay attention to changes in temperature, textures, and sounds that may arise in your perception. These sensations can offer clues about the current state of the habitat.
   - Look for energy patterns that represent the interaction of natural forces—such as the flow of water, the movement of winds, or the cycles of day and night. These energy patterns contribute to the vitality of the ecosystem.
3. **Observe the Wildlife**
   - Pay attention to the animals within the habitat. What are they doing? Are they active, at ease, or stressed? How do they interact with their environment and one another?

- Look for any signs of imbalance in the animal population, such as unusually high or low numbers of certain species, or signs of illness or unusual behaviour. This could indicate stress within the habitat, whether from environmental changes, human interference, or the presence of predators.
- Notice the emotional and energetic state of the animals. Are they thriving in harmony with their environment, or are there signs of distress that suggest the habitat may be in need of restoration?

4. **Explore the Interconnectedness of the Habitat**
   - Understand that all elements of the habitat—plants, animals, water, air, and soil—are interconnected. Pay attention to how these different elements interact and influence one another.
   - Look for hidden or overlooked aspects of the habitat, such as endangered species, areas of environmental degradation, or previously unnoticed ecosystems. Sometimes the most critical parts of an ecosystem are those that are less visible.
   - Investigate how human activity or environmental changes may be affecting the habitat. Are there signs of pollution, deforestation, or disruption caused by climate change or other external factors? Remote viewing can provide insights into how these impacts are altering the energy of the habitat.

5. **Reflect, Document, and Maintain Neutrality**
   - After completing your session, take time to reflect on the impressions and insights you received. Document everything you observed about the energy of the habitat, the animals, and the overall health of the environment. This written record can help you clarify the findings and make connections between different elements of the habitat.
   - Ensure that your observations remain neutral and objective. Wildlife habitats can evoke strong emotional responses, so it's essential to stay detached and avoid

personal biases that may colour your interpretation of the data.
- Consider the ethical implications of your findings. If your insights reveal that a habitat is under threat or facing challenges, think about how you can share this information in a constructive and responsible manner. The goal is to use your observations to help raise awareness and support the preservation of these critical ecosystems.

Remote viewing wildlife habitats is a powerful practice that allows you to connect with the energy of the natural world and gain insights into the health and dynamics of ecosystems. By observing how animals interact with their environments, how different ecological elements influence one another, and how human activity impacts the habitat, you can contribute valuable information to conservation efforts and promote greater understanding of the natural world.

However, remote viewing wildlife habitats requires sensitivity, respect, and neutrality. These environments are delicate and interconnected, and the information you receive should be handled with care. By approaching wildlife habitats with an open mind and a responsible attitude, you can explore their hidden energies and help raise awareness about the importance of preserving and protecting these vital ecosystems for future generations.

Workspaces

People often choose to remote view workspaces to gain insights into the energy, dynamics, and effectiveness of a work environment. Whether it's an office, factory, laboratory, or creative studio, the energy in a workspace can have a profound impact on productivity, creativity, and overall well-being. Remote viewing workspaces offers a way to assess the atmosphere, uncover hidden challenges, and identify areas where energy could be improved for better flow and harmony. This practice can be particularly useful for understanding interpersonal dynamics, uncovering inefficiencies, or helping organizations improve their work environments.

Workspaces are often filled with a complex mix of energies—motivating forces, stressors, and even emotional imprints left by past interactions. By remote viewing these environments, you can tap into these energies and assess how they affect individuals working within them. While this practice can offer valuable insights, it is important to approach workspaces with a neutral mindset and respect for the privacy and autonomy of individuals.

Five Steps to Remote View Workspaces
1. **Set Your Intention and Ground Yourself**
   - Before beginning, take a moment to ground yourself and set a clear intention for the session. Do you want to understand the general energy of the workspace, identify any sources of tension, or assess the overall productivity and flow of energy? Clarifying your intention will help you stay focused and avoid distractions.
   - Grounding is essential, as workspaces are often filled with diverse emotional and mental energy. Visualise yourself as rooted to the earth, ensuring that your energy stays calm, centred, and unaffected by the stress or distractions within the workspace.
2. **Tune Into the Energy of the Environment**
   - Focus on the energy within the workspace itself. Is the energy light and free-flowing, or is it heavy and stagnant? Does it feel open and creative, or constrained and stressed?
   - Pay attention to how different areas of the workspace feel. For example, common areas like break rooms or meeting spaces may have different energy compared to private offices or workstations. Are certain areas more peaceful, while others are filled with tension or chaos?
   - Also, notice the flow of energy in the physical space. Is it cluttered or organized? A workspace's physical layout can affect how energy moves, and remote viewing can help identify areas where flow is hindered, which may impact productivity or morale.

Remote Viewing | 237

3. **Observe the People and Their Interactions**
   - Workspaces are primarily places where people interact. Tune into the energy of the individuals present. How are they feeling emotionally? Are they motivated, stressed, or disengaged?
   - Observe the interpersonal dynamics. Are there any conflicts or unresolved tensions between colleagues, or do the individuals appear to be collaborating harmoniously?
   - Pay attention to the emotional imprints that may linger in the workspace, especially if there have been difficult interactions or unresolved issues. These imprints can influence the overall energy of the workspace, affecting how employees feel and perform.

4. **Explore the Impact of External Factors**
   - Consider the influence of external factors that may affect the workspace. This could include elements such as company culture, leadership styles, or even the broader work environment (remote vs. in-office, for example).
   - Investigate how external pressures—such as deadlines, high expectations, or organizational changes—are affecting the energy and dynamics within the workspace. Are these pressures motivating individuals, or are they contributing to burnout and stress?
   - Pay attention to any hidden energy blockages, such as toxic work habits, poor communication, or lack of trust. These factors can significantly affect the overall productivity and health of the workspace, and remote viewing can help reveal areas for improvement.

5. **Reflect, Document, and Maintain Neutrality**
   - After completing your session, take time to reflect on the impressions and insights you gathered. Document any observations about the energy of the workspace, interpersonal dynamics, or external factors affecting the environment. Write down any specific areas where energy may need to be shifted or adjusted.

- Approach your findings with neutrality and objectivity. Remote viewing workspaces can evoke strong emotions, especially if you uncover issues that may be causing distress in the environment. Maintain a neutral stance and avoid becoming emotionally involved in what you observe.
- If your insights reveal areas of conflict or tension, consider how this information can be used constructively. The goal of remote viewing workspaces is to gain clarity and insight, not to judge or criticize. Always aim to provide feedback or insights that can help improve the workspace's energy, harmony, and productivity.

Remote viewing workspaces offers a unique opportunity to gain insight into the energy dynamics that influence productivity, collaboration, and overall well-being in professional environments. By tuning into the emotional and energetic imprints within the workspace, you can uncover hidden challenges, improve workplace dynamics, and promote a more harmonious atmosphere for those who work there.

However, it is important to approach the practice with respect, neutrality, and ethical consideration. Workspaces are deeply connected to the individuals who inhabit them, and any insights should be handled with care to avoid causing unnecessary disruption or discomfort. By using remote viewing as a tool for improving work environments, you can contribute to creating spaces that promote productivity, creativity, and overall positive energy.

World Events

People often choose to remote view world events to gain insights into significant occurrences that impact humanity on a global scale. These events can include political developments, natural disasters, social movements, economic shifts, or moments of historical importance. Remote viewing world events allows individuals to gain a deeper understanding of their underlying energies, potential outcomes, and the emotional currents driving them. It can provide clarity about the broader patterns at play, the intentions behind the actions, and the potential consequences of these events.

World events can be challenging to remote view due to the sheer complexity and magnitude of the energy involved. These events are shaped by a multitude of factors—human emotions, historical contexts, cultural influences, and even unseen energies. Remote viewing can offer valuable insights, but it requires a neutral mindset, sensitivity, and an awareness of the ethical responsibility that comes with observing global occurrences. The goal is to understand, not interfere, and to offer insights that contribute to positive change rather than exacerbate fear or negativity.

Five Steps to Remote View World Events

1. **Set Your Intention and Ground Yourself**
   - Before beginning, clarify your intention. Are you seeking to understand the general outcome of a world event, explore the energy surrounding the event, or uncover hidden motivations and influences? Clear intentions will help guide the session and prevent you from becoming distracted by irrelevant details.
   - Ground yourself by visualizing your energy connected to the earth. This helps ensure that you stay centred and detached from the emotional turbulence that may accompany significant global events. World events are often charged with intense energy, and staying grounded will help you observe the situation from a place of clarity and neutrality.

2. **Tune Into the Event's Energy**
   - Focus on the energetic imprint of the world event. How does the event feel on a global scale? Is there a sense of urgency, tension, or hopefulness associated with it? Notice whether the energy is expansive, constricting, or neutral.
   - Pay attention to the ripple effects. World events often create waves of change that affect not just the immediate area but the broader global community. Observe how the energy

from the event is spreading and how it interacts with the energies of other events occurring at the same time.
- Feel into the emotional undercurrents of the event. Are there widespread feelings of fear, excitement, or uncertainty? The emotional climate surrounding a world event can offer valuable clues about how people are perceiving it and reacting to it.

3. **Observe the Key Players and Their Motivations**
   - Identify the key players involved in the event. This could include political leaders, influential organizations, or even social movements. Tune into their energy and motivations—what are their intentions, and how do they relate to the larger dynamics of the event?
   - Look for underlying currents that may not be immediately apparent. Often, world events are shaped by hidden agendas or motivations that are not disclosed publicly. Remote viewing can reveal the unspoken intentions or dynamics that are influencing the course of the event.
   - Pay attention to the emotional energy of the key players. Are they driven by fear, ambition, hope, or a desire for power? Understanding the emotional motivations behind the event can provide important insights into how it might evolve.

4. **Explore the Impact and Potential Outcomes**
   - Look at the broader consequences of the event. How is it likely to affect not only the immediate parties involved but also the global community? Remote viewing can reveal how the event will ripple through different sectors of society—politics, economics, culture, and the environment.
   - Consider the potential outcomes. Is the event leading toward a positive transformation, or does it hold the potential for negative consequences? Pay attention to any potential shifts in energy that could alter the course of the event.

- Explore the timeline. Does the event appear to be part of a longer trend or cycle? Remote viewing can sometimes uncover patterns that indicate how an event is linked to past occurrences or is part of a broader movement toward change.
5. **Reflect, Document, and Maintain Neutrality**
    - After your session, take time to reflect on the information you've gathered. Document everything—emotional impressions, energy patterns, key players, potential outcomes, and any other significant insights. This record will help you process and analyse the data you've received.
    - Maintain neutrality throughout the session and in your reflections. World events can be emotionally charged, and it's easy to become personally involved or influenced by the energy surrounding the event. However, neutrality is crucial to ensure that your observations remain clear and objective.
    - Lastly, consider the ethical implications of your findings. World events often involve complex, multi-faceted situations that can deeply impact people's lives. Be responsible in how you use the information you've received and remember that the purpose of remote viewing is not to manipulate or control but to understand and offer insights that may help guide positive change.

Remote viewing world events offers a powerful tool for understanding the deeper energy, motivations, and potential outcomes behind significant global occurrences. Whether you're observing political developments, natural disasters, or historical moments, remote viewing can provide valuable insights into how these events unfold and the forces at play.

However, world events are often complex and charged with strong emotional and energetic forces. It's crucial to approach them with neutrality, respect, and ethical responsibility. By maintaining a detached, objective mindset, remote viewers can gain clarity and insight, helping to illuminate the hidden patterns and consequences of these events. Ultimately, the purpose of remote viewing world events is to foster understanding, promote peace, and support a more harmonious future for all.

Zoos

People often choose to remote view zoos to gain a deeper understanding of the environment and energy within animal habitats, the conditions affecting the animals, and the overall energy dynamics of the zoo as an institution. Zoos are complex places, as they serve multiple purposes, including wildlife conservation, education, and entertainment. Remote viewing can help assess the health and well-being of the animals, uncover any hidden stressors in the environment, and even evaluate the ethical practices surrounding the treatment of the animals.

The energy in zoos can be highly varied—ranging from the vitality and playfulness of healthy animals to the more subdued or stressed energy of those in captivity. By remote viewing zoos, you can assess the overall atmosphere, the quality of care being provided, and the underlying emotional energy of both the animals and the humans involved in the zoo's operations. This practice offers insights that can be used for improving the welfare of the animals and ensuring that zoos fulfill their roles in an ethical and sustainable way.

Five Steps to Remote View Zoos
1. **Set Your Intention and Ground Yourself**
   - Before starting your session, set a clear intention for what you hope to explore. Do you want to understand the well-being of specific animals, assess the zoo's energy as a whole, or uncover hidden aspects of the zoo's operations? Having a focused intention will guide the session and help you stay on track.
   - Ground yourself by visualizing your energy rooting into the earth. Zoos can hold a lot of diverse energies—both

positive and negative—so grounding ensures that you remain neutral and unaffected by any emotional intensity in the environment.

2. **Tune Into the Overall Energy of the Zoo**
   - Focus on the energy of the entire zoo, starting with the overall atmosphere. Is the environment calm and nurturing, or is there a sense of tension or discomfort? Pay attention to the general feeling of the zoo—are the spaces harmonious, or is there discord in certain areas?
   - Observe whether the energy feels balanced and whether there are any emotional imprints lingering in the environment. Zoos often contain both natural and artificial elements, and the way these energies interact can influence the well-being of the animals and the visitors.
   - Look for areas that might feel particularly heavy or light. For example, certain exhibits or enclosures might have more stagnant energy if the animals are stressed or if the environment doesn't align with the animals' natural needs.

3. **Observe the Animals' Energy and Well-Being**
   - Tune into the energy of the animals in the zoo. How do they feel? Are they lively, calm, and content, or do they appear stressed, anxious, or lethargic? Remote viewing can help you detect any imbalances in their energy and identify potential signs of discomfort or health issues.
   - Observe the interactions between the animals and their environment. Are the animals able to exhibit natural behaviours, or are they restricted in ways that could lead to stress or mental health challenges?
   - Pay attention to any emotional or physical imprints left by past experiences. Animals in captivity can sometimes carry emotional wounds from traumatic experiences or long-term confinement. Remote viewing can help uncover the lingering effects of these past experiences on the animals' energy.

4. **Explore the Human Element**
   - Observe the energy of the humans involved in the zoo—this could include zookeepers, veterinarians, staff, or even visitors. How are the humans interacting with the animals and the space? Are they respectful, nurturing, and calm, or is there any tension or agitation in their behaviour?
   - Consider the ethical practices of the zoo. Are the animals treated with kindness and care, or do there seem to be areas where improvement is needed? Remote viewing can reveal hidden imbalances, such as areas where the animals are not receiving adequate care or attention.
   - Tune into the collective energy of the zoo staff—are they emotionally aligned with the zoo's mission of conservation, education, and animal welfare, or is there a disconnect that affects the environment? The energy of the staff can have a significant impact on the atmosphere and the well-being of the animals.

5. **Reflect, Document, and Maintain Neutrality**
   - After the session, take time to reflect on the insights you've gathered. Document your findings—this could include the general energy of the zoo, the emotional well-being of the animals, any ethical concerns, and any areas for improvement. Writing down the details will help you process and analyse your impressions.
   - Remain neutral and objective in your observations. Zoos can be controversial institutions, and it's important to stay detached from any judgment or emotional bias. Your role as a remote viewer is to observe and offer insights, not to criticize or influence others' decisions unless it serves a greater purpose.
   - Consider how the insights can be used to improve the zoo environment. If you've noticed areas where the animals are not thriving or where energy could be shifted for the better, reflect on how this information can be shared or applied to promote positive change.

Remote viewing zoos offers a unique opportunity to explore the energy dynamics of animal habitats, assess the well-being of the animals, and evaluate the ethical practices that define how they are treated. Zoos are complex environments with a mix of positive and negative energies, and remote viewing can help uncover areas where improvement is needed for the benefit of the animals and their caretakers.

It's important to approach remote viewing of zoos with a sense of responsibility and neutrality, as the emotional intensity surrounding these spaces can be strong. The goal is to gain understanding, offer constructive insights, and help ensure that the zoo environment fosters the well-being of both the animals and the humans involved. By observing the energy and conditions within zoos, remote viewing can play a role in creating healthier, more ethical, and compassionate spaces for wildlife and their caretakers.

Chapter 9:
Remote Viewing of Your Body

Remote viewing of your body helps to find balance and uncover underlying emotional or energetic blockages that may be affecting your health, enabling a more holistic approach to healing and well-being.

As a medical intuitive and holistic medical doctor, I have found remote viewing to be an invaluable tool in understanding and healing the body. I regularly practice remote viewing and teach others how to do it themselves.

Many people think remote viewing only applies to external places, like a city, building, or forest. In reality, though, the same technique can be used to connect with your own body.

Energetically, we are all connected, and when we enter the energy field, there are no boundaries—whether you're connecting with the energy of a distant place or tuning into your own physical body.

Remote viewing gives us access to the subtle energy systems within, helping us understand imbalances and areas in need of healing. Through this method, you can tune in to what truly aligns with your energy—whether it's selecting the right foods, meditation practices, or even choosing a doctor or healer whose energy resonates with yours.

This approach ensures that the choices you make are in harmony with your body's needs. Ultimately, remote viewing your body enables natural healing, bringing you into balance not only with your internal systems but also with the external influences around you.

How Remote Viewing Can Support Your Health and Healing

1. **It Helps to Understand Your Body:**
   You can use remote viewing to connect deeply with your body, observing its energy, sensations, and any areas that need attention.
2. **It Helps to Understand Your Mind:**
   You can use remote viewing to observe the energy of your thoughts and emotions, allowing you to see them clearly and then transform them.
3. **It Helps to Understand Your Soul:**
   You can use remote viewing to observe the energy of your soul—beyond the needs and desires of your ego. This allows you to connect more deeply with your soul's true purpose.
4. **It Helps You Choose the Right Practitioner:**
   You can use remote viewing to help you select the right health practitioner—whether a doctor, psychologist, healer, or physiotherapist—whose energy aligns with your values and resonates with you.
5. **It Helps to Sense the Energy of Prescribed Medications:**
   You can use remote viewing to assess how a medication's energy aligns with your body, providing insight into its potential effects on your well-being.
6. **It Helps to Sense Treatment Compatibility:**
   Remote viewing helps you intuitively assess whether a treatment, technique, surgery, or procedure aligns with your energy, ensuring it supports your body's natural healing rhythms before committing.

How to Use This Guide to Remote View Organs and Body Parts

1. Identify the specific organ, body part, or system you want to view remotely.
2. Refer to the guide and locate the organ, body part, or system in alphabetical order (see below).
3. Read the steps provided for viewing it distantly.

4. Repeat the process, building on your previous findings until you gain deeper insights.
5. Compare your findings with medical tests if possible. The more physical confirmation you receive, the more accurate and masterful your remote viewing becomes.
6. Before viewing the organ or body part, Google "anatomy of [name of organ/body part]." For example, if you need to remote view your ear, search "anatomy of the ear" on Google, and you'll find many images to guide you. Spend 2 minutes looking at the picture to familiarize yourself with it. You don't need to be an anatomy expert, but remember: "Energy flows where attention goes." The better you understand the anatomy, the easier it will be to perceive it remotely. Try it and see how it works!

When you remotely view a body or organ, you are connecting with its hologram—its energetic representation. To deepen your understanding of this concept, I recommend reading the chapter titled "My Approach to Remote Viewing" in this book. It will help you revisit the foundational principles of holographic viewing. By connecting to a target, including your own organs, you're engaging with its hologram—an energetic reflection of the organ itself.

The same applies to the mind and soul—when you connect remotely, you engage with their current energetic reflections.

A hologram is what you see when you break the body down into its smallest particles. Here's how it works: a body part or organ consists of cells, which can be broken down into molecules, molecules into atoms, and atoms into energy. At this level, you perceive the hologram, which is the energetic representation of the organ or body part.

To access this, you only need to calm your mind and connect to the energetic field.

The calmer your mind, the more attuned you become to sensing the energy within and around you. To practice, try selecting an organ or body part to focus on remotely and explore it through remote viewing.

Don't take yourself too seriously — let go, have fun, and play with energy. Approach it as if you're a child learning something new, with lightness and curiosity.

Good luck!

- Below is a list of organs and body parts in alphabetical order.
- Choose an organ or body part and read the description to learn how to perform remote viewing on it.

Arms

Arms represent our ability to embrace life, handle challenges, and connect with others through giving and receiving. Remote viewing the arms goes beyond physical observation; it allows us to perceive the subtle energy patterns that shape how we reach out, hold on, and manage responsibilities. Remote viewing the arms allows us to explore these energetic dynamics and identify imbalances that may affect how we handle things, give, and receive. When viewing the left arm, you connect to your feminine energy of receiving and nurturing, while the right arm is linked to masculine energy, focused on giving and action.

Here are five steps to remotely view and sense the energy within your arm, with suggested times for each step, to deepen your understanding of its role in your well-being.

1. **Relax and Set Your Intention (3 minutes)**
   Start by taking a few minutes to relax your body and clear your mind with deep breathing. Inhale slowly and deeply, then exhale gently, allowing any tension to melt away. Next, search for "arm anatomy" on Google and spend a moment observing the muscles, bones, and ligaments in the images. Familiarizing yourself with the arm's basic structure will help you focus inward. Set a clear intention to connect with the energy inside your arm. As you continue with deep, calming

breaths to centre yourself, say the affirmation: "I am tuning into my arm," allowing your focus to deepen as you prepare for the remote viewing session.

2. **Visualise a Beam of Light from Your Third Eye (4 minutes)**
Spend 2 to 4 minutes visualizing a beam of light coming from your "third eye" (forehead area). Picture this beam extending out and connecting with your arm, wrapping it in light. This creates an energetic link between your consciousness and the subtle energy within your arm.

3. **Tune into Physical Sensations (4 minutes)**
Focus on your arm's physical sensations. Notice its weight, warmth, tension, or any tingling sensations that arise. Pay close attention to the subtle movements or changes in how your arm feels without overanalysing. Just observe the sensations.

4. **Use Your Inner Eye – Your X-ray Vision (4 minutes)**
Use your focused attention to scan your arm, moving through each layer—skin, muscles, bones, and blood vessels—without judgment or analysis. Simply feel and sense the energy, being fully present as you observe any areas that stand out or need attention. Allow the energy to guide you wherever it needs to go within your body. Over time, you may begin to see your arm's tissue from within, a phenomenon known as the "inner eye"—the ability to observe your organs from the inside.

5. **Document and Reflect on Your Observations (5-7 minutes)**
After observing your arm with no judgment, take note of everything you saw and felt. Record all details, as they may be useful when you remote view your arm again in the future. Repeat the process on the next day and the following days, adding to your observations until you develop a deeper understanding and connection with what is happening inside your arm. Remote viewing your arm is not just a diagnostic tool,

but also a way to promote healing. By sensing energy and visualizing the structures of your arm, you support its healing and help bring it into balance.

While taking notes, observe if you noticed any areas of increased energy or blockages. This reflection will help you refine your sensitivity and deepen your awareness within your body.

The process will take about 23 to 30 minutes in total, but you can extend the session, especially if you begin to feel the energy more strongly. As you connect with the energy, you may feel inclined to prolong the session for healing purposes.

Aorta

The aorta, the largest artery in the body, symbolizes the flow of love, joy, and life force, nourishing both our physical and emotional well-being. Just as it delivers blood to vital organs, it represents the essential flow of energy and life force that sustains us. Remote viewing the aorta allows us to connect with this flow, observing and healing any blockages that may hinder the circulation of love, joy, and vitality.

By following these five steps, you can begin to remote view the aorta, exploring both its physical and energetic aspects to promote balance and healing within your body.

1. **Clear Your Mind and Prepare (5 minutes)**
   Start by sitting comfortably and taking deep, slow breaths to relax your mind and body. Inhale deeply through your nose, hold briefly, and then exhale through your mouth. Set your intention to connect with the energy within your aorta, seeking clarity and balance. Before you begin your remote viewing session, take a moment to Google an image of the aorta to familiarize yourself with its structure and position in the body. This will help direct your focus and enhance your ability to visualise accurately.

2. **Focus Your Attention (4 minutes)**
   Gently direct your awareness to your aorta, sensing the energy flowing through it. Visualise its full structure, extending from the heart to the body's extremities. As you breathe, imagine the air flowing through the aorta, as though you are breathing directly through it. Tune into the sensations that arise, feeling the rhythm of both blood and energy circulating through the body. Allow your focus to deepen as you feel the energy moving and pulsing through the aorta, sensing its steady rhythm and the flow of internal sensations within your body as it circulates.
3. **Tune into Physical Sensations Inside the Aorta (4 minutes)**
   Tune into any physical sensations you may feel inside the aorta. Pay attention to areas of warmth, pressure, or any subtle shifts in energy. These sensations may indicate areas of blockages, flow irregularities, or healing points within the aorta. Stay open to any intuitive impressions that arise during this scan.
4. **Use Your Inner Eye or X-Ray Vision (5 minutes)**
   Activate your inner eye or x-ray vision to look deeper into the structure of the aorta. Visualise its inner workings—its walls, valves, and the flow of blood and energy. See any disturbances or imbalances that may appear in your view. Allow your intuitive sense to guide you as you observe the aorta from a deeper perspective, beyond just the physical.
5. **Document Your Observations (3 minutes)**
   After your session, take a few minutes to reflect on and document your observations. Record any images, sensations, or emotions you experienced during the session. Write down areas that felt strong, blocked, or in need of healing. This documentation will help you track progress and deepen your understanding in future remote viewing sessions.

The entire process of remote viewing the aorta takes about 21 minutes, but as you begin to connect more deeply with the energy, you may find yourself extending the session. The experience of being immersed in the energy field inside your body becomes increasingly enjoyable, and you'll want to spend more time exploring it. Over time, you'll come to realize that remote viewing is not just a diagnostic tool; it is also a powerful healing practice. By engaging with the energy of the aorta, you facilitate a deeper sense of energetic balance and harmony, promoting both physical and emotional well-being.

Adrenal Glands

The adrenal glands play a crucial role in the body, producing hormones like adrenaline and cortisol that help regulate stress, energy levels, and metabolism. They are deeply associated with our sense of responsibility and self-esteem, influencing how we respond to challenges and manage stress. Imbalances in the adrenal glands can manifest as feelings of overwhelm, fatigue, or diminished self-worth.

Remote viewing of the adrenal glands offers an opportunity to explore the energy patterns and emotional connections linked to these glands. By understanding their function and energy flow, you can support healing and balance within your body.

You can follow these five steps to remote view the adrenal glands, enabling you to connect with their energy and promote harmony in both your physical and emotional well-being.

1. **Clear Your Mind and Set Your Intention (5 minutes)**
   Begin by sitting comfortably and taking slow, deep breaths to calm your mind and body. Inhale deeply through your nose, hold briefly, and exhale through your mouth. As you breathe, set the intention to connect with the energy of your adrenal glands, seeking balance, vitality, and insight into your stress response and self-esteem. Before you start remote viewing, take a few minutes to Google an image of the adrenal glands

and observe their structure and location above the kidneys. This visual grounding will help you focus on the right area and enhance your connection during the session.

2. **Focus on the Glands and Sense Their Energy (5 minutes)**
   Gently bring your attention to the adrenal glands, located above your kidneys. Visualise them in their physical location and structure. As you focus, sense the flow of energy inside and around them. Tune into any sensations or impressions that arise, paying attention to how the energy feels in these glands.

3. **Tune into Emotional Connections (4 minutes)**
   Reflect on how the adrenal glands are linked to your emotional state, particularly your sense of responsibility and self-esteem. As you focus on these glands, notice any feelings of stress, anxiety, or overwhelm. Pay attention to how these emotions may be affecting your adrenal glands and whether there are any areas of imbalance or excess.

4. **Use Your Inner Eye or X-Ray Vision (5 minutes)**
   Activate your inner eye or x-ray vision to look deeper into the structure and function of the adrenal glands. Visualise their intricate inner workings, including the release of hormones like adrenaline and cortisol. See any imbalances or blockages that may be affecting their energy. Allow your intuition to guide you as you observe their energetic state.

5. **Document Your Observations (3 minutes)**
   After completing your remote viewing session, take a few moments to reflect on and write down your observations. Record any images, sensations, or emotional insights you experienced during the session. Note any areas of imbalance, stress, or energy that felt out of alignment. This documentation will help you track progress and deepen your understanding in future sessions.

Completing this remote viewing session for your adrenal glands is just the beginning of a deeper connection with your body's energy.

Remote Viewing | 255

Repeating this practice regularly will allow you to develop a clearer understanding of your adrenal glands and their role in your emotional well-being and stress response. As you continue, you'll find that each session brings more insight, and you'll start to enjoy spending time within the energy of your own body. With practice, remote viewing becomes not only a tool for understanding but also a space for healing, balance, and self-discovery.

Bladder

People often choose to remote view the bladder because it is associated with emotions related to relationships—particularly themes of boundaries, holding on, and releasing emotional tension. The energy of the bladder can reflect how we navigate our connections with others, especially in sensing and responding to a partner's energy. By tuning into this area, you can gain insights into relationship dynamics and emotional patterns, helping to foster greater emotional balance and understanding.

Here are five steps to remote view your bladder, incorporating focused attention and sensing the subtle energy within.

Step 1: Calm your Mind (3 minutes)

Begin by sitting comfortably with your eyes closed, taking slow, deep breaths to calm your mind and body. Before you begin, take a moment to Google a picture of the bladder to familiarize yourself with its structure and positioning in the body. This visual reference will help you focus more accurately. Once you've done this, close your eyes again and tune into the subtle energy flowing within, sensing it as a gentle vibration or warmth. This grounding step aligns you with your inner energy field, preparing you for deeper awareness in your remote viewing session.

Step 2: Focus Attention on Your Bladder (4 minutes)

When you calm your mind, direct your attention to your lower abdomen, where the bladder is located. Visualise this area clearly, bringing it to the forefront of your awareness. As you focus, begin to breathe deeply, consciously breathing in and out through your bladder. Imagine the air flowing directly into the bladder as you inhale, and then releasing any tension as you exhale.

Step 3: Feel the Energy Inside the Bladder (3 minutes)
With your focus on the bladder, gently shift your attention to the sensations within it. Notice what you feel—its unique vibration, warmth, or subtle movement. By sensing this energy more deeply, you gain insight into the emotional and energetic patterns associated with this area. Since emotions are forms of energy, tuning into these sensations helps you better understand the emotions connected to the bladder.

Step 4: Scan the Bladder with X-Ray-Like Vision (4 minutes)
Imagine that you're scanning the bladder with X-ray vision. Slowly visualise its structure, shape, and energy flow. Move your inner vision across the bladder, noticing any unusual sensations, blockages, or areas that stand out. Focus on observing with clarity and neutrality.

Step 5: Receive and Interpret Information (4 minutes)
After completing the scan, open yourself to any messages, insights, or impressions that may arise. Whether visual, energetic, or intuitive, allow the information to flow naturally. Receive it with an open mind and conclude the session by noting your observations.

The suggested time to view the bladder is 18 minutes, but as you continue practicing these steps, you'll find that each session helps you connect more deeply with your bladder's energy and its emotional associations, particularly those related to relationships, boundaries, and emotional release. Repeat this exercise regularly, gradually increasing the time spent in each session as you become more comfortable. With consistent practice, remote viewing your bladder can become both a valuable tool for gaining insight and a powerful way to enhance emotional release, energetic balance, and overall well-being within your body.

Brain

People often choose to remote view the brain because it serves as the central control system of the body, influencing everything from thoughts and emotions to physical movements and overall health. The brain is like the body's "computer," processing vast amounts of information and regulating various functions. By remote viewing the brain, you can access deeper layers of awareness, uncover energy imbalances, and identify areas that may need attention, whether they relate to mental clarity, emotional health, or physical conditions. This practice can offer valuable insights into the state of your brain and provide a pathway to enhancing its function and well-being.

Here are 5 steps to remote view your brain, incorporating subtle energy sensing and performing a thorough scan for various conditions, helping you better understand its energetic and physical state.

1. **Calm Your Mind and Centre Yourself (3 min)**
   Begin by sitting comfortably and taking deep, slow breaths. Inhale deeply through your nose, hold for a moment, and exhale through your mouth. As you breathe, allow your mind to settle and your body to relax. Before you begin, take a few moments to look up images of brain anatomy on Google. This will help you visualise its structure more clearly and accurately during your session.

2. **Bring Your Attention to the Brain (3 min)**
   Once you are calm, direct your attention to the brain. Become aware of it as an essential organ within your body. Start breathing through your brain, as if the air is flowing directly into it with each inhale, visualizing the oxygen nourishing every part of it. With each exhale, feel any lingering thoughts being cleared away, creating space for clarity and focus. Pay attention to any sensations you may feel as you focus your energy on this area, connecting deeply with the brain's presence and its vital role in your body.

3. **Sense the Energy Inside the Brain (5 min)**
   Shift your focus to sensing the energy within your brain. The energy you feel are the sensations in your brain, such as subtle vibrations, warmth, or pressure. Notice how the energy flows through different areas, and how this flow can be felt through the sensations you experience. Observe if there are any blockages or heightened sensations. This helps you connect more deeply with the brain's energetic state.
4. **Scan the Brain with X-ray Vision (4 min)**
   Visualise yourself using X-ray vision to scan the brain. Move your mental focus across its different regions, paying attention to both the structure and the flow of energy. Look for any unusual sensations, imbalances, or patterns that stand out. This step allows you to examine the brain in more detail and gain insights into its current state.
5. **Receive and Interpret Information (4 min)**
   As you complete the scan, stay open to any messages or insights that may come through. These could be visual impressions, feelings, or intuitive knowledge. Take note of what you sense and interpret it with an open mind. Trust your intuition as you receive information, and remember that each session offers a new layer of understanding about your brain's energy and health.

In conclusion, remote viewing your brain is a powerful practice that allows you to connect with the energy and sensations within this vital organ. By tuning into its subtle vibrations, warmth, and pressure, you gain insight into its energetic state and uncover any imbalances or blockages. The more you practice, the deeper your awareness of the brain's energy flow will become. Repeating this exercise regularly helps you not only understand your brain's state but also promotes overall energetic balance. With continued practice, you can enhance your connection to your brain and foster a sense of clarity, well-being, and insight.

Colon

People often choose to remote view the colon because it represents the process of letting go of old patterns, releasing emotions, and releasing physical and emotional "junk." Just as the colon plays a key role in eliminating waste from the body, it is also symbolic of the emotional and energetic release we must undergo to free ourselves from outdated beliefs, burdens, and energies that no longer serve us. By remotely viewing the colon, you can gain insight into both your physical health and emotional state, helping you identify areas where release is needed. Below are five steps to help you connect with the energy of your colon and promote healing and emotional release.

Step 1: Calm Your Mind and Centre Yourself (3 minutes)
Start by sitting comfortably with your eyes closed. Take slow, deep breaths to calm your mind and body. Breathe in through your nose, hold for a moment, and exhale slowly through your mouth. Set the intention to connect with the energy of your colon, seeking clarity and balance. Before you begin, take a few moments to Google pictures of the colon to familiarize yourself with its structure. This will help you visualise its form during the session.

Step 2: Focus on the Colon (4 minutes)
Once you are calm and centred, bring your awareness to the area of your colon. Visualise this part of your body, imagining its shape, position, and energy. Focus on the sensations you feel in this region, and breathe through it, imagining that the air is flowing through the colon. Feel any subtle vibrations, warmth, or pressure that might arise.

Step 3: Sense the Energy in the Colon (3 minutes)
Shift your attention inward and sense the energy flowing within the colon. Allow yourself to feel the subtle sensations that arise—vibrations, warmth, tingling, or any other sensations. Notice the energy

flow through the colon, and observe if there are any blockages or areas of heightened sensation. Trust that the energy you sense in this area corresponds to emotions or physical sensations related to release and letting go.

Step 4: Scan the Colon with X-ray Vision (3 minutes)
Visualise scanning the colon, as if you are using X-ray vision to see its internal structure and energetic flow. Observe the colon's shape, size, and any irregularities in its energy. Pay attention to areas that may feel blocked, congested, or strained. With practice, you may sense any emotional imprints or energetic patterns related to your ability to release or hold on to old emotional baggage.

Step 5: Receive and Interpret Information (3 minutes)
As you complete the scan, allow any insights, impressions, or messages to come through. This could be visual, energetic, or intuitive information related to your colon. Take a moment to interpret any sensations or emotional patterns that arise, and trust the process. Write down your observations for later reflection.

The total time for this remote viewing exercise is around 16 minutes. As you continue practicing, you will deepen your ability to sense the energy of your colon and understand its role in releasing old patterns and emotional baggage. Repeating this exercise regularly will help you build a stronger connection to the energy within your body and promote healing. With more practice, you may find yourself extending the time spent in each session, as you grow more attuned to the energy flow and emotional release that takes place. Remote viewing the colon becomes not only a tool for understanding but also a healing practice, supporting emotional release and energetic balance.

Diaphragm

The diaphragm is a powerful muscle that separates the chest from the abdomen and plays a central role in breathing. It symbolizes the process of expansion and contraction, not only physically but also emotionally and energetically. It represents the area of the body where we process feelings related to our ability to take in life—our breath, our space, and our ability to release tension. Often, the diaphragm is where we hold stress, anxiety, and emotional blocks, as it is intricately connected to our respiratory and emotional systems. Viewing the diaphragm through remote viewing techniques allows you to access deeper awareness of the energetic and emotional patterns that reside there. By learning to remotely view the diaphragm, you can facilitate emotional release, restore balance to your energy flow, and support better physical health, especially regarding your breathing patterns. Below are five steps to help you begin remote viewing the diaphragm.

Step 1: Calm Your Mind and Centre Yourself (3 minutes)
Sit comfortably and close your eyes. Take a few deep, calming breaths—inhale deeply through your nose, hold briefly, and exhale slowly through your mouth. As you breathe, focus on relaxing your body and mind. Set your intention to connect with the energy of your diaphragm, seeking to understand any emotional patterns or physical tensions stored there. Before starting, visualise an image of the diaphragm (Google it if needed) to help you focus your attention on this specific area of your body.

Step 2: Focus Your Attention on the Diaphragm (3 minutes)
Direct your attention to the diaphragm, which lies just beneath the ribcage. Visualise its shape and position in your body. Imagine the diaphragm expanding and contracting as you breathe, creating space for life force to enter and exit your body. As you continue to breathe deeply, focus on the subtle sensations in this area, noticing any vibrations, tightness, or areas of tension.

Step 3: Sense the Energy Flow in the Diaphragm (3 minutes)
Shift your attention to the energy within the diaphragm. Begin to sense any subtle vibrations, warmth, or pressure that arise. Notice how energy flows through this area with each inhale and exhale. Pay attention to areas where the energy may feel blocked or restricted. Trust the sensations that come up and be neutral in your perception, without judgment. This step allows you to connect more deeply with the energetic patterns associated with your diaphragm.

Step 4: Scan the Diaphragm (3 minutes)
Now, imagine that you are scanning the diaphragm as if you have X-ray vision, observing both its physical and energetic structure. Focus on any irregularities or areas where the energy feels stagnant or tense. You may also sense any emotional patterns tied to this area, such as feelings of restriction or difficulty in "taking in" life. Look for any energetic blockages that may be preventing the diaphragm from functioning freely.

Step 5: Receive and Interpret Information (4 minutes)
As you complete the scan of your diaphragm, open yourself to any intuitive messages or insights. Allow any emotional impressions, physical sensations, or visions to arise. This could include feelings of stress, anxiety, or other emotions tied to the diaphragm. Reflect on what you sensed and trust the process. Write down any insights or messages you received.

Total time for this remote viewing exercise is around 16 minutes. As you continue practicing, you'll deepen your connection with the diaphragm's energy and uncover new insights. Remote viewing is not only diagnostic, but also a powerful healing tool that can facilitate balance and release blockages. Repeating sessions regularly helps you develop a deeper understanding and connection to your body's energy. As you grow more comfortable, you may find yourself enjoying the process and extending your session time. Consistency will enhance both your healing and your overall well-being.

Elbow

People often choose to remote view the elbow because it represents flexibility, both physically and emotionally. The elbow is the joint that allows movement in the arm, symbolizing how we handle the challenges and tasks in our lives. It's associated with the ability to adapt, make decisions, and express ourselves with ease. By remote viewing the elbow, you can uncover emotional blockages or areas where you may feel stuck, providing insights into how to release those restrictions. Here are 5 steps to remote view your elbow.

Steps to Remote View the Elbow:
1. **Calm and Centre Yourself (2 minutes)**
   Begin by sitting comfortably and closing your eyes. Take slow, deep breaths to calm your mind and body. Inhale through your nose, hold briefly, and exhale through your mouth. Set the intention to connect with the energy of your elbow, bringing awareness to the flow of movement and ease within it.
2. **Focus on the Elbow (3 minutes)**
   Direct your attention to the elbow, visualizing it clearly in your mind. Imagine the structure of the joint, the muscles, ligaments, and tendons around it. As you breathe, focus on the sensations in and around the elbow, sensing its energy and any subtle sensations.
3. **Sensing the Energy (3 minutes)**
   Gently shift your focus to sensing the energy within the elbow. Notice any sensations such as warmth, tingling, or pressure. Pay attention to any areas of discomfort or tightness, as these may indicate emotional blocks or patterns that are affecting your flexibility, both physically and emotionally.
4. **Scan the Elbow with Your Inner Vision (3 minutes)**
   Visualise scanning the elbow with X-ray-like vision. Focus on the internal structure and the flow of energy around the joint. Notice any blockages, areas of imbalance, or energy that feels stuck. Observe how the energy flows through the elbow and if there are any areas in need of attention or release.

5. **Receive and Document Insights (4 minutes)**
   Allow any insights, images, or intuitive impressions to come through. Pay attention to what you feel or sense. Whether it's an emotional memory, a sensation of tightness, or a visual representation, trust what arises. Take note of your observations and consider how these insights may relate to your physical or emotional flexibility.

The total practice time for this remote viewing exercise is about 15 minutes. As you repeat this process, you'll start to connect more deeply with your elbow's energy, noticing shifts and changes over time. Remote viewing is not just diagnostic—it's also a powerful tool for healing. With regular practice, you can address emotional blockages and achieve greater flexibility in both your body and life. As you become more comfortable with the process, you may choose to extend the time you spend during each session. Consistency is key, and as you deepen your connection to the energy of your elbow, you'll foster healing and growth.

Ear

People often choose to remote view the ear because it represents how we listen and process information, both from the physical world and the spiritual or emotional realms. The ear is not just for hearing sounds; it also symbolizes our ability to trust in the information we receive, process it, and make sense of the world around us. By remote viewing the ear, you can gain insights into your relationship with communication, trust, and how you process external influences. Here are 5 steps to help you remotely view your ear.

1. **Calm and Centre Yourself (2 minutes)**
   Begin by sitting in a comfortable position, closing your eyes, and taking slow, deep breaths. Inhale deeply through your nose, hold briefly, and exhale through your mouth. As you calm your mind, take a moment to Google ear anatomy. This will help you visualise the structure of the ear and understand

its different parts, such as the outer ear, ear canal, eardrum, and inner ear. This awareness will enhance your connection during the remote viewing process.
2. **Focus on the Ear (2 minutes)**
   With a calm mind, bring your focus to the ear. Imagine the shape of the ear, the structure, and the intricate details you've just visualised. Begin to feel the energy in and around the ear. Let your awareness flow to this area and allow the sensations to become clear in your mind.
3. **Sensing the Energy (3 minutes)**
   Shift your attention to sensing the energy within the ear. Notice any subtle vibrations, warmth, or tingling sensations. Pay attention to how the energy moves or if you feel any blockages. The ear not only processes physical sounds but also absorbs emotional and intuitive information, so observe any sensations that might relate to emotional or spiritual processing.
4. **Scan the Ear with Your Inner Vision (3 minutes)**
   Now, visualise scanning the ear with X-ray-like vision. Move through the outer ear, ear canal, and eardrum, and deeper into the inner ear. Notice any areas of tension, imbalances, or blockages. Observe the flow of energy and if there are any areas that might need healing or realignment.
5. **Receive and Interpret Insights (2 minutes)**
   Allow any insights, images, or impressions to come through. Trust what you sense, whether it's related to your ability to trust others, communicate, or process the information you receive. Take note of any emotional patterns, messages, or intuitive impressions that arise during this session.

The total time for this remote viewing exercise is approximately 12 minutes. As you repeat this process, you'll start to deepen your connection to the energy of your ear and its role in your life. Remote viewing is not just about diagnosing potential blockages—it's also a healing tool that helps you align the flow of energy, enhancing your ability to trust and process both physical and emotional information. As you practice more, you may choose to extend the time of each session, allowing yourself to explore deeper insights and healing. Regular practice will not only improve your connection to your ear's energy but will also help you better process information in all areas of your life.

Gallbladder

The gallbladder is often associated with emotional health, especially in relation to unexpressed anger and frustration. People choose to remote view the gallbladder not only to diagnose physical imbalances but also to explore these deeper emotional patterns that may be affecting overall well-being. Remote viewing offers a unique opportunity to connect with the gallbladder's energy and emotions, facilitating both physical healing and emotional release. Here's a structured approach to guide you in this process.

1. **Calm and Centre Yourself (2 minutes)**
   Begin by sitting comfortably with your back straight. Close your eyes and take slow, deep breaths. Inhale through your nose, hold briefly, and exhale through your mouth. Focus on calming your mind, allowing any distractions to fade. Once your mind is clear, take a moment to Google the anatomy of the gallbladder. Understanding its location under the liver and its role in bile storage and digestion will help you visualise it more effectively during the session.
2. **Focus on the Gallbladder (3 minutes)**
   With your mind calm, bring your awareness to the gallbladder. Imagine its shape and location on the right side of the body, beneath the liver. Visualise its pear-like structure and its connection to the digestive system. Let your awareness move to this area, feeling its presence and the subtle energy around it. Allow the sensations to become clearer in your mind.

3. **Sensing the Energy (3 minutes)**
   Shift your focus to the gallbladder and begin to breathe deeply, imagining you are pushing the air in and out through it. With each breath, direct your awareness to this area, focusing on the sensation of the breath moving through the gallbladder. As you continue, allow yourself to tune in until you begin to sense tingling sensations. These subtle feelings are your way of perceiving energy—tingling is how your body responds to the flow of energy. Trust these sensations, as they are key to understanding the emotional and energetic patterns within the gallbladder.
4. **Scan the Gallbladder with Your Inner Vision (4 minutes)**
   To activate your inner vision (your own X-ray vision), you need to focus deeply on the gallbladder and visualise it in your mind's eye. Imagine seeing through your body and into the gallbladder, observing its structure from the inside. Look for any areas that appear imbalanced, tense, or blocked with energy. Pay attention to how the bile flows and notice if there are any obstructions that may represent emotional congestion, such as repressed anger or frustration. Trust the images and impressions that arise, as they offer valuable insights into the emotional and energetic state of the gallbladder.
5. **Receive and Interpret Insights (3 minutes)**
   Finally, remain open to any impressions, images, or intuitive messages that come through. These insights may manifest in various forms—pictures, whispers, tastes, smells, visions, energy changes, or even physical discomfort. Pay attention to whatever arises, as it could relate to emotional patterns tied to anger, frustration, or difficulty in releasing these emotions. Take note of everything that comes to mind about how the gallbladder's energy might be influencing your emotional and physical state. Writing down these impressions will help you interpret the full picture and gain deeper insights into the need for emotional release or the restoration of balance.

This remote viewing session of the gallbladder should take approximately 15 minutes. By repeating this process regularly, you'll deepen your understanding of the gallbladder's energy and its emotional significance. Over time, you'll find that remote viewing is not just a diagnostic tool but a healing practice. As you continue to explore, you'll uncover deeper insights and healing, extending the length of your sessions because you'll enjoy being in your energy field more. With consistent practice, you'll not only gain clarity on physical imbalances but also learn to release trapped emotions, restoring harmony within both body and mind.

Hands

The hands are vital for managing daily tasks and responsibilities, and they reflect how we navigate life's challenges—from simple actions to complex decisions. The right hand, often associated with the masculine, is linked to action, logic, and control, while the left hand, associated with the feminine, represents creativity, intuition, and receiving. Emotional patterns like stress, overwhelm, or difficulties with balance between these energies often manifest in the energy of the hands. People choose to remote view their hands to uncover and release these emotional blocks, gaining insight into both their active and receptive sides. This practice helps bring more ease and confidence into handling everyday tasks while promoting emotional healing and personal growth.

Here are 5 steps to remote view the hands:

1. **Relax and Centre Your Mind (3 minutes)**
   Begin by sitting comfortably, closing your eyes, and taking slow, deep breaths. Inhale deeply through your nose, hold briefly, and exhale through your mouth. As you calm your mind, bring your focus to your hands. Take a moment to Google the anatomy of the hands to better understand their structure—the bones, muscles, tendons, and nerves. This knowledge will help guide your visualization as you connect with the energy of your hands.

2. **Direct Your Attention to the Hands (3 minutes)**
   With your mind centred, shift your focus to your hands. Visualise their shape, fingers, palms, and the space between them. Feel the physical sensation of your hands resting. Tune into the energy around them and allow any sensations—whether warmth, tingling, or heaviness—to come through. Simply notice how your hands feel in this moment.
3. **Tune Into the Subtle Energy (3 minutes)**
   Shift your awareness to the energy within your hands. Notice any vibrations, tingling, or shifts in temperature. Pay attention to whether the energy feels light and flowing or if it seems blocked or stagnant. These sensations can indicate emotional patterns such as feeling overwhelmed or disconnected from tasks at hand. Trust these feelings as they offer clues to the underlying emotional states affecting your hands.
4. **Explore the Hands with Your Inner Vision – internal x-ray (3 minutes)**
   Activate your inner vision (third eye) to see your hands from within. Use your inner X-ray vision to scan through the bones, tendons, and muscles. Look for any areas where energy may feel stuck or where tension is present. Notice if there are particular spots in your hands that feel tight, strained, or unbalanced—these physical sensations may reflect deeper emotional blocks related to control, responsibility, or fear of acting. Trust whatever images or feelings arise during this exploration.
5. **Reflect and Receive Insights (3 minutes)**
   Stay open to any insights, images, or intuitive messages that emerge. These may relate to how you approach tasks, handle responsibilities, or express yourself through action. You might sense emotional patterns such as frustration, fear, or uncertainty about making decisions. Write down whatever impressions, sensations, or thoughts arise. This will help you interpret the full picture of how the energy in your hands is influencing your emotional and physical state.

This remote viewing practice for the hands typically takes about 15 minutes. By repeating this process, you will deepen your connection with the energy of your hands and gain valuable insights into how they reflect your emotional state. Over time, you may experience more subtle and profound realizations, not just about blockages but also about healing and growth. Remote viewing the hands is a tool for both diagnosis and healing, empowering you to manage your responsibilities with greater ease and confidence. With regular practice, you'll find yourself enjoying the sessions more, using them for personal transformation and emotional balance.

Hip

The hips are symbolic of the directions we take in life, both physically and metaphorically. They represent our ability to move forward, change direction, and embrace new experiences. Emotional patterns around the hips can reveal feelings about where we are in life, whether we feel stuck, unbalanced, or uncertain about our path. By remote viewing the hips, you can gain clarity about your life's direction, release any emotional blocks, and restore balance to your energy flow. This practice helps you align your physical and emotional states, making it easier to move through life with confidence and purpose. You can use these 5 steps to remotely view the hips.

1. **Relax and Centre Yourself (2 minutes)**
   Sit comfortably and close your eyes. Begin by taking slow, deep breaths, focusing on the breath as it flows through the centre of your body—your spine. Feel the air move in and out, grounding you in the present moment. Keep breathing through your spine and feel the rhythm of your breath as it flows up and down, calming and centring your energy. This is called centring yourself, as the breath helps you connect deeply with your body and the present moment. Let any distractions fade as you bring your awareness to your hips. To deepen your connection, Google the anatomy of the hips to better understand their structure. This will help enhance

your visualization and allow you to connect more fully with this area of your body.

2. **Direct Your Attention to the Hips (2 minutes)**
   With your mind calm, shift your focus to your hips. Visualise their shape and position, including the bones, muscles, and joints. Begin to feel any sensations in the area—warmth, tension, or even a sense of heaviness.

3. **Sense the Subtle Energy in the Hips (3 minutes)**
   Focus on your hips and begin breathing through them, directing your breath into this area. As you do this, stay fully focused on your hips and the sensations you may feel there. Continue breathing deeply through your hips until you start to notice subtle sensations, such as tingling or vibrations. These sensations are your body's way of perceiving and revealing subtle energy. They may reflect emotional patterns related to your sense of direction in life or feelings of being stuck or uncertain. Trust what you feel, as it will provide valuable insights into your emotional state and connection to your life's journey.

4. **Use Your Inner Eye (3 minutes)**
   Activate your inner eye, which is your ability to see inside the body, and imagine scanning the area around your hips as if you have X-ray vision. Visualise the muscles, bones, and energy flow in this area, looking for any tension, imbalance, or stagnation. Observe if there are any obstacles that could indicate emotional blockages or unresolved issues related to your sense of direction in life. Trust what you see, as it may reveal areas that need attention or healing.

5. **Reflect and Record Your Insights (2 minutes)**
   Stay open to any impressions, images, or messages that arise during the session. These may appear as thoughts, feelings, physical sensations, or intuitive insights. Write down anything you observe, as it will help you interpret the emotional and energetic patterns around your hips and your life's direction.

Remote viewing the hips can offer valuable insights into how you feel about your life's direction and the energy you carry through your personal journey. The more you practice, the clearer and more detailed your understanding will become. Repeating this process regularly will help you release emotional blocks, align your energy, and gain a deeper sense of purpose. With time, you will strengthen your connection to your hips, allowing you to move more freely through life and make decisions with clarity and confidence.

Intestines

Viewing the intestines through remote viewing offers a unique opportunity to explore how you digest not only food but also life experiences. The state of your intestines can reveal how you process emotions, handle past events, and perceive your future. By remote viewing the intestines, you gain insights into emotional patterns that affect your relationship with yourself and your outlook on the future. This practice allows you to uncover any blockages or imbalances, helping you align better with your personal growth and healing. People choose to remote view the intestines to understand and address any challenges in moving forward or digesting life's experiences.

Here are 5 steps to guide you in this process:

1. **Calm Your Mind with Deep Breathing (2 minutes)**
   Start by centring yourself. Take deep breaths, focusing on directing your breath through your spine to calm both your mind and body. This process, known as centring, helps ground your energy. Next, find an anatomy image of the intestines on Google and study it for 2 minutes to aid in visualization and remote connection.
2. **Focus on Your Intestines (3 minutes)**
   Bring your attention fully to the intestines, imagining the flow of air as you breathe through them. Visualise the movement of energy as you focus on this area for another 2-3 minutes.

3. **Become Aware of Subtle Energy Inside Your Intestines (3 minutes)**
   Pay attention to the subtle sensations inside your intestines, such as tingling or vibrations. These sensations represent the energetic state of the area and can reflect emotions connected to the intestines, such as anxiety, fear, or difficulty letting go. These emotional patterns may manifest physically in the form of tension or discomfort. By noticing these sensations, you can connect more deeply with the energetic state of the intestines.
4. **Use Your Inner Eye (X-ray Vision) (3 minutes)**
   Engage your inner eye to look deeply inside the intestines. The inner eye is your natural ability to perceive your organs from within. To activate it, focus on your intestines, breathe through them, and remain aware of any sensations such as tingling or vibrations. Practice all of these simultaneously for 3-4 minutes. Over time, you will begin to receive impressions from within your intestines—these may come in the form of images, energetic sensations, or a sense of inner knowing.
5. **Record Your Impressions (3 minutes)**
   After your session, write down everything you perceived—images, sensations, or emotions. These notes can be used to interpret later and serve as a reference for future remote viewing sessions.

In conclusion, remote viewing the intestines is not just a diagnostic tool; it also serves as a powerful healing practice. By engaging in remote viewing of this area, you not only gain insight into its physical state but also connect with the energetic and emotional imbalances that may be affecting its health. During remote viewing sessions, you may receive impressions of emotions such as fear, anxiety, or unresolved feelings, which can contribute to intestinal issues. This awareness allows for deeper healing, as addressing the emotional undercurrents alongside the physical can help restore balance and promote overall wellness.

Jaw

The jaw is an area of the body that often holds tension and is commonly affected by stress, clenching, or other issues. Many people choose to remote view the jaw remotely because problems here are frequent and closely linked to emotional patterns, such as indecision, anger, frustration, and the challenges of "biting down" on life's choices. These emotional patterns can create physical discomfort or alignment issues in the jaw, impacting both our ability to communicate and our sense of personal strength and assertiveness.

By following these five steps, you can connect deeply with the jaw's structure, energy flow, and emotional influences. This process offers insights not only into the physical aspects of the jaw but also into the underlying emotional patterns that may be contributing to tension or discomfort in this area.

1. **Set Your Intention and Focus (3 minutes)**
   Begin by setting a clear intention to remote view the jaw, focusing on its structure, energy, and emotional connections. Visualise the jaw's role in biting, chewing, and decision-making, and tune into its energetic qualities of strength, stability, and flexibility. Spend a few minutes quieting your mind and connecting with both the physical and energetic aspects of the jaw.
2. **Visualise the Structure of the Jaw (3 minutes)**
   Use your intuitive "x-ray vision" to explore the physical structure of the jaw, including the mandible, teeth, temporomandibular joint (TMJ), and related muscles. Focus on the movement of the jaw during biting, chewing, and speech. Notice any areas of misalignment or tension. Spend 5 minutes visualizing and identifying any areas where energy might be blocked.
3. **Sense the Energy Flow (3 minutes)**
   Tune into the energy flow in and around the jaw. Focus on areas where tension or stress may be stored, especially related to decision-making or unexpressed anger. Pay attention to

whether the energy feels smooth, blocked, tense, or relaxed. Spend 15-20 minutes observing these energy sensations.
4. **Explore the Emotional Patterns (3 minutes)**
Investigate the emotional patterns affecting the jaw. Emotions like indecision, anger, and frustration often manifest as tension or discomfort in the jaw. Pay attention to any emotional resistance or clenching, particularly around decision-making and assertiveness. Spend 10-15 minutes sensing these emotional influences.
5. **Evaluate Overall Health and Balance (3 minutes)**
Assess the overall health and energy balance of the jaw. Consider both physical alignment and emotional expression, particularly related to decision-making and communication. Evaluate whether the jaw feels aligned and free-flowing or if there are signs of misalignment and imbalance. Spend 10-15 minutes making a final assessment.

Summarize your findings, reflecting on both the physical and emotional health of the jaw. Consider any areas needing attention and explore steps for improving energy flow, emotional release, and better decision-making. Spend 5-10 minutes consolidating your insights and preparing for any necessary follow-up for healing or balancing the jaw's energy.

Kidney

The kidneys play a powerful role beyond their physical function—they are often associated with deep-seated emotions like ancient sadness and inherited grief. These emotional patterns, which may have been collected over generations, can sometimes influence kidney health. Kidney-related issues are widespread, and treatment can be challenging due to the complex interplay of physical and emotional factors. By using remote viewing, you can gain insight into your kidneys and uncover hidden emotions or energies that may be impacting them. This unique perspective may help you understand what's happening on an intuitive level, opening the door to a deeper awareness of both your physical and emotional well-being. Here, we will guide you through five essential steps to remote view your kidneys, helping you connect to their energy and explore any underlying emotional patterns.

1. **Clear Your Mind and Become Neutral (2 minutes)**
   Begin by calming your mind and removing all thoughts by focusing on your breath 3-4 min. Reach a state of neutrality, where you feel centred, balanced, and without judgment. This neutral mindset is essential to perceive information accurately.
2. **Visualise your Kidney (3 minutes)**
   Bring your awareness to your kidneys and visualise them clearly. To aid in this, find an anatomical image of the kidneys so you can understand their shape, position, and structure within your body. Focus on these details for about 5-6 minutes, keeping your full attention on the kidneys.
3. **Breathe Through the Kidneys (4 minutes)**
   As you hold your focus, imagine you are breathing in and out through the kidneys themselves. Visualise the air gently pushing through them, cleansing and energizing. This breathing helps you build a connection with their energy.
4. **Sense the Energy While Visualizing (4 minutes)**
   With each breath, tune in to any sensations in your kidneys—these may feel like tingling, vibrations, warmth, or subtle movements. Hold the visual image of your kidneys in your mind as you focus on these sensations, which represent the subtle energy within this area.
5. **Receive Impressions and Record Them (4 minutes)**
   Allow any impressions, emotions, or subtle messages to surface naturally. You may sense images, words, or emotions tied to the kidneys. Write down these impressions for future reflection and to deepen your understanding of what they reveal.

To fully benefit from remote viewing, repeat the process regularly. Each session builds upon the last, strengthening your connection to your kidneys' energy field. Over time, this familiar space will become inviting, and you'll find yourself enjoying the process. As you deepen your practice, remote viewing becomes more than just a diagnostic tool; it becomes a path to healing. By recognizing and releasing emotional patterns, you create space for the energy to flow freely, enhancing your physical and emotional well-being.

Knee

Remote viewing the knee can offer valuable insights, not only into physical sensations but also into underlying emotional patterns that may be stored in this joint. Many people choose to focus on the knees due to their connection to emotions like feeling "stuck," resistance to change, and difficulty moving forward in life. These emotions can affect flexibility and physical ease, potentially leading to tension or discomfort in the knee area. By remote viewing, you can connect with these emotions, understand their origins, and promote healing. Here are five steps to help you view the knee intuitively.

1. **Clear Your Mind and Let Go of Thoughts (3 minutes)**
   Begin by releasing all thoughts through deep, focused breathing along your spine. Inhale and exhale slowly, following the breath as it flows up and down your spine. If any thoughts arise, gently dismiss them by saying, "not this thought, not this thought." Continue until your mind is clear and free of thoughts. Once you reach this quiet, thought-free state, you've turned off your logical mind and connected with your unconscious, preparing you for remote viewing.
2. **Visualise the Knee (3 minutes)**
   Focus your awareness on the knee and begin visualizing it. First, find an anatomical image of the knee and study it for about 2 minutes to create a clear mental picture. Understanding the

knee's structure helps you direct your attention effectively, as energy flows where attention goes. This familiarity allows you to connect more deeply with the knee during your remote viewing.

3. **Sense Subtle Energy and Sensations (3 minutes)**
   As you focus on your knee, begin breathing through it and pay attention to any sensations that arise. These could include tingling, vibrations, warmth, or subtle movements. These sensations reflect the body's energy within the knee and can offer insights into its current state. Often, knee issues are linked to feeling "stuck" or having difficulty letting go of the past. These emotional patterns can be sensed during your remote viewing, and by acknowledging them, you can release them, allowing for healing and movement.

4. **Breathe Through the Knee (4 minutes)**
   Start imagining yourself breathing in and out through the knee, focusing on it until you activate your "inner eye"—your intuitive ability to see within. With each breath, deepen your connection to the knee's energy and structure. As you exhale, visualise pushing any negative, stuck energy away from the knee, allowing it to release and clear.

5. **Receive and Record Impressions (3 minutes)**
   As you continue breathing and focusing on your knee, allow any impressions or insights to arise naturally. These may come as emotions, images, or physical sensations. Trust whatever comes up, and be open to receiving messages from your knee. Record these impressions, as they can offer valuable insights for understanding and healing.

To deepen your connection with your knee's energy, repeat this remote viewing practice regularly. As you become more familiar with this space, you may begin to enjoy the experience of being within your own energy field. Over time, remote viewing transforms into not only a diagnostic tool but also a healing practice, allowing you to release emotions and restore balance within your knee.

Liver

The liver is a vital organ closely linked to emotional health and is often associated with holding unexpressed anger. Many people choose to remote view the liver to understand what energy contributed to their liver problems, especially emotional patterns that may be stored within it. Chronic anger or frustration, whether directed inwardly or outwardly, can manifest as physical imbalances in the liver. By using remote viewing, you can connect with the liver's energy, uncover these emotional patterns, and release them. Here are five steps to help you remote view the liver.

1. **Quiet the Mind (3 minutes)**
   Begin by calming the brain chatter. Use deep breathing through your head, focusing on each breath until your mind feels empty or silent. This quiet state prepares you to connect more deeply with the liver's energy.
2. **Visualise the Liver (4 minutes)**
   Bring your awareness to the liver and start visualizing it. First, find an anatomical image of the liver and study it for about 2 minutes to familiarize yourself with its structure. This will help you focus clearly on its shape and position within the body.
3. **Breathe Through the Liver (4 minutes)**
   Begin breathing through the liver, focusing on this area as you inhale and exhale. Continue for about 3 minutes until you begin to sense subtle sensations, such as tingling, vibrations, warmth, or slight movements. These sensations are an indication of the energy within the liver.
4. **Sense the Energy Inside the Liver (4 minutes)**
   As you continue breathing through the liver, keep tuning into the sensations within it for as long as you can—ideally 5-7 minutes or longer. This practice helps you sense the liver's subtle energy. Notice any shifts or changes in sensation, as these indicate energy moving and transforming in the liver.

5. **Receive and Record Impressions (3 minutes)**
   Allow any impressions, emotions, or insights related to liver issues to arise naturally. These may appear as images, physical sensations, smells, tastes in your mouth, or specific feelings. Record everything you receive, as these impressions can offer valuable insights for healing and understanding the emotions trapped within the liver.

Remote viewing the liver offers a powerful way to connect with its energy and uncover any emotional imbalances, such as unexpressed anger, that may be stored within it. By following the steps of quieting the mind, visualizing the liver, sensing its energy, and receiving impressions, you can gain valuable insights into its state and begin the process of healing. Regularly practicing remote viewing can help you release emotional blockages and restore balance, making it not only a diagnostic tool but also an essential part of your healing journey. The more you practice, the more familiar and comfortable you will become with the energy of the liver, allowing you to facilitate deeper healing and emotional release.

Lungs

The lungs play a profound role in our emotional well-being, acting as "emotional sponges" that often absorb emotions from those around us. For this reason, many people are drawn to remote viewing their lungs, seeking to understand and release the accumulated emotional energy that can contribute to lung issues. By connecting with the subtle energy held in the lungs, you can begin to release emotional burdens and feel a renewed sense of openness and relief.

Below are five steps to guide you through remote viewing your lungs, helping you explore and transform the energy that affects your respiratory health.

1. **Centre Yourself with Deep Breathing (3 minutes)**
   Begin by centring yourself through deep breathing, focusing on your spine. Imagine each breath flowing gently up and down your spine, creating a sense of calm and grounding.
2. **Visualise the Lungs (4 minutes)**
   Look at a picture of lung anatomy to familiarize yourself with its basic structure. Bring your attention to your lungs, focusing on them until you can clearly visualise them in your mind. (3 min)
3. **Sense the Subtle Energy Within the Lungs (3 minutes)**
   Start breathing deeply through the lungs, feeling the air move within them. Maintain your focus on the lungs until you start sensing sensations like tingling, vibrations, or subtle movements—these are signs of energy within the lungs.
4. **Perform an Internal Scan (3 minutes)**
   Use an "internal x-ray" to scan the lungs, searching for areas that feel blocked or congested. With each breath, visualise the blockages dissolving and being gently pushed away by the flow of air.
5. **Receive and Record Impressions (3 minutes)**
   Allow impressions to come naturally—whether as visions, sounds, smells, tastes, or physical sensations. Record everything you receive, as these impressions provide insights to interpret later. Consider doing another remote viewing session to deepen your understanding and support healing.

Remote viewing the lungs is a powerful way to explore and release the emotions stored within. The lungs often absorb not only our own emotions but also those of the people we're in close relationships with. By tuning into your lungs, you can begin to balance your own emotions with the emotions of others, creating a clearer sense of personal boundaries and emotional health.

Repeating this process helps you build on each viewing session, allowing you to deepen your understanding of the energy within your lungs. Over time, you'll find yourself more connected to and comfortable within your own energy. With regular practice, remote viewing of the lungs can become not only a diagnostic tool but also a healing process that supports emotional resilience and self-care.

Mouth

The mouth is central to how we communicate, express truth, and share our inner thoughts with the world. People often choose to remote view the mouth to understand the energy surrounding their communication—how they speak their truth, the vulnerability involved in sharing openly, and the impact of words on themselves and others. By tuning into the mouth's energy, we can gain insight into our own patterns of expression and heal any blockages that may affect our ability to communicate authentically.

Here are five steps to guide you in remotely viewing the mouth.

1. **Centre Yourself with Gentle Breathing (3 minutes)**
   Begin by taking a few deep, calming breaths, feeling the air flow up and down your spine—this is called centring yourself. As you connect to your spine, you'll feel grounded and centred. With each breath, release any tension from your body, focusing solely on your centre+- and your breath. Continue breathing until you begin to feel lighter and more at ease.
2. **Visualise the Mouth (3 minutes)**
   Look at an anatomy picture of the mouth to familiarize yourself with its structure. Then close your eyes and bring your attention to your own mouth, visualizing its shape, position, and parts, including the lips, teeth, tongue, and throat area.
3. **Sense the Subtle Energy Within the Mouth (4 minutes)**
   Begin by breathing through your mouth, imagining the air flowing gently through it. You don't need to open your

mouth—simply visualise and feel the breath moving through your mouth. Focus on your mouth and continue breathing through it until you begin to feel sensations. These sensations may include tingling, vibrations, subtle movements, or even warmth.

This is how you sense the subtle energy within the mouth.

4. **Scan Your Mouth like an X-ray (4 minutes)**
   Visualise your mouth and perform an "internal scan" with your focused attention. Explore it layer by layer, as if you're using your own x-ray vision. Look for areas of tightness, tension, or energy blockages. When you find these areas, breathe into them, and visualise pushing the blockages away from your mouth. Imagine releasing the tension and clearing these blocked areas with your breath.

5. **Receive and Record Impressions (4 minutes)**
   Stay open to any impressions that may come to you. These impressions can manifest as feelings, images, tastes, smells, sounds, or visions. Each one can offer valuable insight into how you communicate, as the energy of communication directly affects the mouth. Be sure to record everything you notice, as these impressions can reveal important information about your communication patterns and any underlying emotions.

Remote viewing the mouth allows you to explore the energy of communication, expression, and the vulnerability of sharing your truth. By tuning into the mouth's energy, you gain insight into how you communicate and the emotions that influence your words. Whether it's uncovering blockages in expression or understanding deeper patterns in your interactions with others, this practice helps you become more aware of the energy behind your communication. Regularly remote viewing the mouth can enhance your ability to speak freely and authentically, promoting healing in both your verbal expression and your emotional well-being.

Muscle Tissue

Our muscles are not only responsible for movement and physical strength but also hold deep connections to our emotional and mental states. Tension, stress, and unprocessed emotions can manifest as tightness or discomfort in the muscles, affecting how we carry ourselves and interact with the world. Remote viewing muscles allows you to tune into the energy stored within them, helping to identify areas of tension, release blockages, and promote healing. By exploring the subtle energy within your muscles, you can gain valuable insights into how emotional patterns and stress impact your body, and work towards restoring balance and ease.

Follow these five steps to remote view your muscle tissue.

1. **Centre Yourself and Focus on Your Breath (3 minutes)**
   Start by taking several deep, calming breaths. Direct your attention to your spine and feel your breath flowing through it. Your spine is your centre. As you continue breathing, feel the breath moving within it, grounding you deeply in yourself. With each breath, release any tension and allow your body to relax.
2. **Visualise the Muscles (4 minutes)**
   Bring your attention to the muscles you wish to view. Visualise their structure—think of their shape, location, and how they interact with bones and joints. If you're unsure, look at an anatomy image to familiarize yourself with the muscles' appearance, then close your eyes and visualise them as clearly as possible.
3. **Sense the Energy in the Muscles (4 minutes)**
   Focus on the sensation of your breath flowing through your muscles as you continue breathing deeply. Notice any subtle sensations—tightness, warmth, tingling, or vibrations—as these indicate energy moving through the muscles. Keep breathing into these areas and observe any shifts in sensation;

this reflects changes in the energy within your muscles. Allow your awareness to move through different muscles, noticing any variations—each one is a unique expression of energy (3 minutes).

4. **Scan for Tension or Blockages (3 minutes)**
Perform an internal scan of your muscles, bringing focused attention to any areas where you sense tension, tightness, or discomfort. Imagine this process as your own internal x-ray, using your awareness to carefully examine each muscle. Notice any areas that feel "stuck" or resistant. As you identify these spots, breathe deeply into them, visualizing the energy gently releasing and the muscles relaxing with each exhale. (4 minutes)

5. **Record Impressions and Release (3 minutes)**
Stay open to any impressions that come through, such as images, emotions, or sensations. These may reveal underlying causes of muscle tension, like emotional stress or physical strain. Record everything you notice. With each breath, visualise releasing the tension, allowing the muscles to become more relaxed and freer of any blockages. (4 minutes)

Remote viewing your muscles offers a unique way to connect with the physical and emotional energy stored within your body. By exploring subtle sensations and observing areas of tension, you gain insights into how stress, emotions, or repetitive strain may affect you physically. With practice, this technique can become a powerful tool not only for self-awareness but also for releasing tension and supporting healing. The more you connect with your muscles in this way, the more you'll foster a sense of ease, grounding, and comfort within your own body. Regular remote viewing helps strengthen this connection, turning it into both a diagnostic and healing practice over time.

Nerves

The nervous system serves as the communication network within the body, transmitting signals that affect every thought, feeling, and movement. Our nerves hold the energy of these communications, and over time, they can also store stress, emotional tension, and even trauma. Remote viewing the nerves allows us to connect with this intricate network, gaining insight into how stressors and emotions may impact our well-being on a deeper level. By tuning into the subtle energy of the nerves, we can explore areas where tension or blockages exist, helping to release stored stress and restore a sense of calm and balance within the body. This practice can provide not only valuable self-awareness but also enhance relaxation and healing. You can follow these 5 steps to remote view the nerves.

1. **Release All Your Thoughts (3 minutes)**
   Begin by taking slow, deep breaths. Visualise and feel the breath moving through your spine, the central core of your body. Sense the breath flowing up and down along your spine, grounding you deeply in this connection. Clear your mind of any thoughts, allowing a calm emptiness to settle in. If a thought does arise, gently push it away, repeating to yourself, "Not this thought, not this thought," and imagine the thought drifting away like a passing cloud. Embrace the silence in your mind, feeling it become still and open.
2. **Visualise the Nervous System (4 minutes)**
   Bring to mind an image of the nervous system—think of its web-like structure reaching throughout the body. Imagine the main pathways along the spine, then branching out to other areas. This visualization will help guide your awareness to the nerves you're about to explore.
3. **Tune into the Energy of the Nerves (4 minutes)**
   As you breathe, focus on sensing subtle energy within the nerves. Pay attention to any sensations—such as tingling, warmth, or pulsing—that might emerge along these pathways.

Allow these sensations to build, observing how the energy feels as it flows through different parts of the nervous system.
4. **Scan for Areas of Tension or Blockages (4 minutes)**
Perform a gentle "internal scan" along the nerve pathways, focusing on any areas that feel tight, tense, or blocked. If you identify any "stuck" points, breathe deeply into those areas, imagining the energy flowing smoothly through them. Visualise tension or blockages releasing with each exhale.
5. **Receive and Record Impressions (3 minutes)**
Remain open to any impressions that arise—these might come as images, sounds, emotions, or physical sensations. Each impression can provide insights into areas of stress or stored emotions in your nervous system. Record everything that comes to mind; these observations can guide future sessions and help in understanding and releasing tension in your nerves over time.

Remote viewing of the nerves is a valuable practice for accessing the subtle, often hidden layers of stress and emotional energy within the body's communication pathways. By connecting to this intricate system, you gain insight into how various experiences and emotions may affect your physical and mental well-being. With consistent practice, remote viewing becomes more than an observational tool; it empowers you to release tension, ease blockages, and foster a greater sense of calm and clarity. As you develop a deeper connection to your nervous system, you enhance your ability to listen to your body, encouraging natural healing and balance from wit

Ovary

The ovaries are not only central to reproductive health but also closely tied to the energy of creation, femininity, and emotional balance. Often, they hold onto subtle emotional patterns, especially those related to creativity, nurturing, and personal power. Remote viewing the ovaries allows you to connect with this vital energy centre, exploring any stored emotions, stress, or energy blockages that may affect physical and emotional well-being. By tuning into the energy of the ovaries, you can gain insights that support healing, release tension, and deepen your connection to the creative and nurturing aspects within yourself. Follow these 5 steps to remote view ovaries.

1. **Calm Your Mind and Release Tension (3 minutes)**
   Begin by taking slow, deep breaths through the centre of your body (spine) to relax your body and quiet your mind. With each exhale, let go of any tension, especially in the lower abdomen and pelvic area. Allow your mind to become clear and open, creating a calm space to focus on the energy of the ovaries.
2. **Visualise the Ovaries (4 minutes)**
   Gently bring your awareness to the location of the ovaries, on either side of your lower abdomen. If helpful, refer to an anatomical image beforehand to assist with visualization. Picture the ovaries as small, oval-shaped organs, and imagine them exactly where they are in your body. As you visualise them, allow yourself to not only see them but also feel their presence and energy. When you visualise them within your body, it's as if you are seeing a holographic representation of your ovaries.
3. **Sense the Subtle Energy of the Ovaries (3 minutes)**
   Continue to breathe deeply, directing your awareness to the ovaries. As you breathe, feel the breath flowing through them. You may begin to notice sensations like warmth, tingling, subtle vibrations, or other signs of energy movement. These sensations are indicators of energy flowing through your ovaries. Keep focusing on this energy and continue to feel it within the area of your ovaries.
4. **Scan for Areas of Tension or Blockages (4 minutes)**
   Perform an "internal scan" of each ovary, using your attention to feel for any tightness, heaviness, or other subtle

sensations. If you identify an area that feels blocked or tense, breathe deeply into it, visualizing the breath gently dissolving any tension and allowing energy to flow smoothly through the area.

5. **Receive and Record Impressions (4 minutes)**
   Remain open to any impressions, feelings, or images that come to you during this process. Impressions can emerge as emotions, colours, sounds, or even memories, offering insights into stored energy or emotional patterns within the ovaries. Record everything you notice, as these impressions can guide future sessions and deepen your understanding of the connection between emotional and physical health.

In conclusion, remote viewing the ovaries provides an opportunity to explore the energy and emotions tied to this vital part of the body. By focusing on the sensations and energy flows, you can gain insight into areas that may need healing or attention, whether physical or emotional. This practice helps you connect with the deeper aspects of your well-being and fosters a sense of balance. The more you engage in this process, the more you strengthen your intuitive awareness, allowing for greater healing and harmony within the body and mind. Repeating this practice will enhance your ability to understand and nurture your body's energy.

Pancreas

The pancreas is an important organ not only for its role in digestion and blood sugar regulation but also for its emotional connections to self-esteem, personal power, and our sense of responsibility. Many people choose to remote view the pancreas to explore these emotional themes, as imbalances in this area can reflect issues related to feeling overwhelmed, inadequate, or unsure about one's role in life. By connecting with the pancreas through remote viewing, you can gain insight into the energetic patterns that may be influencing your sense of self-worth and responsibility. Here are five steps to guide you in remote viewing the pancreas.

1. **Release Stress and Ground Yourself (3 minutes)**
   Begin by releasing any tension or stress. Take several deep, calming breaths, focusing on letting go of any tightness in your body. Centre yourself by bringing your awareness to your spine, which is the core of your body, and feel the air flowing through it with each breath. Sense your deep connection to your spine as your centre, grounding yourself in this space. Feel rooted, relaxed, and fully present in the moment.
3. **Focus on the Pancreas' Location and Energy (4 minutes)**
   Bring your awareness to the area of your pancreas, which is located behind the stomach and near the lower part of your rib cage. Visualise its shape and placement in your body. Imagine this area as an energy centre, and allow your focus to rest there, connecting to its unique vibration and energy. Before proceeding with this step, you may choose to refer to an anatomical picture of the pancreas to help you visualise it more clearly.
4. **Breathe into the Pancreas (4 minutes)**
   Take slow, deep breaths, and imagine your breath flowing directly into the pancreas. As you breathe, feel the energy moving through this area. Pay attention to any sensations that arise, such as warmth, tingling, or shifts in energy, which may signal imbalances or emotional blockages.
5. **Scan for Blockages or Imbalances (4 minutes)**
   Perform an internal scan of your pancreas. With your focused attention, look for any areas of tension, tightness, or energy blockages. These may indicate emotional stress related to self-esteem or responsibility. Visualise breathing energy into these areas, clearing any blockages and restoring balance to the pancreas.
6. **Record Impressions and Insights (4 minutes)**
   Stay open to any impressions that arise during the session. These may come as feelings, images, sensations, or insights

about your emotional state and how it might relate to your pancreas. Record everything you experience, as these impressions can offer valuable insight into your emotional well-being and how it affects your pancreas.

In conclusion, remote viewing the pancreas provides an opportunity to explore the emotional and energetic aspects of self-esteem and responsibility. By tuning into this vital organ, you can uncover any imbalances or emotional blockages that may be affecting your sense of self-worth. Through continued practice, remote viewing the pancreas becomes a tool not only for diagnosing energy patterns but also for facilitating emotional healing. As you deepen your connection to this organ, you will enhance your ability to release stored emotions and restore balance, supporting both your emotional and physical well-being.

Pituitary Gland

The pituitary gland, often referred to as the "master gland," plays a crucial role in regulating many essential bodily functions, including hormone production, metabolism, and growth. It is deeply connected to our emotional and psychological states, influencing our sense of balance, intuition, and the way we respond to stress. People often choose to remote view the pituitary gland to gain insight into their hormonal balance, emotional well-being, and to uncover any energetic imbalances that may be affecting their overall health. By connecting with the pituitary gland through remote viewing, you can explore its energy and uncover deeper layers of insight related to your personal growth, emotional healing, and physical vitality. Here are 5 steps to help you begin remote viewing the pituitary gland.

1. **Calm and Centre Yourself (3 minutes)**
   Start by calming your mind and body with deep breathing or meditation. Focus on grounding yourself, allowing your

thoughts to settle and reaching a neutral, non-judgmental state. Visualise yourself connecting with your body's energy, specifically around the area of the pituitary gland, which is located at the base of your brain. (5-10 minutes)

2. **Set Your Intention and Focus on the Pituitary Gland (3minutes)**

   Set a clear intention to remote view the pituitary gland. Direct your focus to the base of the brain where the gland is located. Visualise yourself zooming in on this area, ready to explore the energy and details of the gland. Breathe deeply, imagining the air flowing in and out of the pituitary gland, and feel the breath at the base of your brain. (3-5 minutes)

3. **Energy Sensing in the Body and Pituitary Gland (5 minutes)**

   Continue breathing deeply through the base of your brain, and pay attention to any sensations you feel there—tingling, warmth, vibrations, or pressure. These are subtle energies surrounding the pituitary gland. Notice whether the energy flows smoothly or if there are any blockages or disruptions. Now, focus specifically on the pituitary gland itself. Tune into its energy—how does it feel? Is there a sense of balance or imbalance? Simply observe what you sense as you connect with the pituitary gland. All of these sensations are forms of energy.

4. **Observe the Pituitary Gland Using X-ray Vision (5 minutes)**

   Engage your X-ray vision to gain a clearer view of the pituitary gland. Visualise it as if you could see through its layers. Observe its structure and any details within it. Are there any areas that seem dense or out of balance? Note any irregularities or unusual patterns that you perceive. Intuition is all about noticing the subtle details. In this process, your goal is to become aware of the subtle energies present within your pituitary gland.

5. **Reflect on Emotional Patterns and Physical State (5 minutes)**

   After completing your remote viewing, gently bring your awareness back to the present. Reflect on the energy and emotional patterns you sensed. Consider how your sense of control over yourself might be influencing or being influenced by the pituitary gland. Document any insights or imbalances you discovered. If needed, plan a follow-up session to focus on addressing and balancing these emotional and energetic aspects.

In conclusion, remote viewing the pituitary gland allows you to connect with the subtle energies within this vital part of the brain. By tuning into its energy, you can become more aware of any imbalances or blockages that may be present, which can influence not just physical health, but emotional and spiritual well-being. As you continue practicing this technique, you deepen your ability to perceive and understand the intricacies of your body's energy system. With each session, you cultivate a stronger connection to your inner wisdom, empowering you to maintain balance and harmony within your body and mind.

Prostate

The prostate is not only an important organ in the male reproductive system, but it also symbolizes the masculine principle within a man. It embodies qualities such as strength, power, and vitality—traits traditionally associated with masculinity. However, the energy of the prostate is not limited to just these outward expressions of power; it also reflects a deeper sense of purpose, responsibility, and groundedness. Understanding the prostate through remote viewing allows us to explore how a man connects with his inner sense of masculinity in a balanced and positive way. It provides an opportunity to observe how energy flows through this area, highlighting the health of both the physical and emotional aspects of masculinity. Through remote viewing, we can uncover blockages or imbalances in this energy and restore the natural, empowering flow of the prostate. Here are five steps to guide you in remote viewing the prostate, focusing on the positive and nurturing aspects of masculinity.

1. **Clear Your Mind of All Thoughts (3 minutes)**
   Begin by taking slow, deep breaths, directing your focus to your centre and feeling the breath move through your spine. As you breathe, release any thoughts that come to your mind. If any thoughts arise, simply acknowledge them and let them drift away, saying to yourself, "Not this thought, not this thought." Visualise these thoughts gently floating away like clouds, leaving your mind clear and empty, allowing a peaceful stillness to take over.
2. **Set Your Intention and Focus on the Prostate (3 minutes)**
   Clearly state your intention to remote view the prostate. Visualise the area where the prostate is located, which is below the bladder and in front of the rectum. Direct your mental focus to this region, preparing to connect with the energy and details of the prostate.
3. **Energy Sensing of the Prostate (3 minutes)**
   Now, begin breathing deeply through the area of your prostate, as if you are directing the air into that space. As you do this, visualise the prostate and feel your breath flowing through it with each inhale and exhale. Allow your awareness to settle fully into this area. After a few breaths, you may begin to notice subtle sensations within the prostate. These sensations could include warmth, tingling, gentle pressure, or a feeling of expansion. These are signs of the energy moving through the prostate, and they may vary in intensity. Pay close attention to the sensations you experience, as they indicate the flow of energy. The more you focus on this energy, the clearer the sensations will become, helping you to connect more deeply with the prostate's energetic state.

4. **Explore Emotional Patterns Related to the Prostate (3 minutes)**
   Take a moment to reflect on the emotional patterns linked to the prostate, particularly those connected to masculinity and how one perceives themselves as a man. Tune into any emotions or energies that may arise related to these themes. These could include feelings of strength, vulnerability, identity, or concerns about self-worth and responsibility. Notice if any past experiences, beliefs, or unresolved emotional imprints seem to be influencing the energy of the prostate. As you focus on these emotional patterns, consider how they might be impacting the health and balance of the prostate. Pay attention to any sensations or shifts in energy as you process these emotional aspects.
5. **Write Down Your Impressions**
   After completing your remote viewing, gently bring your awareness back to the present. Reflect on the energy and emotional patterns you observed. Document your findings, noting any insights about the prostate's energy, its connection to masculinity issues, and overall comfort. If necessary, plan a follow-up session to address and balance any negative emotions or energy imbalances.

In conclusion, remote viewing the prostate is an opportunity to connect with both the physical and emotional energy of this important organ. By tuning into its subtle sensations and exploring any emotional patterns associated with masculinity, identity, and self-worth, we can gain deeper insights into how these factors influence prostate health. Through continued practice, remote viewing of the prostate can serve not only as a diagnostic tool but also as a means of promoting balance and healing. As you refine your ability to sense the energy and emotions tied to the prostate, remember to approach the process with neutrality, compassion, and a willingness to explore the deeper layers of both the body and mind.

Rectum

The rectum, as a part of the digestive system, plays a significant role in the body's process of elimination and detoxification. It is deeply connected to the release of physical waste, but also holds emotional significance tied to the concept of letting go. Issues in the rectum can sometimes reflect emotional blockages or difficulties in releasing both physically and mentally. When remote viewing the rectum, we can explore not only the physical state of this area but also the emotional and energetic patterns associated with it. This process can offer insight into any underlying tensions or imbalances, whether they are related to past trauma, the need for control, or an inability to release what no longer serves us. By tuning into this area, we can promote healing and gain clarity on both the physical and emotional layers that influence the health of the rectum.

1. **Ground Yourself to Your Centre (3 minutes)**
   Begin by taking a few deep, calming breaths. Focus on your breath and let it flow through your spine, grounding you to your centre. Feel the connection between your body and the earth beneath you. As you breathe, release any tension from your body, clearing your mind, and becoming fully present in the moment. Your centre is your spine, and with each breath, feel more rooted and connected to yourself.
2. **Focus Your Awareness on the Rectum (3 minutes)**
   Bring your awareness to the location of the rectum in your body, at the end of your digestive system. Visualise this area clearly in your mind, imagining it in detail as if you were looking at it from the inside. Feel its presence in your body, and allow yourself to become aware of any sensations or energy you sense around this area.
3. **Energy Sensing in the Rectum (3 minutes)**
   Breathe through the area of the rectum, feeling the energy moving in and out with your breath. Focus on the flow of air through this region, noticing any subtle sensations such

as warmth, tingling, or pressure. These sensations represent the energy moving through the rectum. Pay attention to any blockages or disruptions in the flow of energy, as these may indicate areas that need healing or attention.

4. **Explore Emotional Patterns Related to the Rectum (3 minutes)**
   Reflect on any emotional patterns associated with the rectum, such as issues related to release, control, or holding onto past emotional burdens. The rectum can hold energy related to one's ability to let go of what no longer serves them. Tune into any feelings or energies that arise as you focus on this area. Are there any feelings of resistance or difficulty with releasing? Consider how these emotional patterns might be influencing the health of this area.

5. **Clear Any Blockages and Release Stagnant Energy (3 minutes)**
   If you identify any areas of blockage or tension, use your breath to clear them. Visualise the energy being released from the rectum with each exhalation. Imagine the area becoming free and open, allowing the energy to flow smoothly and naturally. Feel a sense of emotional and physical release, as if you are letting go of any stagnant or unneeded energy in your body. Trust the process of release, knowing that it promotes healing and balance.

In conclusion, remote viewing the rectum helps you understand both the physical and emotional energies connected to this part of your body. By grounding yourself and focusing on your breath, you can sense any tension or imbalances in the area. Emotional patterns, such as issues with letting go or control, can affect the health of the rectum. By paying attention to these feelings and using your breath to release blockages, you can help bring balance to both your body and mind. This practice allows you to identify potential physical issues while also understanding the deeper emotional connections that influence your health.

Rib Cage

People often choose to remote view the rib cage because it holds significant emotional and energetic connections to protection, boundaries, and support. The rib cage serves as a physical shield for vital organs, and it can reflect the way we emotionally protect ourselves from the outside world. It is also linked to feelings of vulnerability, control, and security, as it surrounds the heart and lungs, the organs vital for emotional and physical well-being. Emotions such as fear, grief, and a lack of emotional boundaries can become trapped in this area. Remote viewing the rib cage allows you to explore these energies, uncover hidden emotional patterns, and help release any blockages or unresolved emotions that may be affecting your health or sense of security. You can follow 5 steps to remote view the rib cage.

1. **Centre Yourself (3 minutes)**
   Begin by centring yourself with deep, calming breaths. Focus on your breath as it flows in and out through your spine, your core. Feel the air moving gently up and down, connecting you to your centre. Clear your mind of all thoughts, allowing your head to become empty and still. Focus solely on the sensation of your breath and the energy of your spine. This is the process of grounding and centring yourself.

2. **Focus Your Attention on the Rib Cage (4 minutes)**
   Bring your attention to the area of your rib cage. Visualise the ribs as a protective structure surrounding your heart and lungs. You may find it helpful to refer to an anatomical reference beforehand to aid in visualization. As you focus, feel the ribs, their shape, and their connection to the body. Sense the energy around this area.

3. **Breathe Through the Rib Cage (4 minutes)**
   Begin breathing deeply, imagining the air flowing through your rib cage. Feel the breath expanding the ribs and filling the space between them. As you do this, pay attention to any sensations that arise—such as tightness, warmth, or subtle

vibrations—indicating the flow of energy. These sensations help you tune into the rib cage's energy field.

4. **Explore Emotional Patterns Associated with the Rib Cage (3 minutes)**
   Reflect on any emotional patterns tied to the rib cage, such as fear, vulnerability, or the need for protection. Tune into how these emotions might be affecting the energy of the ribs. Are there any blockages or unresolved emotions? Observe how the energy feels—whether it is open and free or tense and constricted.

5. **Clear and Release Blocked Energy (3 minutes)**
   If you notice areas of tension, tightness, or emotional discomfort, focus on releasing them. Breathe into these areas and visualise the energy clearing. Imagine the breath dissolving any blockages or stagnant energy, restoring balance and harmony to the rib cage. Allow yourself to experience a sense of ease, relaxation, and protection within your rib cage.

In conclusion, remote viewing the rib cage provides a deeper understanding of both its physical structure and the emotional energy stored within it. By centring your focus on the breath, energy flow, and the sensations within the ribs, you can uncover any blockages, tension, or imbalances tied to feelings of safety, protection, or vulnerability. This practice offers an opportunity to release emotional weight and physical discomfort, fostering a sense of ease and balance. Through this exploration, you can promote healing, not only in the rib cage itself but also in the emotional patterns that may be influencing it.

Skin

Remote viewing the skin allows you to connect with the body's largest organ, which serves as a boundary between the inner and outer world. The skin not only protects and defines personal space but also reflects our emotional state and interactions with others. It can reveal subtle energy patterns tied to how we create boundaries, experience touch, and express our identity. By remote viewing the skin, you can explore both physical and emotional aspects, gaining insight into how we protect ourselves and relate to the world around us. This practice can offer valuable understanding of emotional blockages or imbalances related to boundaries, sensitivity, and self-esteem.

1. **Calm Your Mind (3 minutes)**
   Start by calming yourself with deep, steady breaths, focusing on the air flowing through your spine, your body's centre. Clear your mind of distractions and allow yourself to feel grounded and present in the moment. A calm and focused mind will help you connect with the subtle energy of your skin.
2. **Visualise the Skin as a Protective Boundary (4 minutes)**
   Visualise your skin as a protective boundary surrounding your body, a shield that defines your personal space. See it as a layer that not only keeps you safe but also regulates the flow of energy in and out. Imagine this boundary as flexible, allowing positive energy to flow in while keeping out any negative influences.
3. **Sense Energy in the Skin (4 minutes)**
   Focus on sensing the energy within and around your skin. As you breathe, notice any subtle sensations like warmth, tingling, or coolness. Feel the energy that moves through the skin as a boundary. Are there any areas of tension, blockages, or areas that feel lighter or more energized than others? Observe these sensations without judgment.
4. **Explore Emotional Energy (3 minutes)**
   Reflect on the emotional patterns related to your skin, particularly those involving your boundaries. How do you feel about your physical space? Are there any emotional imprints tied to protection, vulnerability, or sensitivity? Tune into how your skin might reflect these emotional states, such as areas of discomfort or heightened sensitivity.

5. **Write Down Impressions (3 minutes)**
   Record any impressions, sensations, or insights you experienced during your remote viewing of your skin. These impressions can come in many forms, such as physical sensations (like tingling, warmth, or pressure), emotional responses, or mental images. For instance, you might notice areas of sensitivity or feel certain emotions tied to protection or vulnerability. Be sure to capture any subtle or unexpected sensations, as they can provide valuable insights into your skin's role as a boundary, both physically and energetically. Reflecting on these notes will deepen your understanding of the connection between your skin and your personal boundaries.

Remote viewing the skin can offer profound insights into both the physical and energetic boundaries we maintain. By tuning into the sensations, emotions, and images associated with the skin, you gain a deeper understanding of how it protects and connects us to the world. This practice can help uncover areas where your boundaries may feel strong or vulnerable, offering valuable clues about how you interact with your environment and how you care for yourself. Engaging with the skin in this way enhances your ability to nurture your personal space and foster healthy boundaries, both physically and emotionally.

Spleen

The spleen plays an important role in our body's immune system, filtering blood, recycling iron, and managing the body's energy balance. When remote viewing the spleen, you may tap into emotional patterns tied to protection, self-worth, and the ability to release or hold onto things. People often choose to remote view the spleen to gain insight into how these emotional patterns might affect their physical health, particularly when it comes to feelings of overwhelm, suppressed emotions, or a lack of self-care. Exploring the spleen energetically allows you to better understand the internal dynamics of these emotions and their impact on overall well-being. You can follow 5 steps to remote view spleen.

1. **Bring Yourself to Your Centre (3 minutes)**
   Begin by sitting comfortably and taking several deep breaths. Focus on your breath flowing in and out, allowing yourself to ground into your body. Visualise your spine as the centre of your body and feel the energy flowing through it as you breathe deeply. This helps you become present and focused on the task ahead.
2. **Direct Your Awareness to the Spleen (3 minutes)**
   With your mind calm and centred, shift your focus to the location of the spleen, which is on the left side of the body, just beneath the ribs. Visualise the organ in your body, and allow your awareness to settle on its energetic presence. Picture the spleen in relation to the rest of your organs to better understand its position and function.
3. **Sense the Energy of the Spleen (4 minutes)**
   Breathe through the spleen and focus on any sensations you feel in the area. These could include warmth, tingling, pressure, or even a sense of lightness or heaviness. These sensations are indicators of the energy flow through the spleen. Pay attention to any changes in these sensations as you continue to breathe and focus on the organ.
4. **Explore Emotional Patterns Connected to the Spleen (3 minutes)**
   Consider the emotional patterns linked to the spleen, such as feelings of protection, trust, or emotional release. The spleen often stores unresolved emotions or burdens related to a person's sense of security or ability to let go of past experiences. Tune into any emotional responses you might feel as you observe the spleen's energy.
5. **Record Your Impressions (3 minutes)**
   After you've completed your session, take some time to write down any impressions, feelings, or insights you received

during the remote viewing session. This may include sensations, colours, or emotional patterns that you experienced. Recording these impressions can help you reflect on the energy you sensed and the possible emotional imbalances that may exist.

Remote viewing the spleen can offer valuable insights into the emotional and energetic imbalances that affect a person's sense of protection and self-worth. By tuning into the energy of the spleen, you can identify areas of emotional stagnation or unresolved feelings, which can provide guidance for healing. Whether you are looking to better understand the physical or emotional health of the spleen, this practice allows you to connect deeply with your body's energy, leading to greater awareness and balance.

Stomach

The stomach is a vital organ in the digestive system, responsible for breaking down food and absorbing nutrients, but it is also deeply connected to our emotional well-being. People often choose to remote view the stomach because it holds emotional patterns related to digestion, nourishment, and the ability to "digest" life experiences. Issues such as stress, anxiety, and feelings of insecurity can manifest in the stomach, leading to discomfort, indigestion, or even chronic conditions. Remote viewing the stomach can provide insight into not only its physical health but also the emotional and energetic blockages that might be influencing its function. By connecting with this area, you can better understand how your emotional landscape affects your ability to process and integrate life's challenges.

1. **Preparation and Grounding (3 minutes)**
   Start by finding a quiet, comfortable space. Take several deep breaths to centre yourself and ground your energy. Visualise your energy connecting with the earth to create a stable and focused mental state. Set the intention to observe the stomach with clarity and openness.

2. **Visualizing the Stomach (4 minutes)**
   Picture the stomach within the body, focusing on its location, shape, and structure. Visualise the stomach in detail and create a mental connection with this organ, tuning into its physical and energetic aspects. To help visualise it more clearly, you may choose to refer to an anatomical picture of the stomach before beginning your visualization (4 minutes).
3. **Sensing Energy in and Around the Stomach (4 minutes)**
   Tune into the energy within and around the stomach. Observe whether the energy feels balanced or if there are areas of tension, blockages, or disturbance. Pay attention to sensations such as heaviness or lightness and how the energy flows in this area.
4. **Exploring Emotional Patterns (4 minutes)**
   Investigate the emotional patterns connected to stomach problems. The stomach is often associated with fear of the new and difficulties in assimilating new experiences or changes. Observe any emotions or issues related to these patterns and how they might be influencing the health of the stomach.
5. **Record Your Impressions (4 minutes)**
   After completing your remote viewing session of the stomach, take a moment to write down or record any impressions, sensations, or images that came to you during the process. These impressions might include physical sensations, emotional responses, or visual details about the stomach's energy or state. By documenting what you observed, you can gain deeper insights into the health, emotional patterns, and overall energy flow of the stomach.

Remote viewing the stomach allows you to connect with the energetic and emotional aspects of this vital organ. By focusing on the sensations, energy flow, and emotional patterns associated with the stomach, you can gain valuable insights into its health and well-being. This process helps you become aware of any blockages, imbalances, or emotional influences that may affect the stomach's function. Regularly practicing remote viewing of the stomach can deepen your understanding of its energetic state and support healing by fostering awareness of underlying issues.

Teeth

The teeth are not only vital for chewing and digestion but also symbolize our capacity to "bite" into life, assert ourselves, and stand our ground. They are a source of personal power, representing the strength to break through obstacles and express our individuality. In remote viewing, exploring the energy of the teeth can reveal how well one is tapping into their own sense of power, ability to take action, and communicate their needs. Emotional imbalances such as fear of confrontation, feeling powerless, or unresolved issues related to self-expression may manifest in the teeth. By tuning into the energetic state of the teeth, remote viewing can offer insights into these areas, helping restore balance and empowering you to reclaim your strength and voice.

1. **Ground and Centre Yourself (3 minutes)**
   Begin by grounding yourself with deep, calming breaths. Focus on your spine as the centre of your body, feeling the air flow through it. Clear your mind of any distractions, allowing yourself to be fully present and centred. This helps you tune into the subtle energies of the body and prepare for remote viewing.
2. **Visualise the Teeth (3 minutes)**
   Direct your attention to your teeth, imagining them as a powerful structure connected to your capacity to bite into life and assert yourself. Visualise the teeth in detail, paying attention to their shape, position, and overall health. If necessary, reference an anatomical image to assist with your visualization.
3. **Tune into Energy Sensations (3 minutes)**
   As you continue to focus on your teeth, begin to sense any energy or sensations in this area. This may include tingling, warmth, pressure, or vibrations. These sensations represent

the flow of energy in your teeth, which could indicate areas of strength or blockages. Trust your intuition as you sense any imbalances.
4. **Explore Emotional Patterns (5 minutes)**
   Reflect on the emotional patterns tied to your teeth. These may include issues related to self-expression, fear of confrontation, or personal power. Tune into any emotions that arise as you focus on the teeth and observe whether there are any unresolved feelings or energy blocks that might be affecting your sense of empowerment.
5. **Record Your Impressions (4 minutes)**
   Take a moment to record any impressions, sensations, or insights you experienced while remote viewing your teeth. These could be physical sensations, emotional patterns, or intuitive messages. Writing them down will help you gain clarity on any areas that need attention, healing, or further exploration.

Remote viewing the teeth provides valuable insights into your ability to assert yourself, express your needs, and tap into personal power. By tuning into the energy and emotional patterns of the teeth, you can identify blockages or imbalances that may be affecting your strength and self-expression. Regularly practicing remote viewing of the teeth can promote healing, self-awareness, and a deeper understanding of your inner power.

Throat

The throat is a powerful energy centre in the body, linked to communication, self-expression, and the ability to speak your truth. Remote viewing the throat offers insights into how freely you express yourself and how well you align with your authentic voice. Blockages in this area may relate to issues such as fear of speaking up, repressed emotions, or a lack of self-confidence. By exploring the throat through remote viewing, you can tap into its energetic patterns and uncover any emotional or physical imbalances that may be hindering your communication. In this practice, you'll learn to connect deeply with the energy of your throat, helping you clear any blockages and embrace your full self-expression. You can follow these 5 steps to remotely view the throat.

1. **Centre Yourself in Silence (3 minutes)**
   Begin by grounding yourself through deep breathing. Focus on your breath as it flows through your centre, feeling the air move through your spine. Clear your mind of distractions and allow yourself to reach a state of calm, creating a quiet space to connect with the energy of your throat.
2. **Set Your Intention for View Throat (3 minutes)**
   Mentally state your intention to explore the energy of your throat. Focus your awareness on this area, visualizing its location at the base of your neck. See it as an energy centre, open to the flow of communication and self-expression.
3. **Sense the Energy Flow in the Throat (3 minutes)**
   Tune into the sensations in your throat as you breathe. Feel the energy as it moves through this area. Notice any sensations such as tightness, warmth, tingling, or even areas of blockage. These are signs of energy flow or stagnation, revealing insights into your communication patterns.
4. **Reflect on Emotional Ties to Expression (4 minutes)**
   Consider any emotional patterns related to self-expression and communication. Is there any fear, hesitation, or confidence tied to your throat? Tune into these feelings, as they might affect your ability to speak freely and clearly.
5. **Document Your Insights (4 minutes)**
   After completing your session, take a moment to record your impressions. Write down any feelings, sensations, or insights you received about your throat. Reflect on any blockages or areas of free flow that might relate to your personal expression or emotional state. (4 minutes)

Remote viewing the throat can provide profound insights into how you express yourself and communicate with the world. By tuning into the energy and emotions connected to this area, you can uncover any blockages that might hinder your ability to speak your truth. With focused awareness, you can support the free flow of expression, helping to clear any limitations in communication and fostering a deeper connection with your authentic voice.

Thyroid Gland

The thyroid gland is closely connected to the ability to speak your truth and express yourself authentically, particularly within family dynamics. It plays a vital role in communication and self-expression, so when there are imbalances, they can manifest as difficulty speaking up or fear of being silenced. Often, issues related to the thyroid arise when one feels humiliated or rejected by family members for their beliefs or individuality. Remote viewing the thyroid can offer valuable insight into these emotional patterns, helping to uncover any energetic blockages that may be preventing you from expressing your true self or standing firm in your personal beliefs. It provides an opportunity to heal these imbalances and restore the flow of energy that supports confident, truthful communication. You can remotely view the throat using these 5 steps.

Step 1: Ground Yourself (3 minutes)
Start by grounding yourself to your centre with deep, steady breaths. Focus on your spine, your core, and feel the breath moving through it with each inhale and exhale. Connect deeply with your spine, becoming aware of the flow of breath as it moves in and out, grounding you and creating a sense of balance and wholeness.

Step 2: Visualise the Thyroid Area (4 minutes)
Bring your awareness to the area of your thyroid. Visualise its shape and structure as though you can clearly see it inside your body. To

enhance your visualization, you may choose to look at an anatomical image of the thyroid beforehand. Remember, energy flows where your attention goes. As you focus on this area, allow your awareness to deepen and settle into the sensations of the thyroid.

Step 3: Tune into the Energy of the Thyroid (5 minutes)
Breathe gently through the area of your thyroid and notice any senSsations that arise. Focus on subtle vibrations, warmth, or pressure that indicate energy flowing through and around the thyroid. Pay attention to areas that may feel blocked or restricted, as these could signal emotional or energetic imbalances.

Step 4: Explore Emotional Connections to the Thyroid (4 minutes)
Reflect on emotional patterns tied to the thyroid, such as challenges related to speaking your truth, issues with self-expression, or feelings of powerlessness. Observe any feelings that arise related to these concerns, especially emotional imprints tied to fear, shame, or self-doubt.

Step 5: Record Your Impressions (3 minutes)
After your remote viewing session, take a moment to write down any impressions, sensations, or emotions you experienced. Note any energy shifts or physical sensations you observed. This helps you process your insights and identify areas that may need healing or attention.

Remote viewing the thyroid can provide profound insights into our self-expression and personal power, particularly in areas where we feel restricted, unheard, or disconnected. By tuning into the energy of the thyroid, we can uncover emotional patterns that affect our ability to communicate and embody our truth. Recognizing these blockages can facilitate healing, realignment, and restore balance in the thyroid, supporting clearer expression and a more empowered sense of self.

Tongue

The tongue is a vital organ involved in speech, taste, and even the process of swallowing, playing an essential role in how we interact with the world. It is deeply connected to our ability to communicate both verbally and non-verbally, and it can also be an indicator of emotional and physical imbalances. Remote viewing the tongue allows you to gain insight into how we express ourselves, both through words and sensory experiences. By tuning into the energy of the tongue, you can uncover any emotional blockages or imbalances tied to communication, self-expression, or even how we experience the world around us through taste

1. **Centre and Ground Yourself (3 minutes)**
   Begin by taking a few deep breaths, bringing your awareness to your spine and your centre. As you breathe, feel the air flowing through your body, grounding you. Let each breath bring you more centred, balanced, and connected to your core. Clear your mind, allowing any distractions or thoughts to dissolve as you focus solely on your breath and your connection to your body.
2. **Visualise the Tongue and its Role (3 minutes)**
   Direct your attention to your tongue, picturing its shape, structure, and position within your mouth. Visualise it as part of your sensory system, playing a role in your ability to communicate, taste, and swallow. Imagine the energy around the tongue, how it feels in your mouth, and its connection to the rest of your body.
3. **Tune into Sensations in the Tongue (4 minutes)**
   Focus your attention on the subtle sensations in your tongue. Do you feel warmth, pressure, or vibrations? Is there an area of the tongue that feels more active or tense than others? Allow yourself to be sensitive to the flow of energy through the tongue, noticing if there are any blockages, excess energy, or discomfort.

4. **Explore Emotional Patterns Linked to the Tongue (4 minutes)**
   Reflect on the emotional aspects tied to the tongue, such as self-expression, communication, and the power of words. Pay attention to any feelings or memories that arise related to speaking your truth, fears of judgment, or challenges in communicating effectively. Notice if there are emotional imprints related to past experiences of being silenced or misunderstood.
5. **Record Your Observations (3 minutes)**
   After your remote viewing session, take a moment to write down any impressions or sensations you experienced. Capture details of any energy, emotional patterns, or physical sensations related to the tongue. This helps to solidify your observations and identify areas that may need further attention or healing.

Remote viewing the tongue can reveal insights into how we express ourselves, both verbally and non-verbally. It may uncover emotional blockages or challenges related to speaking our truth, fears of judgment, or difficulty in communicating. By understanding these patterns, you can begin to address any imbalances and promote clearer self-expression, emotional healing, and better communication in your life.

Ureter

The ureters are a vital part of the urinary system, connecting the kidneys to the bladder and playing a crucial role in transporting urine. When we engage in remote viewing of the ureter, we are not only connecting to its physical structure but also tuning into the subtle energy that flows through it. This process can reveal emotional or energetic patterns associated with issues related to release, cleansing, or letting go—whether physical, emotional, or psychological. Remote viewing the ureters can also provide insights into the body's capacity to eliminate toxins, both on a physical and energetic level, helping to uncover areas that might be blocked or in need of healing. By examining the ureter's energy, we can better understand how this part of the body relates to the flow of life and the act of releasing what no longer serves us.

Here are 5 steps to remotely view the ureter.

Step 1: Prepare and Centre Yourself (3 minutes)
Begin by grounding yourself with deep, slow breaths. Focus on your spine and centre, feeling your breath moving through your body and into your core. As you centre yourself, imagine becoming one with your body, allowing a deep sense of calm and stillness to wash over you. This will help you access a state of awareness where you can focus on the subtle energies of your body.

Step 2: Visualise the Ureter (3 minutes)
Direct your attention to the area where the ureters are located. Visualise them as two narrow tubes running from the kidneys to the bladder, transporting urine. Picture their structure clearly in your mind, and if needed, reference an anatomical image to support your visualization. See them as energy channels, connected to the kidneys and bladder, and allow your mind to settle into this awareness.

Step 3: Tune into the Energy Flow (4 minutes)
As you breathe gently, focus on the energy flowing through the ureters. Feel any subtle sensations that arise, such as warmth, vibrations, or pressure. Pay attention to any areas where the flow feels restricted or blocked. Notice if there are any imbalances or disturbances in the energy, as these can be reflections of physical or emotional blockages.

Step 4: Explore Emotional and Energetic Connections (4 minutes)
Reflect on the emotions tied to the act of elimination and release. The ureters play a role in the body's detoxification and clearing

process, so consider if there are any emotional patterns related to the ability to let go—whether it's holding onto old emotions, past traumas, or outdated beliefs. Tune into any feelings that arise around release and cleansing, and see if there are any patterns you might be holding in your body that need to be cleared.

Step 5: Record Your Impressions (4 minutes)
After the session, take some time to write down your experiences. Record any sensations, images, or emotional insights you gathered during your remote viewing. Reflect on how the energy of the ureters felt, any blockages or disruptions you sensed, and any emotional themes that emerged. This practice of documenting your impressions helps to solidify your insights and aids in identifying areas that may require healing or further attention.

Remote viewing the ureters can reveal much about how your body processes and releases both physical and emotional energies. By connecting to the subtle energy of the ureters, you can uncover blockages or patterns tied to the ability to cleanse and let go. Whether it's emotional baggage, past experiences, or physical toxins, understanding the energy flow in the ureters can help you release what no longer serves you and promote overall healing.

Uterus

People often choose to remote view the uterus as it holds significant emotional and physical connections to creativity, nurturing, and personal boundaries. As the centre of reproduction and creation, the uterus can be a powerful reflection of one's emotional state and ability to manifest or release. By remote viewing this area, individuals may gain insights into any emotional blockages, unresolved feelings, or physical issues that may be impacting their overall well-being. This practice allows for a deeper connection to the self, revealing not only health patterns but also the underlying emotional dynamics related to the uterus, such as past trauma or the ability to create and nurture life. Follow these 5 steps to remotely view the uterus.

1. **Ground and Centre Yourself (3 minutes)**
   Begin by grounding yourself through deep, steady breaths. Focus on your spine and feel the breath move through it with each inhale and exhale. This will centre your energy and create a calm, balanced foundation before you begin your remote viewing.
2. **Focus Your Awareness on the Pelvic Area (3 minutes)**
   Gently bring your awareness to the lower abdomen, specifically to the pelvic region where the uterus is located. Visualise the shape, size, and position of the uterus within the body, allowing your attention to settle on this area. Trust that as your focus sharpens, you will begin to sense the energy of the uterus.
3. **Tune Into the Energy Flow (6 minutes)**
   As you breathe, begin to feel for any subtle sensations or vibrations in the area of the uterus. Does it feel warm, cool, tingling, or perhaps heavy? Pay attention to any blockages or areas where energy feels stagnant, as these may indicate emotional or physical imbalances.
4. **Explore Emotional Patterns Linked to the Uterus (6 minutes)**
   Reflect on emotional connections tied to the uterus. Consider themes such as creation, nurturing, and femininity, as well as any feelings of trauma, fear, or joy that may relate to the reproductive system. Tune into any memories or patterns that might be affecting the energy in this area.
5. **Observe and Record Your Impressions (5 minutes)**
   After your remote viewing session, take a moment to write down the sensations, emotions, or insights you experienced. Did you notice any energy shifts or blockages? Recording these observations helps you track what you've sensed and provides valuable insights for future healing or understanding.

Remote viewing the uterus can offer profound insights into our emotional and physical health, especially regarding issues of creativity, femininity, and reproductive health. By tuning into the energy of the uterus, we can identify any emotional patterns or blockages that may be affecting its well-being. Recognizing these energies provides an opportunity for healing and restoring balance, both energetically and emotionally.

Veins

People often choose to remote view the veins to explore the flow of energy and blood throughout the body, as well as to uncover any energetic blockages or imbalances. The veins are not only essential for circulation but also play a significant role in the release and reception of energy. By remote viewing the veins, individuals can gain insight into how the body's energy flows, whether it is unimpeded or obstructed, and how emotions and mental states might influence the circulatory system. This process helps promote the flow of joy through the veins, clearing any stagnant energy and restoring balance. Remote viewing the veins can reveal underlying issues that affect both physical and emotional health, aiding in healing and supporting a free and harmonious flow of energy throughout the body. These 5 steps can guide you in remotely viewing your veins.

Step 1: Establish a Grounded State (3 minutes)

Start by grounding yourself deeply into the present moment. Take a few slow, deep breaths and feel your feet connected to the ground, imagining roots growing down into the earth. This will help you connect to your body and centre your energy before moving into the remote viewing process.

Step 2: Focus on the Circulatory System (4 minutes)

Shift your awareness to the circulatory system as a whole. Imagine the veins carrying blood and energy throughout your body, connecting all parts in a constant flow. Visualise this network of veins as a vast, interconnected system, moving energy through every part of your body.

Step 3: Tune Into the Energy Flow (5 minutes)
Focus specifically on the flow of energy within the veins. Feel the rhythm of the blood flowing, and notice how it feels to the touch or within your body. Pay attention to any areas where the energy might feel blocked or stagnant, and explore where the flow feels smooth and unimpeded. (4 minutes)

Step 4: Sense Emotional Imprints (5 minutes)
While observing the veins, reflect on any emotional or mental patterns that may affect your circulatory system. Emotions like stress, anxiety, or anger can impact the flow of energy through your veins. Tune in to any feelings that arise, and notice if there are areas in the veins that seem to hold or reflect certain emotional states.

Step 5: Write Down Impressions (5 minutes)
Write down any impressions you received during your remote viewing of the veins. These can include sensations like flow, warmth, coldness, or areas that feel blocked. You may also notice emotional patterns tied to energy flow.

If needed, repeat the remote viewing to add to your observations. The more you practice, the deeper your connection will become. Remember, remote viewing is a healing process. By staying in the energy state, you can transform and restore balance within your body through practice and awareness.

    Remote viewing the veins allows you to gain valuable insights into the energy flow within your body, revealing blockages, imbalances, and emotional imprints. By tuning into the circulatory system and observing these areas, you can enhance your awareness of how physical and emotional states influence one another. This practice promotes healing by clearing stagnant energy, supporting balance, and fostering a harmonious flow of energy throughout the body.

Wrist

People often choose to remote view the wrist to explore the balance of movement, flexibility, and support in the body. The wrist plays a crucial role in connecting the hands to the forearms and facilitating a wide range of motion. Emotionally, the wrist can be linked to how we handle responsibilities, grasp opportunities, or let go of things. Remote viewing the wrist can provide insights into how these elements of control, flexibility, and letting go are present in our lives. This process can reveal both physical imbalances, like stiffness or pain, and emotional patterns tied to attachment or the ability to adapt. Follow these 5 steps to remotely view your wrist.

Step 1: Ground Yourself and Centre Your Energy (3 minutes)
Start by grounding yourself through deep, steady breaths. Focus on your spine and feel the breath moving through your core, calming your mind and bringing you to the present moment. As you do this, feel your connection to the Earth and become centred, which helps to enhance your intuitive abilities.

Step 2: Visualise the Wrist's Structure (4 minutes)
Bring your awareness to your wrist. Imagine its shape and structure in detail, as if you can see it inside your body. Visualise the bones, ligaments, and tendons that make up the wrist, and allow your attention to deepen as you picture these elements clearly. To enhance your visualization, you can look at a picture of the wrist, perhaps from Google, for about 2 minutes before beginning. The more familiar you are with the structure, the easier it will be to visualise it.

Step 3: Sense the Energy in the Wrist (4 minutes)
Focus on the energy surrounding and flowing through your wrist. Breathe gently and notice any sensations that arise in this area—vibrations, warmth, or subtle pressure. Pay attention to any blockages or sensations of freedom and ease, as these can indicate emotional or physical patterns tied to the wrist.

Step 4: Use Your Inner Eye for X-ray Vision (3 minutes)
Activate your inner eye or intuitive vision to see the energy and physical state of your wrist in more detail. Imagine using x-ray vision to explore the internal workings of the wrist, looking for any irregularities, energy blocks, or emotional imprints that may be affecting its functionality or flexibility.

Step 5: Record Your Impressions (3 minutes)
After the session, write down any impressions, sensations, or visuals you experienced. This could include physical sensations, emotional insights, or energy flows you detected. Recording these observations helps process the information and gain clarity on the condition of the wrist, whether physical or emotional.

Remote viewing the wrist offers insights into how we handle responsibilities, adapt to changes, and experience flexibility in life. By sensing the energy and using intuitive tools like x-ray vision, you can uncover blockages or emotional patterns tied to holding onto things or releasing them. This practice helps you connect more deeply with your body's energetic flow and supports healing by restoring balance and releasing tension in the wrist.

Conclusion: Every Organ and Body Part Can Be Explored through Remote Viewing

You can remotely view any organ or part of the body. While I've listed some of the most common organs, there are countless possibilities to explore. You might choose to focus on something very specific, like small bones, individual areas of the brain, or even specific fingers or toes. The possibilities are endless.

The technique remains the same: calm your mind, focus on the organ or body part, sense the energy within, scan it with your inner "x-ray" vision, and record your impressions. These impressions may come in various forms—images, sensations, feelings, colours, dreams, vibrations, sounds, smells, or even tastes.

This practice allows you to view your body from the inside and activate your "inner eye." It is not a special talent reserved for a few; it is a skill anyone can develop with practice.

If you find it challenging to see inside your body at first, don't give up. Keep practicing, and with time, you'll awaken and strengthen your inner eye.

Trust yourself and remind yourself:

- "I am right in my own way."
- "There is no right or wrong. There is only what I am aligned with."

These affirmations reflect the truth—your energetic alignment with your body is your truth. Remote viewing can help you deepen this alignment, not just with your body but with all aspects of life.

Celebrate small steps of progress and keep practicing. With patience and persistence, the results will come.

Chapter 10:
The Future of Remote Viewing

Remote viewing is not just a tool for accessing hidden information—it is an evolving skill that empowers individuals to navigate life with clarity and alignment.

As we move into an era where personal discernment is increasingly critical, Remote Viewing will become an indispensable practice for making choices that resonate with our unique needs and values.

This chapter explores how Remote Viewing can transform everyday decision-making, integrate with diverse disciplines, and foster the development of consciousness, ultimately paving the way for a better world.

The Most Important Question: "What is right for me?"

In the future, remote viewing will be a crucial tool for answering one of life's most pressing questions: What is right for me? 'Right' means being aligned with my energy and my body.

Imagine choosing the perfect diet that aligns with your body's needs, discovering hobbies that truly bring you joy, or selecting the right health practitioners—be it doctors, psychologists, or healers. Remote viewing allows you to tap into the energetic resonance of these options, bypassing external influences and focusing on what is personally beneficial.

For example:
- **Food Choices**: By remote viewing the energetic compatibility of specific foods with your body, you can intuitively select meals that nourish you on a deeper level.
- **Healthcare**: Instead of relying solely on recommendations or credentials, you can remote view potential practitioners to sense who aligns with your energy and has the right approach for your healing.
- **Activities and Hobbies**: Remote viewing helps identify hobbies and interests that truly uplift your spirit and foster creativity.

In a world where even trusted professionals may not fully understand your individual needs, remote viewing offers a way to reclaim personal agency in decision-making. It ensures your choices are guided by your inner wisdom and aligned with your highest good.

Integration with Other Disciplines

Remote viewing is not confined to personal decisions; its applications are expanding into a wide range of fields, enhancing outcomes and fostering innovation.
- **Medicine**: Remote viewing can be used to assess subtle energy imbalances, explore emotional roots of illnesses, and guide treatment plans tailored to individual needs. It complements practices like medical intuition, offering a holistic approach to healing.
- **Business**: Entrepreneurs and executives can use remote viewing to identify market trends, evaluate business opportunities, and make strategic decisions. It also aids in understanding team dynamics and optimizing productivity.
- **Environment**: Remote viewing supports environmental sustainability by providing insights into the energetic impact of human activities. For instance, it can help locate areas in need of conservation or assess the energy of potential development sites.

- **Education and Personal Growth**: Schools and personal development programs are beginning to incorporate intuitive training, teaching individuals how to harness their consciousness to enhance learning, problem-solving, and creativity.

By integrating remote viewing into these disciplines, we are not only improving processes but also fostering a deeper understanding of interconnectedness across various domains.

Developing Consciousness and the Mind

Remote viewing is more than a skill—it is a practice that accelerates the evolution of consciousness. As you engage in remote viewing, you cultivate a heightened awareness of the energetic field that connects all things. This awareness fosters unity and compassion, breaking down the barriers of separation.

The practice also sharpens your intuitive abilities, enhances mental clarity, and strengthens your ability to remain neutral and objective. Over time, remote viewing helps align your mind with your heart, creating a harmonious inner state that supports better decision-making and a more fulfilling life.

The development of consciousness through remote viewing also contributes to collective growth. As more individuals access their intuitive potential, society becomes more attuned to shared values of connection, empathy, and sustainability.

The Role of AI and Technology in Remote Viewing

The integration of Artificial Intelligence (AI) and technology is transforming remote viewing by enhancing training, analysis, and application. AI offers personalized training programs, instant feedback, and randomized target selection, helping practitioners refine their skills while maintaining objectivity. Tools like machine learning and statistical validation analyse session data, uncover patterns, and assess success rates, bringing scientific rigor to the intuitive practice. Virtual reality and AI-driven simulations further allow immersive training environments, augmenting perception and sharpening accuracy.

Despite these advancements, the heart of remote viewing remains human intuition and consciousness. While AI can support and validate intuitive insights, ethical considerations like data security, privacy, and potential misuse are critical. Striking a balance between technology and intuition ensures that remote viewing remains a deeply personal practice, with AI serving as a collaborative tool to enhance its potential without replacing its core human essence.

Striking a Balance Between Intuition and Technology

Striking a balance between intuition and technology in remote viewing is essential to preserving its human essence while embracing modern advancements. Technology, particularly AI, can enhance the practice by providing tools for analysis, training, and collaboration, but it cannot replicate the deeply personal, intuitive connection that lies at the heart of remote viewing. Practitioners must use technology as a supportive tool, not a replacement, ensuring that their innate abilities remain central. Maintaining this balance also involves addressing ethical considerations, such as privacy and the responsible use of technology, to ensure remote viewing remains a respectful and empowering practice. By harmonizing intuition with technological aids, remote viewers can expand their capabilities without compromising the core spiritual and human aspects of their work.

Misuse of Technology in Remote Viewing

The misuse of technology in remote viewing, particularly when enhanced by AI, raises serious ethical concerns. Tools designed to augment intuitive practices could be exploited for purposes that conflict with established guidelines, such as unauthorized surveillance, invasion of privacy, or manipulation of sensitive information. AI's ability to analyses and predict outcomes amplifies these risks, as it could be weaponized to gather intelligence or monitor individuals without their consent. Practitioners must remain vigilant, adhering to ethical principles and ensuring that technology is used responsibly. By fostering transparency and accountability, the remote viewing community can safeguard the integrity of the practice and prevent its misuse for harmful or intrusive purposes.

Conclusion: Remote Viewing as a Tool for a Better World

The future of remote viewing is not just about individual empowerment—it is about creating a better, more unified world. Remote viewing reveals the interconnectedness of all things through the energy field, reminding us that our choices and actions ripple outward to affect others.

As the world becomes more complex, it is up to each of us to take responsibility for our decisions. Remote Viewing offers a way to navigate this complexity with confidence and alignment, ensuring that we act in harmony with our true selves and the greater whole.

By embracing remote viewing, we are not just enhancing our lives but contributing to a global shift toward unity, compassion, and awareness. It is a tool for the future—a future where humanity thrives through interconnectedness and conscious living.

Chapter 11:
Reflecting on Your Progress

Assessing Your Growth and Achievements
As you reach the final pages of this journey, it's time to pause, reflect, and look ahead. Remote viewing is not just a skill you learn—it is a practice that grows with you, deepening your understanding of yourself and the world. Let's take a moment to assess your progress, set intentions for the future, and embrace the profound impact remote viewing can have on your life.

What Actions Should You Take?
Think back to where you began. Perhaps remote viewing was a completely new concept, or maybe you already had some intuitive abilities that you wanted to refine. Regardless of your starting point, take a moment to acknowledge how far you've come.

- Have you gained greater clarity in your decision-making?
- Are you more in tune with your own energy and the energies around you?
- Have you noticed an improvement in your ability to remain neutral, calm, and focused during your sessions?
- Are you beginning to trust your intuition more deeply in everyday life?

Celebrate your achievements, no matter how small. Growth in remote viewing often happens in subtle but significant ways, like increased confidence in your intuitive insights or a heightened sense of interconnectedness with the world.

Setting Goals for Continued Practice

Your journey with remote viewing doesn't end here—it is just the beginning. Use this moment to set meaningful goals that align with your aspirations.

- **Skill Refinement**: Continue practicing and honing your remote viewing techniques. Explore different protocols, target types, and advanced applications.
- **Broader Applications**: Consider how you can integrate remote viewing into more areas of your life—whether it's improving relationships, advancing your career, or contributing to community projects.
- **Personal Growth**: Use remote viewing as a tool for inner exploration. Focus on expanding your consciousness, overcoming limiting beliefs, and cultivating a deeper connection with your intuition.
- **Teaching and Sharing**: If you feel called, consider sharing your knowledge with others. Whether through mentorship, teaching, or participating in community projects, your journey can inspire others to embark on their own path of discovery.

Final Thoughts

The Transformative Power of Remote Viewing

Remote viewing is not just about seeing beyond physical limitations—it is a profound practice that transforms the way you interact with the world. It fosters self-awareness, enhances your decision-making, and opens doors to new possibilities.

By learning to trust your inner wisdom and connecting with the energy field that unites us all, you have tapped into a wellspring of potential that extends beyond what you once thought possible. This journey is as much about self-discovery as it is about acquiring a skill.

The beauty of remote viewing lies in its limitless nature. Each session is an opportunity to learn something new—about yourself, about others, and about the intricate web of life that binds us together.

Encouragement to Keep Exploring and Expanding Your Abilities

As you continue your journey, remember that growth in remote viewing is ongoing. Be patient with yourself and embrace the process of learning. There will be moments of breakthrough and moments of challenge, but each step forward brings you closer to mastering this powerful tool.

Stay curious and open to new experiences. Allow yourself to explore beyond your comfort zone, and don't be afraid to experiment with different approaches. Trust in your abilities and the guidance that comes through them.

A World of Possibilities

Remote viewing is more than a practice; it is a gateway to a more intuitive, connected, and conscious life. By incorporating it into your daily decisions and embracing it as a path of growth, you are not only transforming your own life but contributing to a collective awakening.

Remember: the journey is yours, but the impact is universal. By continuing to explore and expand your abilities, you are playing a vital role in creating a world where intuition, interconnectedness, and conscious living guide our decisions and actions.

The future is bright—and it begins with you.

Chapter 12:
Appendices

This chapter provides additional resources to support your journey with remote viewing. Whether you're seeking to understand key concepts, explore further learning opportunities, or access practical tools, this section has you covered.

Glossary of Terms:

To deepen your understanding of remote viewing, here are key terms and concepts explained in detail:

Core Concepts
- **Remote Viewing (RV)**
  The practice of accessing information about a distant or unseen target using intuitive perception beyond the five senses. This skill allows individuals to perceive details about people, places, objects, or events without physical proximity to them.
- **Target**
  The object, place, person, or event being observed during a Remote Viewing session. The target serves as the focus point and can range from physical objects to abstract concepts.
- **Protocol**
  A structured set of steps or guidelines followed during a remote viewing session to ensure neutrality, focus, and repeatability. Protocols like Controlled Remote Viewing (CRV) are designed to standardize the process and improve accuracy.
- **Session**
  A single attempt to remote view a target, including all impressions, sketches, and notes gathered during the process. Each session is an opportunity to refine skills and learn from feedback.

- **Intuitive Mind**
  The aspect of consciousness that perceives information beyond logical reasoning. It bridges the subconscious and unconscious minds, offering insights that are not accessible through conventional thought processes.
- **Neutrality**
  A mental state free from judgment, bias, or emotional influence. Neutrality is essential in Remote Viewing to avoid projecting personal beliefs or expectations onto the target.
- **Signal Line**
  The metaphoric stream of information from the target to the viewer's awareness. It represents the intuitive connection that allows details about the target to surface in the viewer's mind.
- **Gestalt**
  A holistic or overall impression of the target. Gestalts often arise as the initial sense of the target before specific details become clear.
- **Feedback**
  Information provided after a session to validate or improve the accuracy of the viewer's perceptions. Feedback helps refine skills and build confidence.
- **Energetic Field**
  The interconnected web of energy that links all things in the universe. This field is often considered the medium through which intuitive perception and Remote Viewing occur.

Mind and Energy Concepts

- **Unconscious Mind**
  The part of the mind responsible for automatic bodily processes (e.g., respiration, digestion) and deeply embedded memories or instincts. It is believed to play a foundational role in intuitive perception by processing information beyond conscious awareness.

- **Subconscious Mind**
  The layer of the mind that governs emotions, habits, and automatic behaviours. In remote viewing, it acts as a bridge between conscious thought and intuitive impressions, often revealing insights that bypass logical reasoning.
- **Subtle Energy**
  A term used to describe the non-physical energies that exist within and around all living things. These energies are thought to carry information and influence health, emotions, and intuitive perception.

Types of Remote Viewing
- **Controlled Remote Viewing (CRV)**
  A formalized methodology developed during military programs to teach Remote Viewing as a repeatable skill. CRV uses specific protocols to guide the viewer through distinct stages of perception, from general impressions to detailed insights.
- **Associative Remote Viewing (ARV)**
  A technique used to predict future outcomes by associating each potential outcome with a specific target image or concept. ARV is often used in decision-making and forecasting.
- **Extended Remote Viewing (ERV)**
  A less structured approach that involves entering a deep meditative or altered state to access intuitive impressions about a target.
- **Technical Remote Viewing (TRV)**
  A system of Remote Viewing developed as an offshoot of CRV, incorporating detailed protocols and procedures.

Scientific and Theoretical Concepts
- **Quantum Entanglement**
  A theory in quantum physics where two particles become interconnected, such that the state of one instantly influences the state of the other, regardless of distance. This concept is often

referenced in Remote Viewing as a possible explanation for how information is accessed across time and space.
- **Distant Connection**
The intuitive link between the viewer and the target, regardless of physical or temporal separation. This connection is believed to occur through the energetic field or collective consciousness.
- **Sixth Sense**
A term often used to describe intuitive perception or extra-sensory abilities, including the ability to access information without relying on the five physical senses. Remote Viewing is considered a form of sixth-sense ability.
- **3D (Third Dimension)** of consciousness refers to a reality focused on physical, material existence, where time and space are perceived as linear and separate.
- **5D (Fifth Dimension)** of consciousness expands beyond these limits, embracing interconnectedness, energy, and a heightened awareness of non-linear time and infinite possibilities.

Practical Applications
- **Object**
Any tangible item that serves as the focus of a remote viewing session. Objects may include personal belongings, artifacts, or unknown items hidden from the viewer.
- **Decision-Making**
The process of using remote viewing to gain clarity about choices in daily life, such as selecting the right health practitioner, identifying beneficial activities, or determining optimal solutions in challenging situations.

By familiarizing yourself with these terms and concepts, you'll deepen your understanding of remote viewing and enhance your ability to practice it effectively.

Recommended Resources

For those looking to expand their knowledge and skills, here are some valuable resources:

Books
- *The Seventh Sense* by Lyn Buchanan: A foundational guide to remote viewing and its applications.
- *Remote Viewing Secrets* by Joseph McMoneagle: A comprehensive overview of the techniques and theories behind remote viewing.
- *Limitless Mind* by Russell Targ: Explores the science and spirituality of consciousness and remote viewing.

Websites
- **IRVA (International Remote Viewing Association)**: www.irva.org
  Offers a wealth of resources, events, and community support for remote viewers.
- **Farsight Institute**: www.farsight.org

A hub for research and training in remote viewing.

Courses

- **"Remote Viewing with Intuitive Healing"** – Dr. Irina Webster's Membership Program: A Space for Regular Learning, Practice, and Exploration of Remote Viewing (via Zoom and Online) http://www.intuitive-healing-power.com/
- **Intuitive Healing Practitioner 11-week course:**
  Dr Irina Webster's 11-week Intuitive Healing Practitioner course focuses on developing intuitive abilities and mastering remote viewing techniques to enhance your capacity for healing and understanding energy on a deeper level.
  https://dririnawebster.com/courses/
- **Empath's Diploma Course (Intuitive Healing for highly sensitive people)**
  The Empath's Diploma Course is specifically designed for empaths, teaching intuitive healing techniques to manage energy, build emotional resilience, and harness their sensitivity as a powerful gift.
  https://dririnawebster.com/intuitive-healing-for-empath-diploma/

Join Dr. Irina Webster's exclusive membership program, designed for individuals who are eager to learn, refine, and deepen their remote viewing skills. Through regular online sessions and Zoom meetings, participants will have the opportunity to practice remote viewing, explore new techniques, and engage in guided exercises under Dr. Webster's expert guidance. Whether you're a beginner or an experienced practitioner, this program provides ongoing support, structured learning, and a community of like-minded individuals dedicated to advancing their intuitive abilities.

Sample Exercises and Templates

Guided Exercises to Hone Your Skills

To strengthen your remote viewing skills, it's essential to practice regularly. The following exercises provide guided steps that will help you tap into your intuitive mind and learn to trust your perceptions.

Exercise 1: Sensory Awareness and Energy Sensing

1. **Find a Quiet Space:** Start by settling into a quiet, comfortable space free from distractions. Sit with your back straight and your body relaxed.
2. **Breathe Deeply:** Begin by taking several deep breaths, inhaling through your nose and exhaling through your mouth. This will help calm your mind and tune you into your intuition.
3. **Focus on Sensory Awareness:** Close your eyes and bring your awareness to your physical senses—what you can hear, feel, smell, and even taste. Pay attention to any subtle sensations or impressions that may arise, like a shift in temperature or energy.
4. **Energy Sensing:** Visualise an energy field around your body, and practice sensing its boundaries. This exercise helps you connect with the subtle energies that surround you, which is

critical for remote viewing. Tune into areas of higher or lower energy within your field.
5. **Expand Your Awareness:** After a few minutes of focusing on your own energy, try to expand your awareness outward. Imagine that your energy is extending beyond your body, reaching out to the environment around you. Stay attuned to any intuitive impressions, feelings, or thoughts that arise.

This exercise will help you develop your sensitivity to energy and prepare your mind to interpret subtle cues that are essential in remote viewing.

Exercise 2: Remote Viewing a Target

1. **Prepare a Target:** Choose a target for your remote viewing practice. It could be an object, a person, or even a location. If you have a practice group, one person can select a target without sharing it with the group, while the others will attempt to remotely view it.
2. **Clear Your Mind:** Sit comfortably and clear your mind of any distractions. Focus on your breathing and allow any thoughts to fade away.
3. **Engage Your Intuition:** Gently ask your subconscious to help you connect with the target. Let your mind open to impressions, colours, shapes, textures, and emotions. Allow your thoughts to flow freely without judgment or analysis.
4. **Describe the Target:** As the impressions come to you, write them down or speak them out loud. Do not censor or filter what you receive, even if it feels abstract or unrelated to the target. Trust that each piece of information is part of the whole.
5. **Review the Target:** After a set amount of time (e.g., 20-30 minutes), stop the session and reveal the target to yourself. Compare your impressions with the actual target. Note any matches or surprises, and reflect on the experience.

This exercise helps you practice gathering intuitive impressions and translating them into a coherent view of a target. With repeated practice, your ability to describe targets will improve, and you will develop confidence in your intuitive skills.

Exercise 3: Remote Viewing of a Person's Energy Field

1. **Prepare Your Space:** As always, begin by finding a quiet space and centring yourself through deep breathing.
2. **Visualise the Person:** Imagine the person you wish to view. If you're practicing with a partner, ask them to send a mental image of themselves to you (without revealing specific details), or use a photograph if available.
3. **Tune into Their Energy:** Begin by focusing on their energy field. Imagine that you are reaching out to connect with their emotional, mental, and physical states. Let yourself receive impressions about their current state of being. You may sense emotions like calm, tension, or joy, or physical sensations such as warmth or coldness.
4. **Identify Patterns:** As you receive these impressions, pay attention to any recurring patterns. Are there any areas of energy blockages or excess? What does the energy tell you about this person's well-being?
5. **Share Your Impressions:** After the session, share your findings with the person and compare your impressions with their experiences or state of mind. This practice is valuable for honing your ability to assess the energy fields of others, a skill that is especially useful in medical intuitive remote viewing.

This exercise helps to develop empathy and refine your intuitive abilities to sense others' emotional and physical states. It also helps strengthen the accuracy of your remote viewing skills in human energy assessments.

Setting Up Practice Groups and Sessions

Remote viewing is a skill that thrives on collaboration and mutual support. By setting up practice groups, you can share experiences, gain new insights, and refine your abilities in a safe and supportive environment.

Creating a Remote Viewing Practice Group
1. **Find Like-Minded Individuals:** Look for people who share your interest in remote viewing and are committed to practicing regularly. You can find remote viewing groups online or create one with friends or colleagues who are also interested in the practice.
2. **Set Clear Expectations:** When forming a group, make sure everyone agrees on the goals of the practice. Will the group focus on improving individual skills, exploring specific targets, or enhancing group dynamics? Setting clear expectations will ensure that everyone is aligned in their practice.
3. **Designate Roles:** Within the group, assign roles to ensure smooth sessions. One person can act as the target generator, selecting the targets for the group. Others can act as remote viewers, while a scribe can record impressions. It's important to rotate these roles periodically to give everyone a chance to practice different aspects of remote viewing.

4. **Establish Ground Rules:** To ensure a positive and productive practice environment, establish ground rules. These may include respecting one another's experiences, avoiding judgment, and maintaining confidentiality about personal information.

Holding Regular Practice Sessions

1. **Choose a Time and Place:** Determine a regular meeting schedule that works for everyone in the group. Consistency is key to developing your remote viewing skills.
2. **Prepare for the Session:** Before each session, make sure everyone is in a relaxed state. Allow for a few minutes of grounding exercises, like deep breathing or meditation, to clear the mind and prepare for the practice.
3. **Select Targets:** For each session, select different types of targets to practice. These can include objects, places, people, or even abstract concepts like emotions or energy fields. It's important to vary the types of targets to keep the practice dynamic and challenging.
4. **Review and Reflect:** After each practice session, take time to reflect on the results. What was accurate? What was unclear? Discuss the details and share feedback with one another. This reflective process helps refine your understanding and improve your skills.
5. **Challenge Yourself:** As you progress, challenge yourself by remote viewing more complex targets or increasing the difficulty level. You can practice with more ambiguous or distant targets to stretch your abilities.

Conclusion

The practical application of remote viewing is not only about gathering information but also about developing a deeper connection to your intuition. By engaging in regular exercises and participating in practice groups, you'll gradually strengthen your abilities and deepen your understanding of the remote viewing process. Remember that patience, consistency, and a commitment to neutrality are essential as you progress in your remote viewing journey.

Through these exercises and practice sessions, you will not only hone your skills but also learn to trust the subtle cues your intuition provides, helping you tap into the vast potential of your mind.

Available from Dr. Irina Webster:

1. **"Remote Viewing with Intuitive Healing" – Dr. Irina Webster's Membership Program**

    Join Dr. Irina Webster's exclusive membership program designed for regular learning, practice, and exploration of remote viewing. This program offers a supportive environment where you can refine your remote viewing skills, connect with like-minded individuals, and explore new techniques in a structured format. Sessions are held regularly via Zoom and online, providing continuous guidance and opportunities for growth. http://www.intuitive-healing-power.com/

2. **Intuitive Healing Practitioner 11-Week Course**

    A comprehensive 11-week course designed to guide you in mastering the art of intuitive healing. Through this course, you will learn how to tap into your intuitive abilities to support others in their healing journey. The program combines theory with practical exercises to build confidence and skill in applying intuitive healing techniques. http://www.dririnawebster.com/

3. **Empath (Highly Sensitive Persons) Practitioner 11-Week Course**
This specialized 11-week course is tailored for empaths and highly sensitive individuals who wish to develop their intuitive healing skills. It offers practical tools and strategies to manage sensitivities and harness them for healing purposes, empowering you to help others while maintaining your own well-being. http://www.dririnawebster.com/

4. **Intuitive Healing / Remote Viewing Meditations**
Access a range of guided meditations designed to enhance your intuitive healing and remote viewing abilities. These meditations will support you in strengthening your connection to your inner wisdom, expanding your intuitive perception, and deepening your healing practice. https://intuitive-healing-shop.sellfy.store/

Dr. Irina Webster's Books:

- **"The Secret Energy of Your Body"**
  Discover the hidden energetic influences that shape your physical and emotional well-being. This book explores how to access and understand your body's energetic system to promote self-healing and balance.

- **"How to Heal Using Intuitive Healing"**
  A guide to integrating intuitive healing techniques into your life, offering practical advice on how to use your innate intuitive abilities to facilitate deep healing on physical, emotional, and spiritual levels.

- **"Healthy Pregnancy from A to Z"**
  This comprehensive guide provides essential information and insights for a healthy pregnancy. It includes tips on

maintaining physical, emotional, and spiritual well-being, as well as intuitive healing practices to support both mother and baby.

- **"Cure Your Eating Disorder: 5-Step Program to Change Your Brain"**
  A transformative guide to overcoming eating disorders by addressing the subconscious patterns and emotional blocks that contribute to disordered eating. This 5-step program helps rewire your brain to foster healthier relationships with food.

- **"Chromotherapy Healing Cards: The Secret Energy of Colour"**
  This set of healing cards taps into the power of colour therapy, offering a unique tool to balance your energy and enhance your emotional and physical health. Each card is infused with the healing power of specific colours to support your well-being.

Explore these resources and deepen your knowledge of intuitive healing, remote viewing, and energy work today.

www.ingramcontent.com/pod-product-compliance
Lightning Source LLC
Chambersburg PA
CBHW041135110526
44590CB00027B/4019